AND STONES

STICKS AND STONES

and

Other

Student

Essays

SEVENTH EDITION

EDITED BY

RISE B. AXELROD
UNIVERSITY OF CALIFORNIA,
RIVERSIDE

CHARLES R. COOPER
UNIVERSITY OF CALIFORNIA,
SAN DIEGO

BEDFORD/ST. MARTIN'S
Boston • New York

BP45

For Bedford/St. Martin's

Developmental Editor: Cecilia Seiter
Production Editor: Jessica Skrocki Gould
Production Supervisor: Ashley Chalmers
Marketing Manager: Molly Parke
Art Director: Lucy Krikorian
Copy Editor: Diana P. George
Cover Design: Marine Miller
Composition: Ewing Systems
Printing and Binding: Haddon Craftsmen, Inc.,
   an R.R. Donnelley & Sons Company

President: Joan E. Feinberg
Editorial Director: Denise B. Wydra
Editor in Chief: Karen S. Henry
Director of Development: Erica T. Appel
Director of Marketing: Karen R. Soeltz
Director of Production: Susan W. Brown
Associate Director of Editorial Production: Elise S. Kaiser
Managing Editor: Shuli Traub

Library of Congress Control Number: 2010928023

Manufactured in the United States of America.

5 4 3 2 1 0
f e d c b a

For information, write: Bedford/St. Martin's, 75 Arlington Street, Boston,
MA 02116   (617-399-4000)

ISBN-10: 0-312-59622-7
ISBN-13: 978-0-312-59622-4

2/23/11

Preface for Instructors

Sticks and Stones and Other Student Essays is a reader designed to accompany *The St. Martin's Guide to Writing*. Now in its seventh edition, *Sticks and Stones* continues the tradition of its predecessors: to celebrate student writing.

Enduring features of *Sticks and Stones* include:

- *37 student essays* written in each of *The Guide*'s 9 genres, from "Remembering Events" to "Interpreting Stories."

- *Chapter introductions* that motivate students to write in each genre. In each chapter introduction, we aim to increase students' interest and investment in the featured genre by showing them what is distinctive about it, how it relates to and builds on the others, and what they will gain academically and personally from working in it.

- *Headnotes for each essay* that invite students to become attentive readers of each genre. Headnotes help students approach the essays as models for their own writing by spotlighting some of the writers' achievements working in the genre and by inviting students to notice other achievements. (In some cases, "as you read" sentences direct students' efforts.) Where necessary, headnotes also supply context, such as the background information students need to understand Eve Lee's essay on the case of adventurer Chris McCandless.

- *Two final sections, "A Note on the Copyediting" and "Sample Copyediting,"* that explain the role of editing in published writing and let students see the editing process in black and white.

- *An essay submission form* designed to encourage students to submit their own essays. As an instructor, you should feel free to provide extra encouragement to a student who writes an outstanding essay. Few students have ever thought their assigned essays could be published for a national audience to read. You might work with a student on further revision and assist with filling out the submission form.

NEW TO THE SEVENTH EDITION

Important new features enhance this edition:

- *More new essays than ever before.* To the 17 most popular essays from the sixth edition, we have added 20 new ones. These include essays on topics sure to excite students' curiosity (such as dragon boating, social phobia, and proxemics) as well as essays on topics that students will have much to say about (such as video-game violence, Starbucks and other mega-chains, and the tobacco industry).
- *Essays written in response to a new chapter in* **The St. Martin's Guide to Writing,** *"Finding Common Ground."* Chapter 5 of *Sticks and Stones* offers three new student essays, specifically written to establish common ground among opposing positions on topics of contemporary debate.

SUGGESTIONS FOR USING *STICKS AND STONES*

Sticks and Stones is an ancillary that can be used alongside *The St. Martin's Guide to Writing.* You could ask students to read a chapter in *Sticks and Stones,* select a favorite essay, and analyze how it exemplifies the genre as outlined in the relevant *Guide* chapter's Basic Features section. Because the essays in every chapter of *Sticks and Stones* vary so much in subject and approach, you and your students could explore essays that model the many different ways writers organize ideas, structure sentences, use vocabulary and tone, address an audience, and center themselves in a genre.

You might want to walk students through a few paragraphs of the copyedited essay at the end of the book. The editing displaces, replaces, adds, and subtracts in order to focus and speed the reading and make the relationships among ideas clearer. Students could learn from speculating about reasons for some of the edits, not all of which are so local as they seem (as you will readily recognize).

To inspire thoughtful revision and editing, you could have your students submit essays that were based on assignments in *The Guide* —or even inspired by essays in *Sticks and Stones* itself—to be considered for publication in the campus newspaper or the next editions of *The Guide* and *Sticks and Stones*. You will find a submission form at the end of this book.

These suggestions address but a few of the numerous possible uses of *Sticks and Stones*. We would be delighted to learn how you use this book, as well as what you would like to see in the next edition. Please feel free to send comments and suggestions to us by way of the editorial staff at Bedford/St. Martin's:

> *The St. Martin's Guide* Editor
> Bedford/St. Martin's, 10th Floor
> 33 Irving Place
> New York, NY 10003

ACKNOWLEDGMENTS

We are grateful to many people who made this edition of *Sticks and Stones* a reality. Most of all, we would like to thank the hundreds of students who have conceived, drafted, written, revised, and polished the essays we have received over the years. Although we cannot include every essay submitted to us, we have read each one with interest and care.

We also thank the instructors who encouraged their students to submit their work for this collection or who submitted their students' work themselves. *Sticks and Stones* would not exist without the generous efforts of these instructors.

Many thanks go to the instructors whose students' work is published in this seventh edition for the first time: Sandra Baringer, University of California, Riverside; Christine Baumgarthuber, Brown University; Kristin Brunnemer, Pierce College; Sean Connelly, Chaffey College; Rob d'Annibale, University of California, Riverside; Michelle Dowd, Chaffey College; Shelley Garcia, University of California, Riverside; Scott Geisel, Wright State University; Sean Henry, Mt. San Jacinto College; Chandra Howard, University of California, Riverside; Lisa Martin, University of Wisconsin—Baraboo/Sauk County; Gray Scott, University of California, Riverside; Megan Stein, University of California, Riverside; Shannon Tarango, University of California, Riverside; Hannah Tenpas, University of California, Riverside; Ruthe Thompson, Southwest Minnesota State University; Janice Zerfas, Lake Michigan College.

Many thanks also go to the following instructors, whose insightful reviews of the sixth edition helped to shape the seventh: Lawrence Barkley, Mt. San Jacinto College; April Carothers, Chemeketa Community College; Marilyn Clark, Xavier College; Scott Geisel, Wright State University; Carol Johnson, Virginia Wesleyan College; Lisa Martin, University of Wisconsin—Baraboo/Sauk County; Michael Montgomery, Life University; Bob Pontious, Brunswick Community College; Jude Roy, Madisonville Community College; Mary Werner, Madisonville Community College; and Xuewei Wu, Century College.

We would also like to extend our sincere appreciation to Cecilia Seiter of Bedford/St. Martin's for her thoughtful guidance, invaluable editorial suggestions, and careful organization of this project. And, of course, we thank Ruthe Thompson, Elizabeth Rankin, Paul Sladky, and Lawrence Barkley, whose fine work on previous editions of this book set the standard for everything that followed.

Rise B. Axelrod
Charles R. Cooper

Contents

STICKS
AND STONES

To the Student 1

The essays in *Sticks and Stones* were written by students like you in writing classes like yours across the country. If you're thinking, "I'm not like the students whose essays appear in this book; I could never write that well—or get my writing published," take heart. The truth is, the essays in this book didn't always look like they do now. They began as a few sentences of invention writing, some notes taken from a research source, a phrase written on the back of an old receipt while waiting in the grocery checkout line, a tentative paragraph in a first draft, a comment written by a classmate reading a draft. And when they began to take shape, it was a rough shape. Some essays shifted from one rough shape to the next for a long time. But the writers persisted. They tested the advice of their peers and instructors. They gathered more material, whether that meant interrogating their memories; returning to a profile place; consulting more books and electronic databases; or re-viewing a film. And they pushed themselves to think of new ways to say what they wanted to say.

There's no question that writing something good enough for publication is hard work. But there's also no question that doing so is possible for every student reading this book.

Want a tip? Here's an easy way for you to increase your chances of getting published: As you write, ask yourself, "What can I do to help the readers of *Sticks and Stones*—other students like me—understand what I am trying to say in this essay?" A metamorphosis will begin. You will no longer think of yourself as someone who is merely completing an assignment for your writing class; you will begin to think of yourself as a writer in conversation with your readers.

You will notice that the writers whose work is collected here are determined to seize their readers and provoke a response. The tone of their writing is not, "Hey, would you mind reading my work?" nor is it that of a class assignment written for an audience of one— the instructor. Instead, these essays clearly belong to writers who have something to say, who are writing for an audience they know exists beyond themselves and those grading their work.

We can't wait to hear what *you* have to say.

Remembering Events 2

You can't escape narratives like the ones you will read and write in this chapter, and you wouldn't want to, because they give such pleasure. In fact, your sense of who you are—your personal identity—depends on narratives: the stories told and retold in your family and among your longtime friends, the stories you tell and retell yourself in moments of reflection. These stories may calm and center you, or they may alarm and agitate you, but together they define who you are and provide the foundation for your future.

Listening to gossip, watching a film, or reading a short story are enjoyable activities. But to be on the shaping end of a story—to tell or write a story about your own life—is even more rewarding. Telling about an event might allow you to discover its particular significance in your life: for example, by writing about her first construction job, Julia Barojas discovered new respect for her hardworking brother. Or it might enable you to articulate the event's lessons: Aubrey E. Smith's experience as an EMT, for example, taught her to trust her training during a crisis. Or it might help you see more clearly how the past shapes the future: Aaron Forshier's story about a tragic accident can be seen as a case study in how an event can alter personalities and relationships.

To tell a story is to re-form an event in your mind and examine it from your current perspective, through the greater knowledge you have gained from more education and a larger life experience. As you write and revise your remembered-event essay, take advantage of this perspective: take time to see your story anew, to read each draft as if you didn't already know its details. That way you can look for contradictions and inconsistencies in your thinking, and examine

3

and reconsider any initial, rapid conclusions you may have drawn about the experience. Sharing drafts with classmates and your instructor will give you even more perspective on the event and your response to it, and will refine and deepen your insight into the event's meaning.

Whatever you do, as you cull your memory for details of a remembered event, keep an open mind. Re-seeing events can lead to self-judgment and judgment of others: "I wish I had done this," or "if only she hadn't said that!" But these seemingly useless reflections can be important, allowing you to notice unresolved tensions below the surface of your memory and teaching you to reserve judgment as you struggle to understand the event.

Although language is slippery and imperfect, writing about your past is a powerful tool, allowing you to revisit remembered events, bring together your scattered thinking about them, and achieve significant insights. Your revised essay will document this voyage toward understanding.

Sticks and Stones

Nicole Ball

Niagara University
Niagara, New York

This is a story about bullies. We have all known bullies; the boy in Nicole Ball's story, with his drumsticks and his taunts, is a classic example. It is also a story about words—both their power and their all-too-frequent failure. The title alludes to a familiar saying from childhood: "Sticks and stones will break my bones but words will never hurt me." As Ball's story reminds us, words *do* have the power to hurt, and the child's claim "words will never hurt me" is really a false front, thrown up to hide the very wounds that cruel words have caused. At the same time, Ball's story reminds us of the failure of words. Here the narrator's words fail, the parents' words fail, and the principal's words fail. Indeed, language harms and fails everyone but the bully, who enjoys the effects not only of his words but also of his sticks—his drumsticks.

As readers, we find this essay memorable in part because Ball's experience denies us the story's expected conclusion: the triumph of Nicole and her brother in the banishment of their tormentor. Happy endings are like truisms, the author seems to suggest: tempting because they are easy but too often *un*true.

"Sticks and Stones" is both a challenge to common knowledge—words *do* hurt; endings are not always happy—and a coming-of-age story, a record of the narrator's dawning realization that we must all learn to rely on ourselves, both to confront conflict in the present and to evaluate and comprehend the consequences of experiences past. As a remembered-event essay, it is a confirmation of the power of words to enable the writer to challenge assumptions and strengthen the self.

James Nichols was short and scrawny, the smallest kid in the entire eighth grade class. But he had a foul mouth and a belligerent attitude to make up for it. And he was a bully. 1

James sat in the front seat of the school bus, relegated there by the bus driver after some infraction or other. The driver, a balding, heavyset man who paid little or no attention to the charges he shuttled back and forth, rarely spoke and, except for that act of discipline, seemed disinclined to do anything else. The punishment, however, didn't seem to faze James; in fact, he reveled in it. Sitting in the front put him at the head of all the action and surrounded him with easy victims: those too timid or meek to trespass into the "tough" zone at the back of the bus. 2

I was a year older than James and, though not very tall myself, was at least a foot taller than he was. But by my last year in junior high school, I had a terrible complexion, a mouthful of braces, and a crippling shyness. I sat in the second seat on the school bus, only because I couldn't get any closer to the front. 3

My brother, Greg, who was a year younger, generally sat with me because while he was a bit shorter, and much more confident, he had no more desire to mix with the cigarette-toting crowd in the back of the bus than I did. And although we didn't always get along well at home, we both felt that it was nice to have someone to sit with on the bus, even if we didn't talk much. 4

In our junior high, as in all junior highs, skill at socializing outranked skill in classes. And since Greg and I were both social outcasts, we endured our share of teasing and taunts. But James Nichols set out to top them all. 5

At first, of course, his words were easy to ignore, mostly because they were nothing new. But as his taunts grew louder and nastier, he developed the habit of kneeling on his seat and leaning over the back to shout his unrelenting epithets down upon us. The kids in the back of the bus relished every moment of our humiliation, often cheering him on. James puffed up with pride over his cruelty. The bus driver never said a word, though he could not have helped but hear the barrage of insults. Inside, I seethed. 6

"Ignore him," my parents insisted. "He'll eventually stop when he realizes that you're not going to react." Their words were well meant, but didn't help. The taunts continued and even intensified when we got to school. Upon arrival, the buses lined up in front of the school building, waiting until exactly 8:10 to release their passengers. Those long moments sitting in the parking lot, staring at the red plastic seat in front of me, praying for the bell to ring so I could escape James, were pure torture. 7

Each morning, Greg and I would flee from the bus. "I can't 8 take this much more," I would rage under my breath. Oh how I longed to tear James to pieces. And although I knew I would never physically attack James, I felt better imagining myself doing so. Greg, though, would never respond to my frustrated exclamations, which only added to my wrath. After all, didn't he hate James too? But more often than not, I was just too furious to care what Greg might have been thinking.

The showdown, I suppose, was inevitable. 9

One morning as we sat in the school parking lot, James took 10 his taunting too far. I don't remember what he said, but I remember what he did. He pulled a long, slender wooden drumstick from his pocket. He started to tap Greg on the top of the head, each hit emphasizing every syllable of his hateful words. My brother stared straight ahead. James laughed. The kids in the back of the bus laughed. The bus driver ignored everything.

My anger boiled over. "Don't you touch him!" I shrieked, 11 striking out and knocking the drumstick from James's hand. At that moment, I didn't care that my parents had advised us to ignore James. I didn't care that everyone turned to gape at me. I didn't care that even the bus driver glanced up from his stony reverie. I only wanted James to leave my brother alone. As the stick clattered to the floor, audible in the sudden silence, I bit my lip, uncertain of what I had done and afraid of what might result.

My mistake, of course, was thinking my screams would end the 12 taunts. The crowd at the back of the bus waited to see James's reaction. With his authority threatened, James turned on me like a viper. "Shut up, bitch!" he hissed. Coming from a home where "shut up" was considered strong language, James's swear word seemed the worst of all evils.

My eyes wide, I shuddered but didn't respond. Words were 13 words, and if I had done nothing else, at least I had caused the bully to revert to words instead of actions. I turned my face to the window, determined to ignore his insults for the few remaining minutes before school. But a movement from Greg caught my eye, and I looked back.

In one swift movement, Greg reached into the front seat, 14 grabbed James by the coat, yanked him out into the aisle, pulled him down, and delivered two quick, fierce jabs to James's face. Then he released him without a word and settled back into his seat.

James, for once in his life, was speechless. His cheek flaming red from where the blows had struck, he stared at my brother without moving until the bus driver clicked open the doors a moment later, indicating we could go into school.

My parents heard about the incident, of course, and called the 15 assistant principal about the entire matter. When the vice principal questioned my brother, Greg's explanation was simple: "He called Nicole a swear word, and no one calls my sister that." Greg had never said anything more touching.

I have heard it said that violence never solves anything, and it 16 didn't. The bus driver was advised to keep an eye on James, but no admonition would have spurred the driver to interfere in anything. The teasing went on, cruel as ever, until James threatened to slit our throats with a knife he swore he had hidden in his locker at school. After that, even though a locker search turned up nothing, my parents drove us to school every morning, and my mother talked to us about what to do if James ever pulled a knife on us at school.

But for me an imagined weapon paled when compared with the 17 vivid memory of the complete silence on the bus, the blazing red mark on James's face, the calm little smile that tugged at the edges of my brother's mouth and the click of the bus doors as they opened to free us.

Flashing Lights and Sirens
Aubrey E. Smith

Wright State University
Dayton, Ohio

Have you ever studied hard for a test, only to have your mind go completely blank once the exam starts? Aubrey E. Smith describes a similar, but much more serious, experience during her first major medical emergency as an EMT. In her essay, Smith adds detail to the scene by incorporating medical jargon, but she's careful to avoid using so much that she bores or confuses the reader. Smith also includes a description of her more experienced partner, whose calm efficiency contrasts starkly with Smith's rookie panic. In reflecting on her experience, Smith notes that although "the fear would never go away," she had survived one of the most difficult tests of her life, and ultimately proved the value of her training and her own courage.

After almost five months of classes, endless hours of clinical time at [1] Greene Memorial Hospital and Xenia Fire and Rescue Station 1, and an incredibly long application process, I found myself at EMT Inc., one of the largest ambulance transport companies in the tri-state region. My sense of accomplishment swelled for having survived the months of training and hiring procedures, and I was ready to begin working as a real EMT. My first-ever 24-hour shift arrived and I cantered into work, beaming and ready to "help people." My partner, Miranda, was a petite twenty-something with thick-rimmed glasses and a dry sense of humor. Miranda had been a paramedic for almost five years, so little fazed her. The daylight hours held little excitement for us—just a normal mixture of hospital discharges and dialysis transports. As the afternoon waned, calls became fewer and farther between, which left us sitting around, waiting, for hours. As evening turned into night, I remember lounging, sleepy-eyed on the station couch, expecting a boring night that included some decent sleep and maybe an early morning hospital discharge. Drowsy, my head bobbed as I began to drift off into a light sleep.

Waaahh Waahh Raar Raar Raaar. "Medic 223, I need you to respond to Trinity Nursing Home for a female patient with altered mental status and lower extremity edema. Patient is going to Miami Valley Hospital. Clear the tone and please give an ETA." My heart jumped into my throat. I was terrified, but thrilled. I flew off the couch, halfway out the door before Miranda even peered over her glasses at me, unimpressed. Her nonchalance really bugged me. On our way to the call, with Miranda behind the wheel, running stop-lights and passing cars pulled onto the roadside, it suddenly hit me, lights and sirens ablaze. "Oh my God, I have never been on a real emergency call before! What the heck am I doing here? I don't re-member anything! Clinicals? *What are clinicals?*" After six months of class and training, I couldn't remember a thing. My mind went *blank.* "It's not fair," I thought. "Months of training, and all I ever did was watch someone else do it. I didn't do anything! I can't!"

When we arrived on the scene, Miranda casually tossed me a gear bag and quipped, "You're in charge of patient care, chief." I froze, my mouth gaping wide. "What?" she questioned, "I thought you were *ready* for this?" Before I could protest, she turned toward the front door, leaving me dry in the mouth, sweat flushing my forehead. I hauled the gear bag over my shoulder, trying to look like I knew what I was doing. Down the dark halls of the nursing home I could smell the unforgettable odors of loneliness, urine, and death, and I felt even more unprepared for whatever crisis awaited me. I took a chokingly large breath before walking through the doorway into the patient's room, the kind of dramatic breath that children take before they pencil-dive into the deep end, unsure whether they will continue to sink deeper after jumping. I felt like I was sinking.

"Hello, ma'am, I'm Aubrey. I'm an EMT, and I'm here to help you. Can you tell me what is going on with you tonight?" As she began to speak, I began to work. *OK, take her blood pressure, pulse oximetry, and palpate the edema. Hmmm, vitals seem within normal range, and palpation of the lower peripheral extremities shows pitting edema* (squishy skin that stays dimpled after being pressed in), *cool and diaphoretic to the touch. And she's got some labored breathing* *and a low oxygen saturation, so I should fix that with an O_2 nasal cannula at 4 lpm. The patient's altered mental status seems related to blood sugar, so I'll take an Accucheck and provide oral glucose or insulin.* I was on autopilot for several minutes before I even realized what I was doing: I was saving a life.

Miranda and a nurse stood at the door, poised to assist me if needed. "Can we get a medication list?" I questioned. "And when was her last meal?" The nurse trotted off on her mission, and I continued probing the patient for more information. "Do you know the last time you ate a meal, ma'am? Are you with me? Stay awake. Ma'am, do you know if you're a diabetic?" I got no answer, only some grunts and signs that the patient's consciousness was fading. I looked to Miranda. "We need that medication list so we can package her and get her out of here—fast. I think she's got CHF [congestive heart failure] and is probably in diabetic shock."

"I'm on it, chief. Get your patient ready to go," Miranda returned, now feeding off of my adrenaline and enthusiasm. We packaged the patient onto the stretcher, and I jumped into the back of the medic to continue working her up.

Miranda pulled up to the hospital and we transferred the patient to the Emergency Room. My heart was racing with fear and excitement, and something else: confidence, maybe even pride. Helping my first emergency patient in the field made me realize that I had learned my lessons well. I was still afraid—and the fear would never go away—but I proved I could do the job. I was an honest-to-goodness EMT.

Worse Than a Lump of Coal

James Ziech

University of Wisconsin, Baraboo/Sauk County
Baraboo, Wisconsin

In this humorous essay, James Ziech's idea of the perfect Christmas
Eve is ruined by something "worse than a lump of coal": a trip to
the emergency room. His memories of pleasurable anticipation of
celebrating Christmas with his family are suddenly replaced by his
memories of the fiercest stomach pain he'd ever known. Ziech
builds the story around his increasingly painful symptoms, and uses
time markers to let the reader see the progression of symptoms over
several days. Ziech's figurative language makes the reader feel his
pain; fortunately, his good humor makes the essay fun to read,
rather than actually painful.

---

1   I was only fifteen, but I was about to stare fate right in the face. It
was just a week before Christmas Eve, the time of the year I antici-
pated the most. As I came home from school that Friday, I kept
thinking about the events of Christmas Eve: People would carol in
the streets while the snow collected on the trees; our family would
gather around to eat in front of a tree that sparkled like a thousand
gold and silver goblets. It was going to be the perfect Christmas
Eve.

2   That evening, however, my stomach began to growl and ache.
Maybe it was gnawing on itself in anticipation of Christmas. Whatever the feeling was, it did not stop. Thinking it wasn't serious, I
brushed it off and tried to get some sleep. That night I tossed and
turned enough times to turn my sheets into a straitjacket. I decided
to tough the stomach pain and insomnia out, hoping that it would
pass and sleep would come. It never did.

3   After spending I'm not sure how long inventing a new kind of
yoga, I hurried to the toilet before the stomach pain could squeeze

me like an overstuffed tube of toothpaste. I threw up. I flushed, wiping the half-digested lasagna from my chin. Even after a thorough clean, I still tasted the residue on the back of my tongue. I even felt the smell lighting a match to my nostrils. I still told myself it wasn't serious and went back to bed.

The morning came, sooner than I wished. I went to lie on my mom's bed, under a dozen or so blankets. My arms were frosty and pale, while my legs lay still like dead weights.   4

"Does this hurt?" my mom asked me, feeling the area between my belly button and my waist. I couldn't feel any difference in the pain when she poked me. Since I didn't answer, she guessed I had a bug that was going around her workplace, or something that I caught at school. Stomach flu, maybe.   5

"Here, eat some soup," she said, sitting next to me on the bed.   6

"You want me to throw up?"   7

"We need to get some liquid down."   8

"Yeah, down on that floor. . . ."   9

Every once in a while she would feed me. Even though I knew it was a bad idea, I tried to eat. I still could not keep food down, but by mid-afternoon I was on the road to recovery—or so I thought.   10

On Sunday, even though the good snowy weather was on its way, the fever I had had since Friday night was getting worse. Eventually I was able to sleep again. When seven o'clock came around, every pain I had was gone, my temperature stabilized, and, best of all, I could eat without any nasty side effects.   11

Mom intervened when I hurried off to the door with my book bag.   12

"Where are you going?" she asked.   13

"To school. It's seven, and I'll be late for the bus!" I said, about to brush her aside.   14

"You're not going anywhere. It's seven p.m.—on Sunday."   15

I couldn't believe I had gotten so confused. I was actually relieved because I didn't finish any of my homework for the weekend. I got some of it done and went to sleep. The bug was gone now and I accepted Monday morning as it came. Despite it being a normal school day, I was colder than usual, and that night the vicious cycle of squeeze and squirm started again. I even considered sleeping in the bathroom to avoid climbing a flight of stairs in between the trips. I couldn't handle the pain any longer. I had to get help.   16

"Mom, something's terribly wrong with me. . . ."   17

"When did you get that idea?" Mom asked.   18

"Midnight," I said.   19

"Why did you wait so long to tell?" she exclaimed, fumbling   20
around in her bedroom for some slippers or tennis shoes. She knew
that if I complained about being sick, I was serious about it. She dialed
the hospital right away.

Lying down on the couch, I thought about Christmas Eve. The   21
caroling, the snow, the food, the family traditions . . . everything
was going down the drain and I couldn't stop it.

We left for the hospital in the dead of night. As soon as we en- 22
tered the emergency room, several nurses sprang into action. They
moved me to a wheelchair, wheeled me to an examination room,
and started to do a few oral tests.

"Does this hurt?" asked the nurse, pushing on my abdomen. "I   23
want you to rate it on a scale from one to ten."

I don't remember what number I said, but it was in the double   24
digits.

After she was done, she gave me a chalky vanilla substance to   25
drink and a small dish tub if I needed to throw up. Since I had no
other option, I drank almost half of it before I needed the tub.

The nurse wheeled me into a room with a CAT scan machine in   26
it, and I climbed onto the slab. The machine made several passes
and the technician looked at all the images that spat up onto the
computer screen. He poked the region between my belly button and
my waist—right where my mother had poked me days before. . . .

The next thing I knew doctors were wheeling me down a   27
bright hallway.

"What's happening to me?" I asked.   28

The doctors continued their jargon-filled conversation until   29
one of them answered me.

"Your appendix ruptured. I want you to be strong for me, can   30
you do that?"

I nodded.   31

"We're going to give you some anesthesia," one of the voices   32
said. "Could you count backwards from ten?" Someone slung a
mask around my nose. I looked to my left and my right. My mom
was disappearing from sight. Door signs and figures became mi-
rages. Ten, nine, eight. . . .

Some time later, I woke up from the anesthesia. I was lying in a 33 hospital bed bound by tubes and cords. My stomach was red and stapled shut from the belly button to the waist, and I had a temperature of 106 degrees. The doctor was there, waiting with my mom and grandparents. I felt lucky to be alive.

Lying in my hospital bed, I thought about the Christmas Eve I 34 had hoped for. Instead of playing in the snow, I saw it from a three-story window. Instead of eating a traditional dinner and drinking eggnog, I ate tasteless Jell-O and drank lukewarm water. Instead of excitement and glee, I got something worse than a lump of coal. I spent all of Christmas confined to my hospital room, and by the time I was out, only a few days remained of my winter break. Maybe next year I'll pick a less scary time of year to look forward to—like Halloween.

The Accident: A Grand Day Turned Tragic

Aaron Forshier

Des Moines Area Community College
Ankeny, Iowa

"I chose the subject that I did because it shows how a tragic event that lasts only a few seconds can have a profound, lasting impact on the lives and futures of the people involved," notes Aaron Forshier. Remembered-event essays often present people, and Aaron Forshier's paper about a tragic automobile accident introduces us to a very real, very complex character—Forshier's grandfather, who was profoundly affected by the crash. Forshier writes about his grandfather with the same tenderness that seems to have characterized their relationship. He refers to him not as "my grandfather" or even "my grandpa" but simply and affectionately as "Grandpa," and sketches the contours of their mutually gratifying relationship with both general examples (a list of their favorite activities) and specific ones (the events of the morning of the accident). Forshier's attitude toward his grandfather is not only tender but also non-judgmental, especially in the aftermath of the accident. When he shows, rather than tells, what his grandfather must be feeling, Forshier accomplishes a difficult feat for the autobiographer: He steps outside the personal experience of the event and examines it from a perspective unaffected by his own sorrow.

I began spending summers with my grandparents on their farm   1
when I was three years old. What began as three- or four-day visits gradually turned into most of the summer by the time I was seven years old. Time spent with Grandpa was always fun and exciting. Riding side-by-side in the tractor cab as Grandpa cultivated fields of beans and corn, harvested oats, or put up hay; hauling water and

ground corn to the cattle in a distant pasture; repairing fences and farm equipment; helping in the garden; constructing and running his model train; fishing in the neighbor's pond; and relaxing on the porch swing at the end of the day, laughing over the stories he told about my mom when she was growing up: these were just a few of the wonderful things that Grandpa and I did together. This all changed in the months and years following the accident; the time that I spent at the farm wasn't the same—Grandpa wasn't the same. As a result, visits to my favorite childhood place became fewer and fewer as the years passed.

I was eleven years old on that hot July day in 1999. It began as many days did on the farm, with Grandpa sticking his head into my bedroom and calling, "What? There's work to be done and my best farmhand is still in bed? Rise and shine, sleepyhead." I jumped out of bed, excited for the day to begin. It was the first summer that Grandpa had let me drive a tractor by myself, and we had started putting up hay the day before. I had spent most of the afternoon proudly hauling loads of hay from the field to the farmyard and unloading them onto two growing haystacks, and I was eager to get back on the tractor and continue my first grown-up job on the farm.

Grandpa and I finished the hay by lunchtime. After devouring my favorite lunch—Grandma's crispy fried chicken; creamy mashed potatoes covered with thick, savory gravy; and a big slice of juicy, sweet watermelon—Grandpa and I headed to town to deliver eight loads of bulk feed to the local Kent Feed and Supply business. Since he owned a big grain truck, Grandpa earned extra income by delivering feed to area farmers once or twice a month. We had made seven deliveries and were going back to town for the final load when Grandpa said, "It sure is hot—must be ninety-eight degrees in the shade. What do you say to stopping at the Dairy Den for an ice cream cone before making our last delivery?"

"Great idea! You always know what I'm thinking," I eagerly replied. "There's nothing I'd like more right now than an ice cream cone." But I never got an ice cream cone that afternoon.

With visions of the cool, delicious treat filling my head, I was almost unaware of the passing countryside until Grandpa began slowing down. I then noticed the four hayracks parked in a single row on the right shoulder of the highway a few hundred feet in front of us. A farmhouse and outbuildings flanked the right side of the highway, and three farmers were baling hay in a field on the left side.

When our truck was almost even with the first hayrack, a little girl suddenly darted onto the highway from between the third and fourth hayracks. Grandpa screamed, "Oh, God, no! Hang on, Aaron." I remember screaming, and then everything happened so fast. Slamming on the brakes and turning sharply to the left, Grandpa tried desperately to avoid hitting the child. Sounds of squealing brakes and screeching tires filled my ears as Grandpa managed to whip his powerful stallion to the left side of the highway, but not quickly enough; the right rear wheel hit something with a heart-stopping thud that sent a chill through my body on one of the hottest days of the year. Barely missing a car approaching from the opposite direction, Grandpa continued to rein in his steed, which left the highway, stumbled across a shallow ditch, tore through the wire fence surrounding the hayfield, and was finally stopped by a huge, round hay bale.

Stunned, Grandpa and I both sat as though we were momentarily paralyzed. After a few seconds, Grandpa asked in a shaky voice, "Are you hurt?" 6

Still trying to catch my breath and waiting for my heart to stop pounding, I replied, "No, I think I'm okay, but I'm really scared. Did the truck hit that little girl?" 7

Grandpa didn't answer my question; once he knew that I wasn't hurt, he became silent and stared straight ahead, as though he were dreading what he had to face next. Without saying a word, Grandpa slowly opened the driver's door and stepped out of the truck, and I did the same. I watched Grandpa walk to the highway on trembling, jellylike legs. He collapsed beside the girl; picked her small, limp body up in his arms; and held her close. As I came a little closer, I saw tears streaming down Grandpa's face. He was sobbing softly and moaning, "No, dear God, no! What have I done?" 8

I stood frozen in my tracks, suddenly unable to move closer. This was a side of Grandpa that I was seeing for the first time; I'd never seen him cry before. Grandpa had always been so strong—an unsinkable ship. I didn't see him cry at Great Grandpa's funeral, when Grandma was very sick and in the hospital for weeks, or when he heard the news that his neighbor's son had died in a hunting accident. Seeing Grandpa break down surprised and upset me. I didn't know what to do. 9

As I continued to stand there, immobilized by what I was witnessing, the girl's mother ran onto the highway crying, "My baby, I want my baby! Please, dear God, help my baby!" 10

As the mother grabbed her daughter from his arms, Grandpa 11
somehow choked out the faint words, "I . . . I . . . am . . . so . . . so . . .
sorry."

Suddenly, there seemed to be people everywhere. The farmers 12
who had been baling hay, including the girl's father, rushed to the
scene. Witnesses to the accident were trying to help in any way they
could. A highway patrol car had just pulled up and another was
close behind. Traffic was at a standstill, but police officers from
town had arrived and were starting to detour vehicles onto nearby
gravel roads. When I began walking toward Grandpa, a man took
me by the arm and led me to his car, even though I kept telling
him, "I want to be with my grandpa. Let me go."

The stranger was very persistent and insisted that I wait in his 13
car. He kindly explained, "You can help your grandpa the most
right now by staying here. The highway patrol officers are here, and
they need time to talk to your grandpa and everyone who witnessed
the accident. The ambulance will be arriving soon. The medics
need to work quickly, and they can't do that if lots of people get in
their way. I promise that I will come and get you as soon as you can
be with your grandpa." Finally convinced that he was probably
right, I agreed to wait in the car.

As I sat and waited, I noticed that my shirt was wet; I had been 14
crying along with Grandpa and hadn't even realized it. Tired and
concerned about Grandpa, I closed my eyes and tried to push both
the picture of him crying and the accident out of my mind. I heard
people talking and crying, the muffled voices of officers questioning
witnesses, a siren blaring to announce the arrival of the ambulance,
tractors idling impatiently in the hayfield, and the distant, lonely
howl of a dog. Mixed with these sounds were the pungent aroma of
freshly cut hay, the overpowering odor of a nearby hog farm in ninety-
degree temperatures, and the smell of hot rubber from smoldering
tires that had left their outer layer of skin on the highway in a desperate attempt to stop the truck in time. The combination of the sounds
and smells, along with the intense heat, had almost lulled me to sleep
when a loud wail of despair suddenly brought me back to reality.

When the stranger finally came back to his car, he said, "The 15
ambulance is almost ready to leave, and the police officers are finished with their reports, so you can go to your grandpa now."

I immediately ran over to Grandpa, who was still sitting beside 16
the highway, and gave him a big hug. At the same time, I asked,

"Grandpa, are you all right? Can we go home now?" When he didn't answer, I looked at him more closely and saw that he seemed to be in some sort of trance. I sat down beside him and held his hand, waiting for him to return to me from wherever he had gone. Watching the ambulance slowly leave, I remember wondering why it wasn't speeding away from the scene with its siren blaring or its lights flashing. Even though I knew in my heart that the girl probably would not survive, I wondered why the medics weren't rushing her to the hospital. Wasn't that their job? I learned later that the girl had died in her mother's arms shortly before the ambulance arrived. It had been the mother's wail of despair that I heard while sitting in the stranger's car.

Grandpa and I walked to his truck and sat beside it, but he still 17 didn't give me any indication that he knew I was there. I said, "Grandpa, I'm here. Can you hear me?" Although he didn't answer me, he did squeeze my hand to let me know that he heard me and knew that I was there. I was worried about Grandpa. Even with a summer tan, he seemed too pale, as though the life had been drained out of him. His eyes looked hollow and distant, giving me the eerie feeling that he was in a place shut off from the rest of the world—a place where I could not be with him. Pain and guilt glazed his eyes, from which tears continued to ooze and trickle down his cheeks, etching mournful trails through layers of dust and sweat. Not knowing what else to do to help Grandpa, I sat silently beside him, holding his hand and resting my head against his arm while he dealt with the pain in his own silent way. I had my own pain to deal with—what had happened to the Grandpa I'd always known? Why wasn't he talking to me?

After we had been sitting beside the truck for a while, my 18 mom, grandma, and uncle arrived. Grandpa rode home with Grandma, and my uncle drove the truck home. Before leaving, Grandma took me aside and said, "I'm sorry that you were with Grandpa this afternoon. Are you okay?"

With trembling lips, I replied, "I guess I'm okay, but Grandpa 19 won't talk to me. Did I do something wrong?"

Grandma returned my question with a hug and said, "Why 20 would you think that? You did nothing wrong. Grandpa is hurting very deeply right now, but he still loves you very much. Go home with your mom, and I'll call you in a few days and let you know how Grandpa is doing. Don't worry; he'll be okay."

I gave Grandpa a good-bye hug and said, "I love you, Grandpa." He managed to give me a weak hug but still didn't say a word. He seemed to be drained of every ounce of strength he had. It had been a long, horrible afternoon for both of us.

I cried myself to sleep that night, not only for the little girl and her family, but also for Grandpa and me. Grandpa had always been so strong and full of life, but today he reminded me of a deflated balloon. Even so, I truly believed that everything would be better in a few weeks—but it wasn't. The grandpa that I'd bonded so closely with for more than eight years never really came back to me; a special part of who he'd always been died with that little girl. He lost interest in most of the activities that we had always loved doing together, such as fishing, farming, and model railroading. His truck collected dust in the machine shed for two years before he finally sold it. He changed from a man who had enjoyed every moment of life to a man unjustly imprisoned by guilt.

Nearly six years have passed since the accident occurred, and I've come to realize that Grandpa will probably never be able to forgive himself for what happened that day. Unable to forgive himself, he has become unable to reach out to others like he once did. I still have a grandpa, and I know that he still loves me; that will never change. But a part of him is missing—the part that made the two of us such a special team. I continue to spend time with Grandpa now and then, but we never recaptured the close bond that we once shared. Today, I cherish many unforgettable memories of the summers I spent with Grandpa, and I am grateful for the powerful bond we shared. Yet at the same time I feel cheated out of what could have been. Fate—that invisible something that brought Grandpa's truck and a little girl to the same place at the same moment in time—cheated me out of many more special years with Grandpa and cut short a wonderful chapter in my life.

Almost Quitting

Julia Barojas

University of California, Riverside
Riverside, California

Julia Barojas's essay is about perseverance. Barojas vividly describes the physical experience of suffering through a difficult first day as a construction worker—the hot sun, the blisters on her hands, the overpowering smells, and the pain in her back. Just as she is about to quit because the work is too hard, a comment by her supervisor makes her change her mind. You won't be surprised at this turn of events—the essay is called "*Almost* Quitting," after all. Barojas is not trying to create suspense about whether she will quit, though; she is writing about an event that ultimately filled her with confidence in her own abilities.

I awoke to the loud drone of my alarm as it rang directly next to my head. My eyes opened instantly, but it took me quite some time to understand what was going on. Then it finally clicked: it was 4 a.m. and I needed to get ready for my first day of work as an apprentice carpenter for a concrete company called Shaw & Sons. Somehow I found the strength in my feeble arm to turn off the alarm. The ringing echoed in my ears for a few seconds. 1

I sat up in bed and was surrounded by a piercing silence. The room was pitch black and I staggered out of bed, waving my hands in front of me as I frantically searched for the light switch. After what seemed like hours, I found the switch and flipped it; my eyes slammed shut instantaneously. It took me some time to grow accustomed to the brightness, but little by little I regained my sight. 2

I began to get ready for work. As I laced up my black work boots and put on a bright green shirt with the company name "Shaw & Sons" written on the front in bold black letters, I heard 3 the loud rumble of my brother's truck and realized it was nearly time to go. I made my way through the dark hallway, out the front door, and into the truck.

My brother and I talked the entire way to work. 4

"Are you excited?" he asked. 5

"Of course I am! I'm going to be making my own money," I 6 responded.

"Well, you know it's not going to be easy, right?" 7

"What are you talking about? Of course it's going to be easy! 8 Anything you can do, I can do better. If you can manage, then so can I."

I felt very confident in myself and expected work to be a piece 9 of cake. In my mind, I would simply show up, do some simple work, go home, and then get a paycheck at the end of the week.

The drive went quickly and before I knew it we had arrived at 10 the work site, located on the Pacific Coast Highway in the city of Huntington Beach. We parked and as I opened the truck door an aroma of salt and fish filled my nostrils.

My brother and I walked for a few minutes and passed dozens 11 of boutiques and restaurants. Soon the massive foundations of hollow, unfinished buildings came into sight. I followed my brother as we made our way to our work location. There, he introduced me to the other workers and my new boss, Gilbert Gomez. Gilbert gave me a quick tour and went over some basic rules and expectations. Then he led me to the orientation room, located in what would soon become an underground parking structure. There I was given my hard hat and safety glasses, and strict instructions to wear them at all times.

After the orientation I made my way back to the work site but 12 got lost in the maze of pilasters that sustained the heavy foundation above. I eventually found an exit and it led me straight to our location.

I was put to work right away. It was almost 9:00 a.m. and the 13 heat of the sun was warm and comforting. My first task was to glue half-inch-thick strips of foam all along the base of the buildings. At first the task seemed simple, but after a while the strong smell of the glue spray started to get to me. My legs began to quiver from squatting and standing repeatedly. My back began to ache tremendously. My knees felt as though they would break soon from all the pressure I was placing on them. A small red blister formed on the tip of my index finger from spraying adhesive onto the foam and the building. I checked the time on my cell phone and the clock read 9:47 a.m—I had been working for less than an hour.

After I finished gluing the foam, my next task was to nail plastic 14 devices called Speed Dowels onto the wooden framework. One by one I nailed the Speed Dowels. After I nailed about twenty of them the hammer began to feel heavier and heavier. I picked up the third-to-the-last dowel and placed it against the wood. I put the nail in its proper position and swung the hammer with a mighty force. As I hit the nail, my finger slipped and the hammer smashed down on my middle finger. The hammer dropped to the ground as I shook my hand in a desperate attempt to alleviate the pain.

As the day dragged on, the heat coming from the sun grew 15 more intense. The initial comfort I had felt that morning was long gone. My forehead was soaked with sweat and my head was throbbing viciously.

I stood up from my workplace and decided it was time for a 16 break. Without realizing it, I took a step back and stumbled over a broomstick that had been left on the floor. I landed heavily on my right hip and elbow.

That was the last straw! This job was more than I could handle. 17 I was sweaty and tired. Both my hip and elbow ached. Despite the fall, the hammer remained in my hand. I threw it and it hit the ground with a loud "thud." I stood up and marched over to Gilbert, preparing a long speech about why I would not be returning to work the next day.

As I neared my destination, I looked to my right and caught a 18 glimpse of my brother. I stopped dead in my tracks and just stared at him. He was on his knees, his face smeared with black streaks of concrete and blotches of white powder all along his shirt and pants. He had been working at this job for nearly two years and I could not remember ever hearing him complain about how difficult work was.

As I stood there, transfixed in admiration, I was startled by a 19 loud voice that came from behind me.

"He's a hard worker, isn't he?" 20

I nodded my head in agreement. I turned around and saw that 21 it was Gilbert.

"Hey Gilbert, you're just the person I was looking for," I said. 22 "So . . . um I . . . I . . ."

I wanted to tell him that I quit, that I was hot and hungry and   23
frustrated, but somehow the words just wouldn't come out.

After an awkward moment of silence I suddenly blurted out "I   24
want to thank you for hiring me . . . and I want you to know that I
truly appreciate it."

"It's my pleasure," he responded.   25

We exchanged smiles and I made my way back to my workplace.   26
The hammer I had thrown to the ground was still there, waiting for
my return. I picked it up and resumed my duties. My index finger
still had a painful blister on the tip, I was still hot. My middle finger
continued to throb. I was sweating profusely. However, things didn't
look as bad as they had just a few minutes ago. This wasn't the
most exciting job in the world, or the easiest, but it could be worse.

I began to work intensely and before I knew it, my phone read   27
3 p.m.; the day had finally ended. As my brother and I made our way
back to the truck I removed my safety glasses and hard hat. With the
back of my dirty hand I wiped away the ring of sweat that had
formed on my forehead. I looked at my brother's dirty clothes and
then looked down at my own. The layers of dirt that had accumu-
lated throughout the day would have repulsed me a few days ago,
but today I felt a sense of accomplishment; I hadn't given up. I simply
smiled and climbed into the truck, and away we went.

3 *Writing Profiles*

The essay you write for this chapter will almost certainly be the one you least expected to write in this class. It will not draw you back into memory, as the remembered-event essay did (chapter 2), nor will it lead you to the library, as the other kinds of essays in this book will likely do. Instead, it will take you off-campus to see someone else's place of work or play and—stranger still—require you to ask that person about it and capture what he or she says as a primary source for your essay.

It may seem daring or even reckless to walk into some unfamiliar place and ask strangers about their activities. Countless students given this assignment have done so nevertheless, gaining self-confidence and satisfying their curiosity about some unfamiliar corner of the everyday world—such as the soup kitchen, supermarket, printing press workshop, drive-in movie theater, and dragon boat festival visited by the student essayists in this chapter. The biggest surprise for many profilers is how willing strangers are to talk about their work and other interests.

You may find your expectations about the people and place confirmed, but more likely you will be surprised or even astounded by what you learn—so surprised you may need to make a second visit to gather more information and to figure out how it all fits together. What you need in this special situation of observing and writing is an open mind—or better, a curious mind. Cultivating and stocking a curious mind should be a major goal during your college years, for curiosity is a defining characteristic of a civic-minded citizen in a democracy and a requirement for thinking productively in any writing situation you encounter in college and later in your career. Anticipate that you will be surprised at what you see and hear in your visit and interviews. Embrace that surprise, use it in your essay, and continue to cultivate the curiosity that inspired it.

Our Daily Bread
Linda Kampel
Pennsylvania State University, York
York, Pennsylvania

A two-room cinderblock building in York, Pennsylvania: It's the center of the world for the nearly three hundred people who depend on Our Daily Bread soup kitchen—people like tall, heavyset Andy in his dark cap, who yells at an unseen companion while waiting for lunch in the food line; and Carol, who thinks of Our Daily Bread as more of a social club than a breadline, though that perspective seems optimistic, if not distorted, when contrasted with her "worn-out clothes" and her admission that she has frequented the soup kitchen for about two years. Colorful characters like Andy and Carol surprise us and engage our attention, but they are not the focus of Kampel's essay. Instead, Kampel's spotlight is reserved for Joe and Marie, the self-described "business manager" and "inventory-control specialist" of Our Daily Bread—in short, the operation's human backbone. To diners "so lost that they can't find themselves anymore or [who] have accepted this daily routine as the reality of a bad hand they've been dealt in life," Joe and Marie provide not only hot food but also a daily portion of hope.

To anyone who has the luxury of regular meals and a safe place to call home, walking through the entrance of Our Daily Bread soup kitchen is like stepping into a different world. Our Daily Bread operates out of a two-room cinder-block building in York, Pennsylvania, that has been transformed into a kitchen and dining area, where nearly three hundred poverty-stricken people come every day to eat. The front doors open at 10 a.m. on a large room with rows of six-foot metal tables, dim lights that cast gray shadows, and walls that are painted in 1970s "harvest gold," which has dulled with time. 1

In the back of the room there is a stainless-steel, cafeteria-style 2
serving counter, where people line up to be served hot coffee and
donuts. As gloomy as the surroundings may sound, the majority of
the people in the place seem to be comfortably familiar with the
daily routine of standing in line, waiting for a meal. Occasionally,
someone tells a joke or a funny story and one or more people
laugh, making the atmosphere seem almost cheery.

A tall, heavyset black man wearing a dark cap suddenly starts 3
yelling at an invisible companion who has obviously upset him. "F—
you! I'll do what I want!" he yells. Everyone else in the room goes
on with their business. "I said I'm going to do what I want. Just
leave me alone!"

At first, it seems like this man could be a real threat, but when I 4
ask him what his name is, he very calmly says, "My name's Andy."

There is something sad about the look in Andy's eyes, and 5
within a few minutes, he's arguing again with whomever it is that
has made him so unhappy.

At 11 a.m., the crowd grows to about 80 people, and volun- 6
teers are preparing to serve lunch. By 11:30, the number increases
to 120, and by 12:15, there are close to 250 men and women, and
a handful of children, making their way into the line that moves like
a well-rehearsed act in a play. Today's meal consists of vegetable
soup, broccoli, bread, and tuna-noodle casserole, with a choice of
either lemonade or coffee to drink. People of every age, gender,
and race move through the line. No one is turned away.

Carol, a thirty-five-year-old black woman dressed in clean but 7
worn-out clothes, says that she has been coming here for about two
years. "Most people who come here aren't homeless," she says.
"We all have a place to live and all. It's just that sometimes meals
are a problem. Some people come here because it's a social thing,
you know. You take a break from whatever you're doing. You come
in here and have some food and talk to people you know."

A tall white man, about sixty-five years of age and dressed in 8
dirty, old clothes, walks past us. He has donut powder all over his
mouth and chin. "That's so sad," Carol says. "He doesn't even
know it's there. That poor man. Now he needs help. At least he's
here in a place where he'll be taken care of."

At first it's easy to think that Carol's problems aren't all that 9
bad, perhaps because she has become so good at convincing herself

that this way of life is normal. I fall right into her train of thought. But later, thinking back, I can't help realizing that the majority of the people who come to Our Daily Bread do need help of some kind or they wouldn't be there. They're either so lost that they can't find themselves anymore or have accepted this daily routine as the reality of a bad hand they've been dealt in life.

Around 12:30 p.m., a volunteer worker walks over to a micro- 10 phone at the end of the serving counter and asks, "Has everyone gotten the food they need to eat?" No one says a word. "If anyone needs more to eat, please come up and get as much as you want."

A few people return to the counter for second helpings, but most 11 people are beginning to leave. They've been well fed and maybe somehow given the boost they need to make it through the day.

At the helm of this well-run operation are two people, Joe Mc- 12 Cormick and Marie Rohleder, both of whom seem to have a gen- uine and unconditional interest in making sure that for at least two and a half hours a day anyone who needs a hot meal or emotional support in a warm, dry place can find it within these walls.

Joe McCormick, the business manager, is a tall, white-haired, 13 sixty-year-old man whose smile lets you know right away that he is a very special human being, the "real thing." Joe cares about every inch of this place and about the people who come here for help. Joe is semi-retired now, but he still takes care of all the expenses of Our Daily Bread, keeps track of the donations, and sends out thank-you notes to all those who contribute food or services. Every Monday, Joe is in charge of food preparation and serving.

"We've been here for seven years now," he says. "We're open 14 Monday through Friday from 10 a.m. to 12:30 p.m. You should have seen the place we were in before we moved here. It was hell on earth, in the basement of Cristo Salvador, a local Spanish church. The kitchen was about a third of the size of this one here. There was barely enough room for a dishwasher and a stove. That place used to get about 150 degrees in the summertime when we were making food, and there were times when the water on the floor from rainstorms was six inches deep. We were afraid to use anything electric." Joe lights a cigarette. "Back then we were serv- ing about 107 people a day. Now we're serving around 300. It used to be 400 before September House started its senior citizen outreach program, but I'll let Marie tell you about that later."

Cartons of pastries arrive through the back door, so Joe goes   15
over to help bring them in. When he returns, he leans against a
stack of crates.

"Last Thanksgiving we were really sweating it out because we   16
supply Helping Hands with their turkeys, and we hardly had any
turkeys at all. Then right after the holidays, we got a call to come
and pick up fifty of them. It's feast or famine around here. When
Chuck E. Cheese closed down last year, I got two truckloads of
pizzas and birthday cakes. Boy, were they good. People still come
in here and ask, 'Do you have any more of those birthday cakes?'
We're never at a loss for resources for food, it seems. It's not always
the greatest, but it's out there. York County is a very giving place."

Joe tells me, "Just a second," and when he returns, he is with a   17
dark-haired woman about thirty-five years of age, wearing a blue
nylon jacket. She has the same welcoming smile that Joe has, and I
can't help thinking how lucky everyone here is to have these two
people on their side. Joe introduces the woman as Marie, who is, by
her own definition, the inventory-control specialist.

"In other words, I make sure that all the food gets put in the   18
freezer, which explains the jacket. I also rotate the food on the
shelves so that nothing stays around too long."

Marie also takes on the responsibilities of food preparation and   19
serving on Thursdays and Fridays.

"There's a guy named Charlie who takes care of Tuesdays and   20
Wednesdays, but he's not here right now. Anyway, an organization
called September House started an outreach program a couple of
years ago. They go and pick up our senior citizens and take them
for meals at their senior citizen center. They're much better off
over there because they get the attention they really need. That's
why the number of people we serve here has dropped off slightly.
It's a wonderful organization. It's hard not to get involved sometimes. There are some people you can't help but get involved with.
They need that. And there are some people who come and go. We
just found out today that one fellow we get involved with a lot just
got sent to jail last night. Busted for drugs. It's heartbreaking
sometimes because you know how hard they've been trying. There
was one guy who used to do dishes for us. Lester. He tried so hard
to stay sober, and he just couldn't do it. Eventually he died from alcohol poisoning."

"That's the hardest kind," Joe says. "You see these people and   21
you know that no matter what the hell they do, they're in a hole.
And they're never gonna get out."

One of the volunteers comes over and asks where to put a tray   22
filled with pumpkin bread.

"That's Pat," Marie says after she points her toward a storage   23
shelf. "She's one of our regular volunteers. She comes in almost
every day, along with the volunteers from at least one church
group. "We get about fifty volunteers a week. The only problem is
that no one wants to clean up—everyone wants to serve or cook,
but as soon as 12:30 hits, boom, they're out the door. York College is sending over a group of students this Saturday to paint these
walls. And the group Up with People is coming in tomorrow, I
think, to help out. I'm glad they're coming because Fridays are the
worst. For some reason, that's the day when the people who really
are in desperate need come in, so that they can load up for the
weekend. We always have extra bread, so we can give out a couple
of loaves to everyone."

When 12:45 arrives, the volunteers are finished serving lunch.   24
There is clean-up work to be done, and Joe and Marie take their
place among the volunteers so that they will soon be able to call it a
day.

True Worker

Erik Epple

Bowling Green State University
Bowling Green, Ohio

Many grocery store department managers would probably avoid the graveyard shift, but Larry Harshman prefers it. Harshman, the subject of Erik Epple's profile essay, takes great pride in his efficiency and energy, which allow him to fill pallets with groceries faster than the stockers can unload them—and then step in to help the stockers when they fall behind. Following Harshman through one of his all-night shifts, Epple witnesses both the man's mythic on-the-job performance and his more vulnerable human side—his loneliness and regret at the end of his twenty-five-year marriage, and his fierce pride in his old-fashioned work ethic, which is in danger of crumbling beneath fatigue (after all, Harshman has spent a quarter century moving up the Kroger employee ranks in physically demanding positions). As you read, notice the range of writing strategies that Epple uses to illustrate his perspective that "Larry Harshman is a far more complicated person than my coworkers would have me believe." For example, he *contrasts* Larry Harshman with his coworkers. He *narrates* a sequence of tasks that Larry performs: first unloading a delivery truck with a pallet jack, then slitting box tops. He explains the *causes* of Larry's preference for the night shift, and reveals the *effects* of his years of hard work—his failed marriage, his bad back. These strategies help Epple give readers a complete and nuanced picture of Larry Harshman, and a very unusual behind-the-scenes look at a very usual place.

I've been working at Kroger supermarket in Springville, Ohio, for two weeks now, and my coworkers keep mentioning Larry Harshman, head of the store's grocery department. Depending on whom   1

I talk to, Larry is either the most solitary, antisocial person on staff, or some kind of mythic hero, like Paul Bunyan or Pecos Bill.

I decide I want to meet Larry for myself. The mystique around him only grows when I learn he works the graveyard shift. I head back to the supermarket at 11:00 one Thursday night and introduce myself to Larry. As we talk, I begin to realize that Larry Harshman is a far more complicated person than my coworkers would have me believe. 2

The chattering of mechanical devices, the smashing of falling crates, and the ripping of cardboard would cause most people to cover their ears. Larry welcomes the noises, though. They prove to him that he is working hard and also ease his loneliness. 3

Sitting across from Larry in the dimly lit break room, I am inspired by his work ethic. Over twenty-seven years, Larry has worked his way up from a bagger to head of the grocery department. Clark Carr, the store manager, has nothing but praise for Larry: "He is a very reliable worker, one that I go to every time I need something done." 4

Larry, however, is beginning to feel his age: "It's my back; I just can't move as quick anymore." 5

Other Kroger employees, however, believe that no one there can outwork Larry, even with his disadvantage of a fifty-year-old body. Whether he is cutting open boxes or unloading a truck, he seems to defy his limitations and works in a flurry of activity, in an environment of ordered chaos. Efficient, practiced, and precise are words that best describe Larry. 6

Larry's days are exact: arise, go to work, return home, sleep. The routine is periodically interrupted when he goes out to eat with a friend, but such interruptions are rare. And while Larry works nine to five, he does not go to work in the morning, like most other Americans, because his workday begins at 9 p.m. 7

"I've never been much of a social person," Larry states with downcast eyes. "That's why I work third shift." Larry prefers to work alone and would rather have just one good friend than many. He likes those nights when only he and Carol—a night cashier and close friend of his—work the shelves. His obsession with work and desire for solitude have destroyed his home life. His wife of twenty-five years filed for divorce, leaving Larry totally dispirited. 8

"I like being alone," he comments, "but alone doesn't mean without anyone to care about you. She was always that one special 9 person in my life and was always there when I needed someone to listen to me. Now she is gone, and all that I have left are my friends at Kroger."

After a moment's quiet, I ask Larry to explain his job. He sips his Pepsi and responds: "After my break, I'll show you." 10

Fifteen minutes later, he hauls himself out of the metal chair and nods toward the door. Following him into the back room, I am surprised by his change of mood. His eyes narrow, and cursing under his breath, he falls into step with another employee as they survey the work left undone by the day crew. 11

"Looks like another long night for us, Oscar," Larry proclaims to his companion, cursing again. 12

"Just once," Oscar growls, "I'd like to see those lazy bastards work a night shift." 13

Grabbing the handle of a pallet jack—a large machine that re-sembles a miniature forklift—and rolling the jack toward him, Larry begins speaking to me over his shoulder. 14

"First, we unload the truck, which usually isn't too bad but can be a pain in the ass at times," he declares, as the twin prongs on the jack slide under the first pallet of groceries. 15

I watch Larry repeatedly maneuver the forklift in and out of the semi's trailer, each time appearing with another pallet stacked with boxes; within a half hour the sixty-foot trailer is empty. When all of the pallets are lined along the back wall, Larry pulls a box cutter out of his rear pocket. 16

I watch as Larry mechanically slits the tops, one by one, off of each box. Although working at a frenetic pace, he never cuts into the groceries inside. After removing each top, he places the open boxes on cartlike devices called wheelers. Four workers appear from the front of the store to take the now-filled wheelers inside. As the night continues, I discover Larry always has a wheeler filled before someone comes back for a new one. 17

Everyone agrees Larry is the key to a successful night. 18

"It worries me sometimes, watching him gimp around the break room, but his age never shows through his work," comments Rita, an employee who works the wheelers. 19

"He gets six weeks out of every year for vacation. During those weeks, Oscar loads up the wheelers and Spencer unloads the truck, and everything just goes to hell," complains Mark, another worker. 20

Returning the box cutter to his pocket, Larry calls break over 21
the loudspeaker. As everyone else begins shuffling toward the break
room for a few smokes or a snack, Larry heads for the front of the
store, buys himself a can of soda, then sits down on one of the register belts.

"It's just not like it used to be around here," Larry mumbles. 22
"Clark takes away all of our help, and the ones who are working
don't take it seriously. It's all a big joke these days. Some of the
workers spend most of their time on the clock talking on the telephone to God only knows who. Others just joke around and never
go beyond what is expected of them. The spirit of working and
earning your pay is gone. That gets to me sometimes."

Glancing around me, I see exactly what Larry means. Empty 23
boxes are scattered up and down the aisles, left on the floor for the
morning crew to pick up. The six workers unloading the wheelers
inside the store cannot keep up with Larry, the only person working
in the back on the dock. Not only are wheelers spread around the
store, still loaded, but many more are choking the back; I weave my
way through a narrow canyon of wheelers to reach the break room.

"He just takes his job too seriously. He needs to lighten up,
enjoy himself," remarks a cocky, tall worker, whom I later find out 24
is Greg. "If you want my opinion," he continues, "he needs a
woman."

As if to add gloom to the picture of Larry's personal life, Rita 25
chimes in: "Oh, you know old Larry will never get himself another
woman; he doesn't even know how to act around one anymore."

The crew falls into its own private thoughts. Through the 26
canyon of wheelers, I can see Larry still sitting by himself in the
front. Half an hour later, everyone is back at work.

"No reason to keep stacking up the wheelers," Larry growls, as 27
he stares at the many wheelers waiting to be taken into the store
and unloaded. "They'll just get so backed up that no one can get
into the back."

Larry turns and begins stacking the now empty pallets and 28
cleaning up the docking area. When he is satisfied that everything is
in order, he takes the remaining wheelers out to the front. Instead
of leaving the work to the other employees, Larry begins to help
them stock the shelves. With Larry helping, the others finish in less
than an hour.

"Now is when I slack because all the work is done," Larry   29
states. "There is nothing left to do, even if anyone wanted to. It
makes no sense to slack before the work is over."

Driving away that night, I realize that Larry Harshman is nei-   30
ther mythic hero nor recluse but someone who represents a time
when how well a person performed his job was a measure of that
person's worth. It is an attitude that his coworkers, both those who
see him as Superman and those who don't, do not seem to perceive
or understand. But in just one night, I learned not only to appreciate him as a hard worker but also to respect him as someone who
refuses to let unenthusiastic coworkers or his own physical decline
stand in the way of getting the job done.

Bringing Ingenuity Back
Linda Fine

University of California, Riverside
Riverside, California

Most of us don't spend much time thinking much about the printing process: When we're working on a computer, we just click "Print," and perfectly aligned, legible documents come out of the printer in a matter of seconds. In this essay, Linda Fine learns about a different way to print by visiting a room in her college library where old-fashioned hand presses are still used. Fine profiles Sara Stilley, the librarian in charge of the presses. Using quotations and paraphrases from her interview with Stilley and careful description of the work required to hand-press a document, Fine helps the reader appreciate Stilley's commitment to her work and the craftsmanship it requires. As you read, analyze Fine's perspective on the printing press workshop, and how it changes over the course of the essay.

As I made my way to a set of elevators in the rear of our sleek new campus library, I passed students and librarians working at monitors wired into the university's online system. I also passed students sitting at tables with their laptops open and books piled nearby. A few students were using the photocopiers to scan pages onto their jump drives, and two printers on a corner table spewed paper as students stood nearby chatting. I was on my way into the past to see hand-printing presses dating from the Civil War. The antique presses were donated to the university by Dr. Edward Petko because he favored the hand-press method over modern laser printing, and he hoped that the university would help keep the traditional process alive.

Entering an unmarked room in the basement, I saw numerous weathered wooden cases stacked twice my height and, beyond them, old iron machines in various shapes and sizes. I stepped into the room clueless but eager to learn about this nearly forgotten printing process. Sara Stilley, a thin, dark-haired woman in her late twenties, works in this room five days a week. After welcoming me, she showed me some samples of artwork she has printed. One of her most recent works was a greeting card she had made for another staff member. The finished product looked very professional. She then proceeded to explain to me the frustration behind this masterpiece.

The preparation work takes hours, and in some cases, days. Sara's difficult task is to carefully align each individual letter by hand. The letters are made up of very thin rectangular prisms, which make them difficult to handle. Not only does Sara need manual dexterity, but she also needs skilled eyes to be able to tell the letters apart. If a wrong letter, font, or size has been used, she has to go back to tediously correct the frame and setup by hand. Familiarity with what the letters will look like is essential for the setup of hand printing because the letters can be confusing. The leaded letters in the printing process work like a stamp. Instead of arranging them the way they are read, the operator must position the letters upside down and backwards, like a mirror image. It takes time and effort to train the eye to recognize letters this way. Letters such as "n" and "u" are easily mixed up, as are "p" and "q," and "b" and "d." Formatting the letters correctly is a critical step in the printing process because any careless error in the setup leaves a noticeable flaw in the printed document.

In addition to the letter conflict, Sara said, "Many times after centering the text, I would find out that I made a mistake in the formation. Instead of making it perfectly centered, I was supposed to align it to the left." I could imagine that going back and correcting the spacing would be a wearisome task.

This old-fashioned printing process has other problems and difficulties, too. For example, humid weather causes the ink to spread out, leaving the text appearing smudgy and smeared. There also may be too much or too little ink used in a working press. Sometimes, Sara will run out of a specific letter for a page. The only solution to this problem is to break apart her work into two printing processes and print half the page at a time.

Sara explained that back in the 1800s, printers did not number their pages when printing a book. In order to keep the pages orderly, they had to use the same word twice. For example, if the end of a page ended with the word "boy," then the following page would have to begin with the word "boy." Not numbering the pages can easily cause the pages to fall out of order.

At this point in the interview, I had to ask her, "If using hand-printing presses can cause so many problems, why would anyone still prefer using them over laser-printing presses?" 7

Sara answered, "I feel better with what I produce. For example, personally baking a cake for someone is better and much more appreciated than simply buying one." 8

After she said that, I got the point. If I were to send out Christmas cards, each individual card would mean so much more if I had personally hand-printed it myself rather than buying a box of pre-printed cards at Wal-Mart. I concluded that craftsmanship adds value and meaning that you can't find in industrialized commodities that you just buy. 9

I walked around the room and explored the shapes and sizes of the various printing presses. I saw that each machine had its own unique maneuvers. Some levers had to be pulled clockwise and pushed down. Others simply needed to be rolled across the printing bed and back. The cases and crates stacked around the presses contained lead-filled letters and hundreds of neatly stored rectangular pieces. There were keys, metal washers, wooden blocks called "furniture" to keep the letters in place, ink, and galleys—all of which, I learned, were required for the printing process. 10

At the very end of my interview, Sara demonstrated one of the many printing presses to me, the "Asbern." First she carefully arranged the lead-filled text blocks on the printing bed and used a key to tighten the furniture securing the letters. After she switched the power button on, the ink rollers began to spin. A low, soft mumbling sound stirred and filled the room. Sara slipped a piece of plain white paper into the slot and steered the machine from left to right. Steering the wheel seemed like a very tough job because she was jerking her entire body to create enough torque to rotate the wheel. Soon she turned off the machine and took the paper out. After a careful examination, she announced that it wasn't perfect. Sara handed the page to me expecting me to see what she saw, but as I looked at it, I found nothing wrong with the printing. 11

Squinting, she told me, "The text is not perfectly centered on the paper. It's a bit crooked because I slipped in the paper at a slight angle." 12

Who would have ever thought that small errors, like slipping in 13
the paper slanted, would make such a big difference? This is one of
the many things that make hand-printing more difficult than using
a modern printing press.

Had Sara not pointed out to me the imperfection of her work, 14
however, I never would have caught it. It is amazing how she can
spot a flaw in her work as quickly as a professional chess player can
call a checkmate. Sara's keen expertise in the area of hand-printing
presses impresses me. I never thought such an old-fashioned job
would provide deep insight into the beauty and value of works made
by hand.

As I left the room filled with irreplaceable treasures, I thought 15
of the time when my sister, Irene, knitted a scarf for her friend on
duty in Iraq. Irene was very worried about making the scarf "perfect." She was so concerned about making a mistake—or not having enough time to finish the scarf—that I wondered why she
didn't simply buy a scarf at Macy's. After interviewing Sara Stilley
and learning more about the ingenuity of her work, I now understand why Irene chose to make the scarf by hand. The scarf she
knitted for her friend had more meaning in it than a typical scarf
purchased at a department store. She expressed her loving care and
support through the gift she made because it took time and effort,
and not just money. There are a few holes and gaps in that scarf,
but I'm sure her friend, like me, didn't see the imperfections and
thought the gift was simply perfect.

Modernizing a Remnant of the Mid-Century

Bonnie Lapwood

Mt. San Jacinto College, Menifee Valley
Menifee, California

Bonnie Lapwood profiles an institution in transition: a drive-in movie theater that is modernizing to meet the needs of the twenty-first century. Lapwood begins the essay by describing the theater from a moviegoer's point of view, but she also interviews the theater manager to find out more about the theater's history and upcoming renovations. Using both of these strategies provided Lapwood with enough detailed information to profile the theater effectively for her readers. As you read, ask yourself whether Lapwood takes a spectator role, a participant role, or both in her profile.

A giant, neon pink Stater Bros. sign looms out of the darkness as we approach Mission Blvd. The glowing letters spill out across the unseen background in a streamlined, atomic-age font. The same sign probably greeted those headed to the drive-in fifty years ago. After turning right on Mission, the sign for the Rubidoux Drive-In appears. The Rubidoux is the oldest operating drive-in theater in Southern California, and still attracts a large following. Roy C. Hunt opened the Rubidoux Theater in 1948. The miniature railroad and petting zoo that once surrounded it have now disappeared, but every night, the screen still leans gracefully over an increasing number of cars filled with expectant viewers.

At night, the large slab of screen one is visible only as a black monolith behind illuminated palm trees. Red-vested teenagers stand joking and laughing when the entrance is empty, but snap to attention when prospective moviegoers approach the stone ticket

41

huts. Our attendant is a fresh-faced young man who jovially asks us which movie we are seeing, and tells us the radio frequency of the audio track for our screen. Radio-broadcast movie soundtracks are a relatively recent innovation, replacing communal speakers and individual speakers. Of course, this means that the quality of the movie audio is only as good as the quality of the car stereo, but the broadcast is clear and static-free. The parking lot is uneven, with raised rows allowing the viewers a form of tiered seating. Once parked, viewers can leave their cars to visit the brightly lit snack bar and restrooms, housed in a pink stucco building with teal trim that sits in the middle of all three screens.

Before the movie begins, people arrange themselves to enjoy it   3
comfortably. People with SUVs generally park with the back of their car facing the screen and sit on the ledge with the hatch open and the radio blasting, using blankets for warmth. Most people with sedans simply park facing the screen and sit in the car as they would if they were driving. Others eschew their car entirely, sitting on lawn chairs close to their sedans or pickups, so they can hear the sound. Some people occupying lawn chairs have neon glow sticks, which they either wear around their wrists or wave in the air. Children run around their parents' cars until chided to sit down and behave. The parking lot is almost full by the time the previews begin, and the constant stream of people moving between their cars and the snack bar has slowed to a halt. The massive screen and lack of distractions make it much easier to get absorbed in the movie than in a regular theater. Sitting in a car, it feels like the movie is being projected just for you.

Although drive-in theaters have become less popular since the   4
1960s, this drive-in theater has grown in popularity over the last six years.

"The drive-in appeals to families because it's a bargain, and   5
there's no worry over parking, or being late," says Frank Huttinger, a vice president at De Anza Land & Leisure,which owns the Rubidoux as well as five other drive-in theaters. Frank decides which movies are appropriate for drive-in audiences, negotiates their purchase with the studios, and groups them together by screen. Family-friendly movies are always included, as are large horror and action releases (Frank says that he personally prefers to see action movies at the drive-in, and light comedies and dramas at a traditional theater). De Anza Land & Leisure itself is a family-owned company, as are

most drive-in companies, and has been operating drive-in theaters in California, Utah, and Georgia since the 1960s. With twenty- five screens spread over six theaters, it is the second largest drive-in corporation in America. Frank is a member of the family, having seen his first drive-in movie—HG Wells' *The Time Machine*—at ten years old. Yet he worked in new media—CDs and the Internet—for over twenty years before joining the company.

"I've been in movies for about six years. It's a fun market," he says. Frank's experience in media has influenced the rebranding of the De Anza theaters, which has been taking place over the last five or six years. "We've completely moved away from newspapers, and now all our advertising is on the Internet," he states proudly. Money has also been put into revising snack-bar menus and improving technology at the theaters. Frank sees the drive-in business in a very practical, realistic light. He buys movies for their mass appeal, and despite the success of a recent series of old films shown through a partnership with Turner Classic Movies, he recognizes that audiences desire twenty-first-century entertainment. "You can't rely on nostalgia—you have to keep up and be current," he affirms. This seems to be somewhat of a personal mantra of his. The Rubidoux, with its retro coral pink and sky blue color scheme, is due for a "serious" remodelling in the next year or two. ⁶

Frank also acknowledges the non-movie side of the business. "We wouldn't be able to keep up without the swap meets," he reveals. Swap meets take place at the Rubidoux from 6 a.m. to 2 p.m. on Wednesday, Friday, Saturday, and Sunday. They form the daylight side of the drive-in business, and make use of the giant parking lot when sunlight prohibits movies from being projected. They have been held since the 1960s, and are an integral part of the drive-in industry—which in part explains why so few drive-ins have been refurbished or newly built. Along with the difficulty involved in buying the large amounts of land and equipment required to run a drive-in, Frank noted that it takes about five years to build up swap meets to the point of being profitable. ⁷

The drive-in experience appeals to many, as it offers low admission fees, the freedom to either bring your own food or buy concessions at lower prices than at traditional movie theaters, and an opportunity to relax in the privacy and comfort of your own car. The potential discomforts of a traditional theater—overzealous air conditioning, babies crying, popcorn on the floor, taller people blocking ⁸

the view, teenagers carrying out public displays of affection, having to sit apart from companions because of a lack of seats—are eliminated at the drive-in, where the air conditioner is adjustable, the seats are comfortable, and the other viewers cannot interrupt.

I was originally attracted to the drive-in theater out of senti-   9
mentality for the design and technological innovations of the American mid-century. However, as Frank told me, nostalgia is not enough to sustain a business. I found the Rubidoux Drive-In to be a worthy rival to the modern movie theater since it has the charm of an older drive-in with the convenience and technologies of today. This drive-in theater's resurgence in popularity may inspire more innovations in the way the American public watches movies, which may lead to more alternatives to traditional movie theaters.

"Paddlers Sit Ready!" The Enduring Sport of Dragon Boating

Katie Diehm

The Catholic University of America
Washington, D.C.

Katie Diehm's profile of dragon boating differs from the other essays in this chapter in an important way. While the other profile authors do occasionally insert themselves into their essays—reflecting on an interviewee's comment, for example, or briefly joining the scene they are describing—for the most part they are detached observers, reporters instead of participants. Diehm, on the other hand, takes us through a brief, action-packed race from the seat of her boat.

Diehm's participant-observer role allows her to offer readers not only the look and sound of the race, but also its feel. Readers experience the tug of the water as the paddlers struggle to hold their boats at the starting line; their rush of adrenaline at the command "Go!"; and the strain on their arms, stomachs, and backs as they paddle through the rainy, windy weather. Diehm's essay brings readers not just into the race but into the bodies of the racers.

As we bob up and down in the river, our arms begin to shake in antic- 1
ipation. Our hands grip our paddles tighter as we hold them down straight into the water, bracing the boat and willing it to stay still despite the rain blowing into us. From my seat on the left side of the fifth bench, I can see the call boat over the heads of my nervous teammates. The timer watches us intently until that exact moment when all four teams are lined up and he can give us the go.

Over the sound of water hitting the sides of the boats, we can 2
hear cheering from the excited spectators on the shore. From the
other side of the river, the spectators appear as a long streak of moving color lined up in front of perhaps the most colorful of festivals.
Tents with various Chinese wares, food, and music cover the lawn,
all part of this joyous celebration of the dragon boat tradition.

Dragon boats first originated more than two thousand years 3
ago in China when, as legend has it, disgruntled Chinese poet and
scholar Qu Yuan committed suicide by jumping into a river after his
village was overrun with enemies. As *Washington Post* journalist
Paul Schwartzman tells us, "local fishermen searched for him in
their boats, pounding drums and beating the waters furiously to
ward off the water dragons they feared might eat him" (2). Dragon
boat racing soon developed in honor of this event, often as part of
the Chinese Festival of the Dragon Boat, meant to honor and ap-
pease the dragon ruling over the river. Today's dragon boat races
are often accompanied by a festival, which generally begins with a
flag-raising ceremony the day before the races. This ceremony, in
which the Chinese flag is raised over the river, symbolizes China's
lasting importance in the event. A far cry from the fishing boats of
Qu Yuan's era, today's dragon boats are forty-five feet long and
made of fiberglass, complete with a dragon's head and tail at either
end. Sixteen paddlers line both sides of the boat and paddle in
synch in a way unique to dragon boating.

"Boat Three draw left!" the timer yells over the wind, and the 4
left-side paddlers on the boat in the third lane begin to work hard,
paddling sideways to move their boat further away from the second
lane.

"Boat Four hold! Paddle back!" the timer yells as the wind 5
shifts and their team begins to pull forward past the starting line.
The paddlers strain to hold their paddles down in the water, keeping the boat still, and then slowly and steadily begin to paddle
backwards.

The beginning of a dragon boat race is often the hardest due to 6
elements like wind and the river current. Getting lined up often
takes the better part of ten minutes—an ironic beginning for a race
that lasts approximately three—and is grueling for the paddlers as
they sometimes paddle constantly just to stay in one place. As the
boats finally pull into place, the timer wastes no time in barking out
orders.

"Paddlers sit ready!" he calls, signaling the time for all paddles   7
to be removed from the water and proper grip on the paddle — the
upper hand gripping the top of the paddle as if in a fist, the lower
hand gripping the lower section of the paddle, directly above the
wide part — to be assumed.

"Attention!" At this call the teams lean forward, arms extended   8
and paddles raised about five inches above the water, ready to
plunge with all intensity into the river. Mike Dojc, a dragon boat
enthusiast, explains that the paddlers stretch their backs out straight,
ready to pull at the paddle with the muscles from their arms, stomach, and back by twisting their bodies and keeping their arms
straight (Dojc 1).

"Go!" Instantly the teams spring into action. Simultaneously,   9
my teammates and I drop our paddles down and forward and pull
back with all our strength. The start time in dragon boat racing is
extremely important — it's a thirty-second chance to gain additional
speed that will last even when the paddlers fall back into a slower
and more constant pace. The tiller — the person in charge of steering the boat — stands at the back and grips the till, willing through
long strokes or skillful dips of the till that the boat stay on course.
The caller, standing on the front of the boat and struggling to keep
her balance despite the surging of the boat, beats out a fast rhythm
on a drum, shouting the counts over the beat.

"One! Two! Three! Four! Watch-your-lead! Two! Three! Four!   10
Keep-it-up! Two! Three! Four!"

As the boats leave the beginning of the race, the quick-start   11
pace subsides and the paddlers begin to pace themselves. At ninety
strokes a second, however, the pace is hardly relaxing. As arms begin
to go numb, the paddlers begin to focus all their energy on keeping
up with the rest of the paddlers in the boat, as they know that even
the slightest delay on their paddle's entrance into the river can mean
a demerit of a couple of seconds. Suzanne Ma, a journalist from the
Hamilton Spectator, tells us that the aim is for the "rhythm of the
boat to be like one collective heartbeat" (1). Each team has a unique
way of keeping everyone in time using some division of the paddlers.
My team divided the sixteen paddlers into two groups. The first ten
paddlers (two per bench) watch the two paddlers in the front (called
the lead strokes); the left-side paddlers watch the lead on the right,
and the right-side paddlers watch the left. The paddlers on the fourth
bench, called the mid-strokes, serve as pacers for the back half of the

boat as they watch the lead strokes and are then watched in the same way by the back paddlers. From my left-side fifth bench position, I sit directly behind the mid-strokes and am dubbed a part of the "engine room," the part of the boat that is relied on for constant, steady paddling. The front of the boat is made up of paddlers who have long, solid paddle strokes. These paddlers must also be very strong, as they are paddling dead water. The rear three benches are made up of powerful paddlers called rockets. These six paddlers are perhaps the most important on the boat, as it is their strength that propels the boat forward. Some describe the feeling of paddling in rhythm as entering a Zen state, and Schwartzman tells us that "if the boat is in tune, you can feel it gliding" (2). Paddling in unison with proper technique and a tailwind, our boat can get up to 6 mph.

As the boat reaches the end of the five-hundred-meter race, 12 adrenaline kicks in to counteract our fatigue. At one minute to go, our designated flag catcher, chosen for her light weight and gymnast-like frame, gets up, climbs behind the tiller, ties her feet into a strap secured from the neck of the dragon, and lies down prostrate over the dragon's head until she is extended a good two feet off the dragon's nose. Her outstretched arm directs the tiller toward the flag that she must catch or the team will receive a hefty demerit on its time.

The last thirty seconds of the race are often the hardest. Clearly 13 fatigued and struggling to maintain the pace, the paddlers rely solely on adrenaline to get to the finish line. The pace accelerates to the beat of a drum, and the caller urges the paddlers to "Finish-it-now!"—a signal to paddle faster and firmer than before. As soon as the boats speed through the finish line and flags are caught, the callers waste no time in yelling, "Hold the boat!" We thrust our paddles straight down into the water and attempt—despite the speed of the boat—to hold them still. Our boat comes to a stop about eight feet away from the grassy shore, and the tiller rapidly begins to spin the boat around and back to the docks. With now-shaking arms and pounding hearts we slowly make our way back, where we unload and trade places with the next team waiting to go out. The races continue all day and into the next, tournament style, until only four teams are left. These last four compete against each other in one final race—the last of the season.

As the teams narrow down, the festivities increase, and teams that 14 are out of the running return to the shoreline to cheer for the teams that are still competing. The smell of Chinese foods cooking fills the air, and ethnic music explodes from all corners of the grounds, reminding the participants just how unique an experience the Chinese Festival of the Dragon Boat really is.

WORKS CITED

Bradley, Theresa. "Students Revel in Asian Tradition: Dragon Boat Race." *Miami Herald* 29 Sept. 2005: 1–3. *LexisNexis.* Web. 13 Oct. 2005.

Dojc, Mike. "Blazing Paddles: Q&A with a Dragon Boat Enthusiast." *Toronto Sun* 26 June 2004: 1–3. *LexisNexis.* Web. 13 Oct. 2005.

Ma, Suzanne. "Pulling Together: Dragon Boat Racing Soothes the Mind, Energizes the Body." *Hamilton Spectator* 7 July 2005: 1–4. *LexisNexis.* Web. 13 Oct. 2005.

Schwartzman, Paul. "In Dragon Races, Team Spirit Sinks In, and That's Not All: Ancient Chinese Tradition Grows with Fourth Year of Competing on Potomac." *Washington Post* 29 May 2005: 1–3. *LexisNexis.* Web. 13 Oct. 2005.

4 *Explaining a Concept*

You've noticed a phenomenon: Many of your friends don't think twice about downloading commercial music from the Internet or burning CDs for one another, even though some of your college instructors have lectured that this practice is unethical or illegal or both, and your parents or employers have discussed installing software on your computer that prevents you from joining in the fun. This phenomenon or other phenomena that have intrigued you or that you've participated in but never thought seriously about may provide just the concept you need for this assignment. Once you have identified a phenomenon, your next step is to gain a quick orientation to it. Let's say you've heard about "participatory culture" and would like to know more. A bit of Web surfing reveals that the term participatory culture names the universe of file sharing networks, blogs, wikis, and other platforms that enable ideas and content to flow among peers; the shared values of these participants; and the participants themselves. Voila: a concept you could learn more about and write about. (A concept is a phenomenon or process like participatory culture, academic failure among college athletes, the dowry system in India, jihad, secular humanism, zero-based budgeting, short-term memory, federalism, mitosis, null space, gravity, seasonal affective disorder, ozone depletion, run-and-shoot offense, the hit-and-run play, bankruptcy, the lemon law, or machismo.)

Writing that explains a concept is not so personal as narrating a remembered event (chapter 2) or profiling a place or activity you have observed (chapter 3). It need not be so accommodating to readers' expected resistance as arguing to support your position on an issue (chapter 6) or proposing to solve a problem (chapter 7). But it does invite you to attune yourself to your readers, precisely measuring what they will already know about the concept: you aim neither to bore them nor to burden them, but to enable them to learn about your concept without too strenuous an effort. No showing off is allowed: of course you know more than your readers about your concept-subject, but to win their ear, you must remain tactful and modest throughout, authoritative yet never talking down.

Every academic discipline, profession, career, sport, kind of work, governmental or political organization, local community, and religion has its concepts. Through concepts, we define, understand, and manage our world. We can't live without them. These are not just big words—they are required words. As a college student, you'll add hugely to your concept hoard. In doing so, you'll gain a wider understanding of the myriad aspects of your life and times, and you'll have the precise words—the concept names—to help you organize and deploy your new knowledge.

The Forgotten Personality

Katie Angeles

University of California, Riverside
Riverside, California

In this essay, Katie Angeles explores personality types, with a particular focus on one type: the phlegmatic. Aware that her audience might not know what she means by "personality types," Angeles briefly explains the history and concept of personality types, along with current ideas about what shapes the human personality. Of course, she had to do research to understand personality types, so she cites her sources. Angeles then explains what the *phlegmatic* type is, by contrasting it with the other personality types and by giving examples of its characteristics. These explanatory strategies ensure that the reader will understand and remember the "forgotten" personality.

The next time you're at a party or any other type of social gathering,   1
look around. Some people are telling stories and making everyone laugh, others are making sure everything is running smoothly and perfectly, and a few individuals are the bold ones who liven things up and "get the party started." These are the obvious personalities—the "life of the party," the "busy bee," and the "leader." Personality experts call these personalities sanguine (the popular one), the melancholic (the perfect one), and choleric (the powerful one). However, there's one personality that's not so easy to spot, and therefore is usually forgotten—the peaceful phlegmatic.

What makes people the way they are? Why do some people   2
command the spotlight, while others are experts at fading into the background? Personality types were first identified around 400 BC, when the Greek physician Hippocrates noticed that people not only looked different, but also acted differently. He believed that each

person's personality type was related to a particular body fluid they had in excess: yellow bile, black bile, blood, or phlegm. These were classified as the "four humors" (Funder 203). Around AD 149, a Greek physiologist named Galen built on Hippocrates' theory, stating that sanguines had an excess amount of yellow bile, melancholics had extra black bile, cholerics had more blood than others, and phlegmatics had an extraordinary amount of phlegm (Littauer 16). In later years, more theories evolved—American scientist William Sheldon believed that personality was related to body type, while people in India said that metabolic body type contributed to the way people behave (Funder 373). Ultimately, these theories were proven incorrect; but we still recognize different personality types. Today, what do we think determines personality?

As *Time* magazine reported on January 15, 1996, D4DR, a   3
gene that regulates dopamine, is usually found in people who are risk takers (Toufexis par. 2). However, researchers suspected that the gene itself wasn't the only cause of risk-taking and that other genes, as well as upbringing, contributed to this phenomenon (Toufexis par. 3). At the time the report appeared, people were worried that parents would use prenatal testing to weed out certain genes that invoked undesirable personality traits (Toufexis par. 6). Since all personalities have their good and bad sides, this would have been a controversial development. Thankfully, parents are not yet able to test for their child's future personality.

Moreover, we know that even though people may be born with   4
a certain personality, the way they are brought up can also contribute to how they relate to others later in life. For example, birth order has been shown to affect personality type (Franco par. 1). Firstborn children tend to be choleric since they have the job of leading their siblings; middle children are usually phlegmatic since they're in a prime negotiating spot; and the youngest are generally sanguine because they're used to being spoiled (Franco par. 2–4). Parents can also influence the way a child's personality turns out.

Each personality type has its strength, but a strength taken to an   5
extreme can become a weakness. While sanguines love to talk, sometimes they may talk too much. Although cholerics are born leaders, they may use their influence in negative ways. Melancholics are perfectionists, but they may prefer being right to being happy, and phlegmatics tend to be easygoing and agreeable, but they may be too passive and have a fear of conflict. Their laid-back attitude can

be very frustrating to the most fast-paced personalities, such as cholerics and melancholics.

Phlegmatic people are hard to notice because they're usually not 6 doing anything to call attention to themselves. While the sanguines are talking and loving life, the cholerics are getting things done, and the melancholics are taking care of the little details, the phlegmatics distinguish themselves by simply being laid-back and easygoing. Even though phlegmatic people tend to fly under the radar, it's very noticeable when they're not around, because they are the peacemakers of the world and the glue that holds everyone together. They are low-maintenance, adaptable, even-keeled, calm, cool, and collected individuals. They are usually reserved, yet they love being around people, and they have a knack for saying the right thing at the right time. Phlegmatics also work well under pressure. However, they hate change, they avoid taking risks, they are extremely stubborn, and it's very hard to get them motivated or excited, which can translate into laziness (Littauer 21). Aside from these traits, the phlegmatic's characteristics are hard to define, because phlegmatics tend to adopt the traits of either the sanguine personality or the melancholy personality.

Most people are a combination of personalities—they have a 7 dominant and a secondary personality which combine the traits of the personalities. For example, some phlegmatics are phlegmatic-sanguine, making them more talkative, while others are phlegmatic-melancholy, causing them to be more introverted. It's not possible to be phlegmatic-choleric, since phlegmatics avoid conflict and cholerics are fueled by it (Littauer 24, 25). People who try to resist their natural personality type can wind up unhappy, since they are trying to be someone they are not.

All personalities have emotional needs. The sanguine needs attention, affection, approval, and activity; the melancholic needs space, support, silence, and stability; the choleric needs action, appreciation, leadership, and control; and the phlegmatic needs peace, self-worth, and significance (Littauer 22). If people don't have their emotional needs met, their worst sides tend to emerge. For example, if a phlegmatic, an easygoing, type B personality, is in a family of all cholerics, or "go-getter," type A personalities, the phlegmatics may find themselves masking their true personality in order to survive. This can be very draining for phlegmatics, and sooner or later, their negative side will emerge.

Phlegmatics are very adaptable—they get along with everyone 9
because they are able to meet the emotional needs of all the individual personalities. They listen to the sanguine, they follow the choleric, and they support the melancholic. In return, the sanguine entertains them, the choleric motivates them, and the melancholic listens to them. However, if phlegmatics feel like they're being taken for granted, they will become resentful. Since they have an innate need for peace, they won't say anything, and people won't know that there's a problem (Littauer 125).

Even though phlegmatics are often overlooked, they have a lot 10
to contribute with their ability to work under pressure, their diplomatic skill, and their contagious contentment. So the next time you're checking out personalities at a party, try looking for the phlegmatic first—it will be the first step to overcoming the trend of the forgotten personality.

WORKS CITED

Franco, Virginia. "Siblings Birth Order and Personality Types." *Essortment*. Pagewise, Inc., 2002. Web. 21 Nov. 2006.

Funder, D.C. *The Personality Puzzle*. 2nd ed. New York: W.W. Norton, 2001. Print.

Littauer, Florence. *Personality Plus for Couples: Understanding Yourself and the One You Love*. Berrien Springs: Baker Publishing Group, 2001. Print.

Toufexis, Anastasia. "What Makes Them Do It." *Time*. Time, 15 Jan. 1996. Web. 16 Nov. 2006.

Proxemics: A Study of Space and Relationships

Sheila McClain

Western Wyoming Community College
Rock Springs, Wyoming

We all understand the power of personal space: someone standing closer than we expect seems to be invading, while someone giving us a wide berth seems rude, literally "standoffish." But did you know that the use of personal space to communicate is the subject of an academic field called proxemics? Sheila McClain discovered proxemics while researching body language. When body language proved too broad a topic for a focused concept essay, she returned to proxemics in part because "it was a little known term and I felt it would prove interesting and easy for readers to relate to." As you read, notice how McClain moves between the two concepts, allowing the larger, more familiar subject (body language, or "nonverbal communication") to lead her into an explanation of the smaller, less familiar one (proxemics).

Every day we interact and communicate, sometimes without even saying a word. Body language, more formally known as nonverbal communication, speaks volumes about who we are and how we relate to others. As Lester Sielski, an associate professor at the University of West Florida, writes, "Words are beautiful, exciting, important, but we have overestimated them badly—since they are not all or even half the message." He also asserts that "beyond words lies the bedrock on which human relationships are built—nonverbal communication" (Sielski). A group of pscyhology students at the University of Texas recently demonstrated just how profound an effect nonverbal communication can have on people. The students conducted an experiment to test the unspoken rules of behavior on elevators. Boarding a crowded elevator, they would stand facing and grinning at the other people on board. Understandably, the people

1

became uncomfortable; one person even suggested that someone call 911 (Axtell 5–6). Why all the fuss? Unspoken elevator etiquette dictates that one should turn and face the door in a crowded elevator, being careful not to touch anyone else and honoring the sacred personal space of each individual by staring at the floor indicator instead of looking at anyone else. Although they are not written down, strict rules govern our behavior in public situations. This is especially true when space is limited, as on elevators, buses, or subway trains (Axtell 5–6).

Patricia Buhler, an expert in business management and associate professor at Goldey-Beacon College, confirms the large role nonverbal communication plays. She asserts that as little as 8 percent of the message we communicate is made up of words. We communicate the rest of our message, a disproportionately large 92 percent, with body language and other nonverbal forms of communication (Buhler). While researchers have long known that nonverbal cues play a large role in communication, for many years they made no effort to learn more about them (Sielski). Amid rising public interest, several scientists pioneered new research in the field of nonverbal communication in the 1950s. Among these experts was anthropologist Edward T. Hall. He focused on a specific type of nonverbal communication called *proxemics*. Proxemics is the study of how people use space to communicate nonverbally. Whether we are conscious of it or not, our use of space plays a major role in our everyday interactions with others.

A review of some of Dr. Hall's main terms will help us better understand proxemics and appreciate just how much our use of space affects our relationships. For example, according to Dr. Hall, in our everyday interactions, we choose to position ourselves to create either "sociopetal" or "sociofugal" space. Sociopetal space invites communication; sociofugal space is the opposite — it separates people and discourages interaction (Jordan). A student in a school lunchroom may sit alone at an empty table in a corner, away from the other students (creating sociofugal space), or directly across from a person he would like to befriend (creating sociopetal space).

Dr. Hall identifies three kinds of general spaces within which we can create either sociofugal or sociopetal space. These are "fixed-feature space," "semi-fixed feature space," and "informal space" (Jordan). Fixed-feature spaces are hard, if not impossible, for us to control or change. For example, because my college English class is too small for the number of students attending, we have a hard time positioning ourselves so that we can all see the overhead projections. We cannot make the walls of the classroom bigger or the ceiling higher, and the overhead screen is likewise "fixed" in place. We must work within the constraints of the space. A semi-fixed feature space is usually defined by mobile objects such as furniture. The couches and chairs in a living room, for example, may face only the television, thus discouraging conversation and relationship building. But we are able to reposition the furniture to create a more social environment. Informal space is by far the easiest to manipulate. We each control our personal "bubble," and we can set distances between ourselves and others that reflect our relationships with them. Take for example the way that people approach their bosses. A man who is afraid of or dislikes his boss may communicate with her from as far away as possible. He might stand in her doorway to relay a message. Conversely, a woman who has known her boss for many years and is good friends with him might come right in to his office and casually sit down in close proximity to him. Individually, we have a great deal of control over our informal space, and how we use this space can speak volumes about our relationship with others.

After observing many interactions, Dr. Hall broke down infor- 5 mal space further, identifying four distances commonly used by people in their interactions with others: "intimate distance," zero to one and a half feet; "personal distance," one and a half to four feet; "social distance," four to twelve feet; and "public distance," twelve feet and beyond (Beebe, Beebe, and Redmond 231). Intimate distance, as the name suggests, is generally reserved for those people closest to us. Lovemaking, hugging, and holding small children all occur in this zone. The exception to this rule comes when we extend our hand to perfect strangers in greeting, allowing them to briefly enter our intimate space with a handshake. Personal distance, while not as close as intimate, is still reserved for people we know well and with whom we feel comfortable. This zone usually occupies an area relatively close to us. It can at times be applied, however, to include objects we see as extensions of ourselves. For instance, while driving, we may feel our personal space being invaded by a car following behind us too closely. We see our own car as an extension of ourselves and extend our "personal bubble" to include it. Social distance is often considered a respectful distance and is used in many professional business settings as well as in group interactions. There is a public distance between a lecturer and a class, or someone speaking publicly from a podium and his or her audience.

As we have seen, in positioning ourselves in relation to others— especially in choosing nearness or distance—we communicate respect or intimacy, fear or familiarity. We can improve a friendly relationship simply by using a warm, personable distance, or drive potential friends away by seeming cold and distant, or getting quite literally too close for comfort. We can put people at ease or make them uncomfortable just by our proximity to them. The study of nonverbal communication, and specifically proxemics, demonstrates the truth of the old adage, "Actions speak louder than words." 6

WORKS CITED

Axtell, Roger E. *Gestures: the Do's and Taboos of Body Language around the World.* New York: Wiley, 1998. Print.

Beebe, Steven A., Susan J. Beebe, and Mark V. Redmond. *Interpersonal Communication: Relating to Others.* 2nd ed. Boston: Allyn, 1999. Print.

Buhler, Patricia. "Managing in the 90s." *Supervision* 52.9 (1991): 18–21. *EBSCOhost.* Web. 29 Sept. 2004.

Jordan, Sherry. "Embodied Pedagogy: The Body and Teaching Theology." *Teaching Theology and Religion* 4.2 (2001): 98–101. *EBSCOhost.* Web. 29 Sept. 2004.

Sielski, Lester M. "Understanding Body Language." *Personal and Guidance Journal* 57.4 (1979): 238–42. *EBSCOhost.* Web. 29 Sept. 2004.

Patriarchy in the Arab World

Muhammad Memon

University of California, Riverside
Riverside, California

Muhammad Memon was inspired to write this essay after taking a course with Reza Aslan, creative writing professor at UC Riverside and author of one of the books Memon uses as a source. Memon takes on the concept of patriarchy, specifically in the Islamic Arab world. His essay focuses on the historical basis for patriarchy, but draws the reader in with a personal anecdote from 2009 to show that the patriarchal society he is going to discuss is still alive and well today. Using varied sources, including a personal memoir, a collection of scholarly essays, and a magazine article, Memon explains the origins, the effects, and the possible future of male dominance in Islamic societies.

As you read, ask yourself how you think Memon feels about patriarchy in Arab Islamic society. How did you know? How did that affect your reading of the essay?

It was the summer of 2009 when my family and I went to Pakistan. [1] On our way we spent three weeks in the Kingdom of Saudi Arabia. Muslims must go to Saudi Arabia for a religious pilgrimage at least once in their lifetime, given that they are financially and physically capable. During my three weeks there, I observed that the men had great authority while the women were highly restricted and their rights were oppressed. The typical Muslim Arab man walked around with a great sense of pride with his wife tagging along behind him covered in a burka from head to toe and a veil over her face like she was his personal property. In most cases, the men had more than one wife. It is quite evident that patriarchy—male dominance and superiority—has spiraled out of control in Arab Islamic society.

Patriarchy in the Islamic Arab world is based on changing historical tradition and different interpretations of the Quran, the Muslim holy book.

Patriarchy is a social system that dates back to the ancient Romans and Greeks (Longman). Patriarchy can benefit a society in terms of evenly distributing the duties between males and females, and providing each sex with a significant role. However, extreme patriarchic societies, which are the social system in some Middle Eastern nations, are unjust. In the Arab world, the males are understood to be dominant and the more "capable" sex. Even though Islam promotes egalitarianism and the Quran clearly states that man and woman are created equal, the Arab world has ignorantly made man the superior gender. Reza Aslan, author of *No god but God: The Origins, Evolution, and Future of Islam* and professor at the University of California, Riverside, emphasizes the fact that Islam is a highly egalitarian religion and "the Quran goes to great lengths to emphasize the equality of the sexes in the eyes of God" (Aslan 60). The founder of Islam, Prophet Muhammad, accepted polygyny because it was his goal to increase the population of his people during the early seventh century in Arabia. This resulted in Islam allowing a man to have up to four wives, provided it is for lawful reasons (such as taking care of widows and orphans) and he can treat them all equally (Aslan 63). Unfortunately, this concept was abused in the following centuries and it remains a problem to this day.

After Prophet Muhammad passed away in AD 632, the heir to continue the teachings of Islam was Abu Bakr. Abu Bakr's reign was only two and a half years long, and Umar was his successor to continue the legacy (Aslan 118). Aslan describes Umar as being a devout Muslim with strong morals and a peerless valor. However, Umar was aggressive and easily aggravated, especially towards women. He is infamous for his misogynistic ways and he brought about many changes in the role of women. Preaching the women of the community to stay in their homes at all times and preventing them from attending the mosque were some of the things he imposed. Umar also introduced the punishment of stoning adulterers to death (Aslan 71). This punishment became widely used in the Muslim world by extremists such as the Taliban today.

The Quran does not mention stoning to death anywhere; it is reasonable to say that as rulers continued the teachings of Islam, they imposed their own laws which convoluted the religion as a whole. According to Aslan, there have been many scholars who have interpreted the Quran with their own meanings. Some scholars aim to empower women with their interpretation of one verse, while others promote the oppression of women by interpreting the same verse in a different way. For example, verse 34 from chapter four of the Quran has been interpreted as, "Men are the support of women . . ." and as "Men are in charge of women . . ." (Aslan 69–70). The first is translated by Ahmed Ali from the Princeton edition. He interprets it as, "Men are the support of women. . . . As for women you feel are averse, talk to them suasively; then leave them alone in bed (without molesting them) and go to bed with them (when they are willing)" (Aslan 69–70). Ali's goal is to promote authority for women and men by providing each sex with certain duties and the right to choice. The latter is translated by Majid Fakhry, published by New York University. Fakhry has interpreted the same verse as, "Men are in charge of women. . . . And for those [women] that you fear might rebel, admonish them and abandon them in their beds and beat them" (Aslan 70). In opposition to Ali's translation, Fakhry's undermines women's rights and grants men authority over them. It goes to great lengths to give males the authority to beat females when they feel it is necessary. The Arabic language varies in its meanings, which is the reason that both translations are correct (Aslan 69–70). Every verse in the Quran has been interpreted with various meanings, leaving one to decide what he/she wants to believe. Unfortunately, when it comes to women's rights, the interpretations suppressing their role in society became widely respected throughout the Muslim world.

Women continued to be oppressed by their role in the "traditional" Arab family as new rulers, clans, and empires continued the Islamic teachings in Arabia. From the seventh century until the nineteenth century, Islam went through a major reformation period which impacted women's rights negatively. According to Judith Tucker, editor of *Arab Women: Old Boundaries, New Frontiers*, the female's role in the Arab family had become powerless and the male controlled all aspects of her life (Tucker 197). In this family model, the female is perceived to be one who does the housework and satisfies her husband. Tucker also explains that females are usually married at a very young age, while they are still seen to be pure and moral. A female child of a middle-class Arab family is usually married to a cousin based on the choice of her father or her brother. However, the marriage of Arab women and their position in the Arab family vary based on their social class (Tucker 198–200). Malika Oufkir, author of *Stolen Lives: Twenty Years in a Desert Jail,* was raised from the age of five in the palace of the King of Morocco. Although Morocco is a relatively liberal society, it is evident that it is also plagued by rigorous patriarchy and male superiority. Oufkir and the other girls and women who lived in the palace had all the luxuries in life, but were merely the king's property, to be treated the way he desired. Oufkir seems very fond of her material possessions when she was a young girl; however, when she transforms into a woman, she realizes that she is not meant to live her life like a prisoner or a woman who is the property of another man. Living in the palace, she observes that the concubines have everything they want, but they do not have freedom. Oufkir repeatedly expresses her desire to have the freedom to live her life and pursue her dreams. She vividly shows that men were clearly the superior gender in that society, and had authority over all aspects of the women's lives.

Oufkir and Aslan both provide insight on women's recent condi- 6 tions in the Arab world. Oufkir states, "In recent years, the concubines' caged regime has become more relaxed. They go about unveiled and without curtains at the windows of their cars" (Oufkir 41). Women throughout the Muslim world are fighting for their rights by providing awareness and a translation of the Quran that promotes equality. Shirin Ebadi won the Nobel Peace Prize in 2003 for her great efforts in defending women's rights in Iran. As she accepted her prize, she said, "God created us all as equals. . . . By fighting for equal status, we are doing what God wants us to do" (Aslan 74). Muslim feminists around the world are striving to transform the society to the way Prophet Muhammad had intended it to be. During Muhammad's prophecy, women prayed with men, made political/religious decisions, and had the authority to reprimand their husbands (Aslan 74). Muslim feminists like Shirin Ebadi highly emphasize the fact that Islam is an egalitarian religion. According to feminists, Muslim men, not the religion of Islam, are responsible for suppressing women's rights.

Although patriarchy in Arab society is being challenged by femi- 7 nists and human rights activists, it may still survive into the future. Phillip Longman, a writer for the New America Foundation, says, "Like it or not, a growing proportion of the next generation will be born into families who believe that father knows best" (Longman).

Longman points out the incentives for patriarchy and he believes that patriarchy is the reason that the human species is still abundant. Fiercely individualistic societies such as Japan, the Scandinavian countries, and the United States suffer from a declining birth rate. These countries promote equality of the sexes, which gives males and females the same authority when it comes to marriage and raising a family (Longman). This results in people not marrying, marrying but not having children, or marrying late and producing fewer offspring. Longman points out that while the population declines in these countries, other countries with a patriarchal society will have an increased population over time. According to Longman, this will result in the people of the patriarchal societies being the majority around the world, because "population becomes power." Islamic Arab patriarchy, based on centuries of tradition and certain interpretations of the Quran, may survive in the future because of the higher populations of patriarchal countries.

WORKS CITED

Aslan, Reza. *No god but God: The Origins, Evolution, and Future of Islam.* New York: Random House, 2006. Print.

Longman, Phillip. "The Return of Patriarchy." *Foreign Policy.* The Slate Group, 17 Feb. 2006. Web. 21 Feb. 2010.

Oufkir, Malika. *Stolen Lives: Twenty Years in a Desert Jail.* New York: Miramax Books, 2002. Print.

Tucker, Judith E., ed. *Arab Women: Old Boundaries, New Frontiers.* Bloomington: Indiana UP, 1993. Print.

The Disorder That Hides Within

Max Wu

University of California, Riverside
Riverside, California

Mental illness can be difficult to explain to those who don't suffer from it. Max Wu, explaining social phobia, begins his essay by calling up a familiar fear: public speaking. He then relates that common fear to a far more extreme form of the same fear: social phobia. By relating his concept to something that readers will likely be familiar with, he draws readers in and awakens their curiosity. Wu then clearly explains the disorder's symptoms, effects, and treatments, and uses research to support his claims. As you read, consider how the title of Wu's essay relates to his description of social phobia and to the examples he provides.

Are you afraid of speaking in front of an audience? Do you get jitters and "butterflies in your stomach" as you approach the stage with weak knees? "Yes," he says. "Of course, all the time," she replies. Do you feel your general social performance in the world is so inadequate that you escape any and every instance where you might face public scrutiny? Ask this question and the room goes quiet. The fact of the matter is, most people get nervous and loathe the idea of public speaking, but some people feel nervous in every social situation. This fear of social scrutiny is referred to by mental health professionals as "social phobia." What separates common stage fright from social phobia is that social phobia is a crippling disorder that can obstruct a healthy lifestyle. However, it is easily treated once the individual realizes he or she needs help. 1

Social phobia is difficult to diagnose because of the way patients seem to subconsciously mask their abnormal behavior and practices. 2

In an article written for *The Irish Times,* Marie Murray describes in great detail the actions that many patients practice that make it hard for the outside world to spot a problem. A clinical psychologist at University College Dublin, Murray has observed many students with social phobia and has made some breakthrough discoveries that have helped doctors around the world deal with the mystery surrounding social phobia. An unfortunate facet of social phobia that Murray observes is that "people become trapped by their false belief of how they appear to other people and . . . are unable to see evidence of when they are being successful in social encounters" (Murray 11). People with social phobia have a distorted view of the world that develops over time to a point where they become clinically depressed and believe that the world is against them. This hazy view of the world grows day by day as normal conversation becomes interpreted as personal attacks time and time again.

Murray also observed that patients with social phobia engage in   3
activities that they feel make them more confident but in reality distance themselves from others and end up hurting their own psychological well-being. Murray knows this disorder is incredibly difficult to cope with and feels that the most important step in curing these people is to allow them to identify their own fears and understand that these fears are common and able to be overcome.

J.A. den Boer, a professor of psychiatry and author of an article   4
on social phobia in the *British Medical Journal,* has dedicated a large part of her career to research about social phobia. Through her numerous studies, she concludes that "social phobia is a poorly investigated and misunderstood condition" (den Boer 796). She finds that social phobia starts when a child is under five years old and "may abruptly follow a stressful or humiliating experience" (797). After years and years of these unfortunate experiences, "the course of the disease is lifelong and unremitting unless treated" (797). Many patients who suffer from the disorder do not realize that the pain they have to endure is that of social phobia and thus further delay their treatment, which den Boer claims leads to increased risks of suicide (798).

Social phobia has not been well documented in the past or well   5
diagnosed, but proper diagnosis and treatment are possible. In order to properly diagnose a patient, doctors need to pay close attention to the patient's medical history for any sign of events that might have triggered symptoms of the condition. The Diagnostic and Sta-

tistical Manual of Mental Disorders, or DSM-III-R, published by the American Psychiatric Association, issues criteria that must be met to diagnose social phobia. Drawing from the DSM-III-R, a doctor would ask questions about how the patient would deal with certain social situations and the responses would determine the severity of the disorder.

After a patient realizes that something must be done to free 6 their lives from social phobia, what treatments are available? What can be done to free a mind from deep-seated nervousness and fear of humiliation that it has grown to accept? One promising form of treatment is being developed in Australia by by Professor Gavin Andrews, the head of the clinical research unit at St. Vincent's Hospital (Fallon 16). Andrews invented a character named John, a first-year college student with social phobia. John has trouble going to class and surviving at school because of the overwhelming case of social phobia that haunts his daily life. By using this generic character in an online treatment program, Andrews manages to help those who feel trapped in their lives that would never have surfaced to receive treatment for their crippling disorder. Using "online exposure therapy, computer-aided training programs, virtual reality technology and enhanced cognitive behavioral therapies" (Fallon 17), Andrews successfully treated the almost 550 patients he received in the first year of his online treatment program, curing half of them completely. It can be difficult for sufferers to seek treatment. In a study Andrews conducted in 2004, he found that 24 percent of Australians with agoraphobia (the fear of public places) and 7 percent of Australians with social phobia surface to receive medical attention from professionals (Fallon 17). The disorder is not difficult to cure, but sufferers must first confront their fears before they can find lasting relief.

Although social phobia was not well documented or often diag- 7 nosed in the past, doctors are becoming increasingly aware of how to identify and treat the disorder. Today, numerous treatment strategies exist, and sufferers are finding relief. Hopefully soon, the excessive fear of social situations will plague only a scarce minority.

WORKS CITED

den Boer, J.A. "Social Phobia: Epidemiology, Recognition, and Treatment." *BMJ* 315.7111 (1997): 796–800. *JSTOR*. Web. 7 Nov. 2009.

Fallon, Mary. "When Fear Takes Over." *Sydney Morning Herald* 28 May 2009, first ed., Health and Science sec.: 17. *LexisNexis Academic*. Web. 7 Nov. 2009.

Murray, Marie. "Anxiety Disorder Leaves You in Fear of Social Situations." *The Irish Times* 1 Apr. 2008: 11. *LexisNexis Academic*. Web. 8 Nov. 2009.

The Art and Creativity of Stop-Motion

William Tucker

University of California, Riverside
Riverside, California

For this assignment, William Tucker knew that he wanted to write on film or animation, but he realized that both "film" and "animation" were far too broad to cover in one essay. Instead, Tucker narrowed his topic to stop-motion animation, a subcategory that caught his interest.

Although stop-motion animation is one of the oldest techniques in film animation, it is still popular both on the big screen and on YouTube. Tucker explains the concept by defining it, explaining its history, narrating the process used to make stop-motion films, and providing examples of popular stop-motion films. The enthusiasm for stop-motion Tucker developed while writing this essay ultimately led him to make his own film. (To see it, search for "Skepsis Stop Motion" at http://video.google.com.) As you read his essay, consider whether Tucker's enthusiasm is contagious: does his explanation of stop-motion animation inspire you to try your own hand at it?

Cinematography and filmmaking are present everywhere in American society today. It is virtually impossible to go about your day without occasionally seeing a motion picture, whether it is a sitcom, an advertisement, or an instructional video. The process of producing films has changed in the past century and many techniques have been invented and perfected. One style of film in particular has proven to stand the test of time. The style can be seen in popular productions such as *Gumby, Chicken Run, Fantastic Mr. Fox,* and the original *Godzilla* and *King Kong* movies. It played a key role in the origin of

1

69

film and continues to be a relevant art form in the filming community, used both by famous Hollywood directors and by independent film students alike. It inspires creativity. This style, stop-motion film, is both the alpha and the omega of film and cinematography.

Stop-motion, also known as frame-by-frame film production, is an animation technique in which a still camera photographs an object which is moved very small distances at a time. When these still images are played back quickly, they create the illusion of movement. The frame rate, or fps (the speed at which the individual photos are shown during the sequence), varies. The original stop-motion films usually never reached over 20 fps, because of the limitations of older technology (Johnson). However, today most stop-motion films vary from 25 fps to as high as 30 fps, depending on how quickly the director wants the inanimate object to appear to move (Johnson). 2

The technique of stop-motion is nearly as old as the motion picture itself. Albert E. Smith and J. Stuart Blackton are credited with being the first to use the technique in their 1898 film, *Humpty Dumpty Circus,* where toys and puppets appear to come alive on screen (Delahoyde). Stop-motion grew in popularity as it allowed directors to depict fantasy and imagination while still providing realistic-looking scenes. For example, before computer-generated imagery (CGI), if a director wanted to make a dinosaur movie, the director could dress humans in dinosaur costumes, hire animators to create a hand-drawn animated film, or use stop-motion with clay dinosaur figurines. Using dinosaur costumes would be easier than using stop-motion, but it would more often than not make the dinosaurs look tacky and unreal. Hand-drawn animation is lovely, but two-dimensional. A stop-motion film takes a long time and meticulous work to create, but it captivates audiences with its more authentic and "real" look. During the beginning years of animated film, stop-motion was critically acclaimed, winning many Oscars in the animated film categories. 3

Stop-motion animators soon began to use clay figurines as the main focus in stop-motion films; this technique is now known as claymation. Clay figurines allow inanimate objects to take on human-like characteristics and are easy to manipulate quickly between individual photographs. Famous claymation stop-motion films include the hit 70s television show *Gumby* and the short film *Vincent,* which helped a young Tim Burton attract the attention of Walt Disney Studios (Dela- 4 hoyde). Burton would go on to revolutionize the stop-motion industry by crafting feature-length stop-motion films, such as *The Nightmare before Christmas, James and the Giant Peach,* and *The Corpse Bride* ("Tim Burton").

Stop-motion not only requires creativity but also patience and precision. With stop-motion films now playing back at as high as 30 fps, nearly 9,000 individual photographs are needed for just 5 minutes worth of footage. Because of this, most stop-motion films, even those with a professional crew, are in production for as long as three years (Delahoyde). Stop-motion directors begin each scene by choosing an inanimate object to be the focus point of the scene. After the object is chosen, it is photographed and moved less than an inch between individual photographs. The camera is placed in a stationary position (a tripod is almost a necessity in order to keep the camera focusing on the same exact location for each photo) (Delahoyde). A major problem that stop-motion enthusiasts face is making sure that the backgrounds of frames are similar to one another. If the background is not exactly the same for each frame, noticeable errors like splotches and blurs can occur. Also, if the background is inconsistent, the film will look less convincing, and may even give the audience headaches from the lack of visual consistency. For this reason most creators shoot inside and make their own backgrounds, either by drawing one or by making a CGI-based background ("Stop Motion Filming Technique").

Those brave enough to shoot a stop-motion film outdoors must take into account all the variables that can hurt the overall presentation of their film. If the film is being shot in a crowded place, the creator cannot allow pictures to be taken with people in the background. People in the background of the shot will cause inconsistency in the frames which will appear as colored splotches in the film, especially if the frame rate is extremely high ("Stop Motion Filming Technique"). Stop-motion directors must also take into account the weather and brightness of the outdoors. Since the process of taking photos for a stop-motion film takes an exorbitant amount of time, people making films may have to plan on being outdoors shooting a scene for many hours. Lighting changes as the sun moves throughout the day. If the outdoor scene doesn't have consistent lighting because of the sun's movements, the scenes may suffer from unwanted shadows and different lighting at separate points in the scene. Consistency and attention to detail are the foundations of stop-motion film. They are perhaps the most important factor separating professional stop-motion films from amateur films.

Stop-motion still plays a key role in the filming world today. It has inspired new film art forms that are heavily used. For example, time lapse photography is a well-known technique used in film to quickly show the passing of time. Stop-motion helped lead to the time-lapse technique by stringing together individual photographs in order to represent movement and time ("Stop Motion Photography"). The time-lapse process does take longer than typical stop-motion. In time-lapse photography, a camera focuses on an object for as long as a year, taking pictures periodically of the slow changes that occur. Then the many pictures are played in quick succession to show the changes. Popular subjects include the growth and blooming of a flower, a day and night's worth of city traffic, and the movement of the sun and moon. These scenes in nature take anywhere from a day to an entire year to take place, but with time-lapse/stop-motion the entire process can be viewed in as little as ten seconds, which creates an interesting illusion for the audience. 7

Although newer forms of cinematography are constantly being invented and revised, stop-motion will forever be important in the film community. It was there at the origin of film, and will likely survive into the future. Although CGI has become the industry standard for movie animation, stop-motion is still flourishing. Popular Internet streaming sites, such as YouTube, allow creators to post their stop-motion videos and let them be viewed by a wide audience. Some of the most popular films on the Internet today are stop-motion films, receiving hundreds of thousands of views daily. This art form will forever captivate viewers and inspire ingenuity, whether it is used for a simple amateur video or a feature-length film of epic proportions. 8

WORKS CITED

"Tim Burton Talking about Animation." *Tim Burton Dream Site*. Minadream .com, n.d. Web. 6 Nov. 2008.

Delahoyde, Michael. "Stop-Motion Animation." *Dino-Source*. Washington State U, 25 Apr. 2006. Web. 7 Nov. 2008.

Johnson, Dave. "Make a Time-Lapse Movie." *Washington Post*. Washington Post, 9 Nov. 2005. Web. 5 Nov. 2008.

"Stop Motion Filming Technique." *Thinkquest*. Thinkquest, 1999. Web. 6 Nov. 2008.

"Stop Motion Photography." *SciFi2K*. SciFi2K, 11 Jan. 2004. Web. 6 Nov. 2008.

5 Finding Common Ground

Every day, high-stakes issues fill the airwaves and the Internet and crowd the pages of newspapers and magazines. Most issues we only glance at, while a few may engage us deeply—either because we are curious or because we recognize that the outcome of these issues is important to us personally: Should prayer be permitted in public schools? Should an underage girl be required to get her parents' permission to have an abortion? Should online search engines release individuals' search records to researchers or businesses? Should phone and cable providers be able to charge Web users differently for different levels of service?

By definition, a controversial issue is unsettled, unresolved. A debate swirls around it. As we read or listen to this debate, we may be inclined at first to take sides. Often, however, if we pay closer attention, we realize that the issues aren't as black-and-white as they sometimes seem. In order to truly understand what's at stake and take a responsible position on an issue, we need to take some preliminary steps: specifically, we need to analyze and explain the debate and then seek common ground among various existing positions.

The analysis and explanation of debates can be informative to readers who want to understand issues of the day. They can also clarify and even help resolve immediate dangers or crises in a business or corporation; inform debate in an elected governing body, like a city council or the United States Senate; or introduce newcomers to an ongoing debate among experts over an important academic discipline, like those from which you choose your college courses.

However, simply explaining the debate is not always enough. If we can identify *common ground* among the stakeholders in the argument—that is, if we can identify points on which they might be able to agree—we can move beyond analysis and move toward *synthesis*. Essays that attempt to find common ground do not simply explain both sides or make arguments in support of one side or another; instead, they analyze the concerns shared by those who argue on one side or another and discuss ways in which seemingly irreconcilable positions might in fact be amenable to compromise or consensus, at least in part.

In "Finding Common Ground," a chapter that's new to the ninth edition of *The St. Martin's Guide to Writing,* we ask students to think more deeply about conflicting opinions. Instead of asking you to merely understand and then write about both sides of the issue, we encourage you to take a closer look into what the stakeholders have in common. If they truly had nothing in common, there would be nothing to argue about. What motivating forces are at work? What is at stake? And what shared values are driving the parties to argue?

You will encounter many disciplinary debates in your college career, whether you focus on sociology, anthropology, cosmology, education, philosophy, botany, geology, aeronautical engineering, or history. By attempting to find the common ground behind these debates, you will hone your analytical skills and broaden your perspective, allowing you to imagine new solutions and acquire greater understanding of your field. Practice in explaining, analyzing, and finding common ground among different positions in a debate will in turn allow you to join the debate, arguing vigorously and responsibly in support of a position of your own.

The three essays in this section were written the first time that this new chapter was taught, at University of California, Riverside. The writers bravely tackled issues that have strong supporters and detractors—the role of the government in regulating gambling in the United States, the controversial case of adventurer Chris McCandless, and whether video game violence adversely affects children. The work these students did serves as a strong model for any serious student attempting to navigate the shoals of a contemporary controversy.

Note: Because we need more essays finding common ground for the next edition of *Sticks and Stones,* we hope you will consider sending us your essay to consider. You will find guidelines for doing so on p. 217.

Gambling and Government Restriction

Luke Serrano

University of California, Riverside
Riverside, California

For some people, gambling is a harmless diversion, and a chance to win a few extra dollars. For others, it is an addiction that draws them away from their families and into unpayable debt. Should people be allowed to have their fun, or should the government step in to prevent them from developing a crippling gambling addiction? In this essay, Luke Serrano examines these opposing positions as presented by a pair of psychologists specializing in gambling addictions, and a financial analyst. Serrano clearly presents the two sides' arguments, but achieves the goal of the assignment by finding what they have in common: a belief that compulsive gambling is real, and serious. As you read, think about how harmful something has to be before you believe the government should ban or regulate it.

Throughout history people have looked for sources of entertainment to temporarily take their minds off of responsibilities and problems. While some people are satisfied with a simple game or a television show, others have the desire to make their entertainment even more interesting by investing money in it. Having something at stake in a game provides people with a rush that does not come from simply playing the game. Archaeological evidence suggests that gambling dates as far back as 2300 BC to ancient China, India, Egypt, and Rome ("The History of Gambling" 1). However, almost as long as there has been gambling, there have been people trying to put an end to it. Authority figures have noticed that gambling can serve as a distraction that keeps people away from what they are supposed to be doing. In medieval England, gambling was outlawed when King Henry VIII discovered that his soldiers were spending more time gambling than working on drills and marksmanship (1). In the United States, gambling was outlawed in Nevada until 1931 when casino gaming was legalized and Las Vegas began its rise as one of the largest gambling hot spots in the world (1). It now brings in over 30 billion dollars in revenue each year (Dunstan 2). Two main views of gambling have arisen from the effects it has had on people. Both sides believe government regulation has a great effect on gamblers, and that gambling addiction is a real problem that requires treatment. Their viewpoints diverge because one side believes that gambling causes serious problems and should be illegal; the other believes that gambling is not a problem and that restrictions do more harm than good.

Those who argue that gambling is a problem point to the personal and social issues created by those who gamble too much. Arnie and Sheila Wexler are both certified compulsive gambling counselors in New Jersey. Sheila developed the compulsive gambling treatment program at the New Hope Foundation in Marlboro, New Jersey (Wexler and Wexler 1). The Wexlers firmly believe that compulsive gambling is a disease similar to drug and alcohol addiction. They argue that "the disease can be much more insidious [than drug or alcohol addiction] because it is more difficult to detect and can have a more devastating effect on friends and families" (2). The devastating effects compulsive gambling can have on people have led the Wexlers to call for the outlawing of gambling in the United States. 2

Some people, however, believe that compulsive gambling is not a pressing issue. Quantitative analyst Guy Calvert represents a Wall Street firm and is an adamant believer that the growing prevalence of compulsive gambling is just an exaggeration (Calvert 1). In his essay "The Government Should Respect Individuals' Freedom to Gamble," Calvert says, "individuals should not be prohibited from gambling just because some people find it addictive" and he claims the "dangers of prohibiting gambling outweigh the benefits" (1). 3

The argument for the prohibition of gambling centers on the detrimental effects that gambling can have on people. The Wexlers argue that compulsive gambling is "a progressive disease" that goes through phases (Wexler and Wexler 3). The first phase of gambling addiction is the phase in which the gambler reports a series of wins or streaks. This phase can reoccur throughout the gambling addiction, but the initial win streak is the hook that draws the gambler in 4

(Wexler and Wexler 3). This hook gives the gambler a taste of wealth and the illusion that the wealth and luck will continue. The next phase of compulsive gambling is the losing phase. The losing phase is the phase in which gamblers lose the money that they might have won and begin to chase their losses (Wexler and Wexler 3). At this point, the gambler begins to borrow money to cover bets that he or she cannot pay. This is when the desperation phase begins. It is the last phase, at which point the gambler will do anything to put down the next bet (Wexler and Wexler 3). Family, friends, and work no longer matter. The desire to get the same rush as from the first big win is the only thing that matters. Families are destroyed, friendships are ruined, and careers are lost because the gambler cannot go without betting long enough to take care of responsibilities. Studies estimate that "the number of compulsive gamblers in this country is between 10 million and 12 million, approximately 5 percent of the general population" (Wexler and Wexler 5). The sheer number of compulsive gamblers and the devastation that comes with them are the reasons that the Wexlers believe the only viable action is the prohibition of gambling.

In contrast to the prohibition argument, the no-restrictions argument says the prohibition of gambling would be detrimental to the United States. Calvert argues that measures to suppress gambling would "usher in a new era of public corruption, compromising the integrity of government officials, judges, and the police" (2). He gives the prohibition of alcohol as an example of what would happen if gambling became illegal (Calvert 1). Crime would rise because of the underground lifestyle that is brought with illegal gambling. In addition to being harmful, Calvert says, the prohibition would be unnecessary because most people do gamble responsibly. Most people who go to casinos "are not crazed, welfare-dependent casino desperadoes; they are in many respects better off than the average American." Studies show that the average household income of casino players is 28 percent higher than that of the U.S. population (Calvert 4). Gambling is used the majority of the time as a source of entertainment, not as a fix for the compulsive gambler. Furthermore, the banning of gambling would not deter the truly compulsive gambler (Calvert 2). It is the nature of an addict to find the next fix no matter what the cost. Illegality would do nothing to stop the compulsive gambler, just as heroin's being illegal does nothing to stop the junkie. Like an alcoholic or drug addict, a compulsive gambler has to want to get help to get better.

Although the two parties disagree on whether the government 6
should regulate gambling, they do agree that compulsive gambling is
a problem and an addiction. In one instance described by the Wexlers,
a man came to a treatment center and seemed to be having with-
drawal symptoms after a gambling binge. He had dilated pupils, he
was sweating and shaking, and he suffered severe mood swings
(Wexler and Wexler 2). The similarities between compulsive gambling
and drug and alcohol addiction are undeniable. Calvert agrees, saying,
"pathological gambling can and sometimes does result in genuine
human misery" (Calvert 5). Both parties agree that this is a problem
that needs to be solved. People who have gambling problems need
treatment because without it there is no stopping the addiction.

In 1996, members of an estimated 32 percent of all U.S. house- 7
holds gambled at a casino, amounting to about 176 million visits to
casinos (Calvert 2). These staggering numbers show that gambling
has a great effect on Americans, whether it is positive or negative.
The arguments both for and against gambling bring forth valid
points. On the one hand, the prohibition argument claims compulsive gambling is a serious problem and the only way to stop it is
by prohibiting gambling completely. On the other hand, the pro-
gambling supporters argue that gambling is a legitimate institution which provides entertainment and economic growth for the
United States; moreover, this party argues that the prohibition of
gambling would cause more harm than good for the American people. Despite the different opinions that exist about gambling, it is a
large part of American recreation and is an issue that should not be
taken lightly.

WORKS CITED

Calvert, Guy. "The Government Should Respect Individuals' Freedom to
    Gamble." *Gambling*. Ed. James D. Torr. San Diego: Greenhaven P, 2002.
    N. pag. Excerpt from "Gambling America: Balancing the Risks of Gam-
    bling and Its Regulation." Cato Policy Analysis 18 June 1999. *Opposing
    Viewpoints Resource Center*. Web. 1 Dec. 2009.
Dunstan, Roger. "Pivotal Dates in Gambling History." *American Gaming
    Association*. American Gaming Association, 2003. Web. 2 Dec. 2009.
"The History of Gambling." *Gambling PhD*. Gambling PhD.com, 2003. Web.
    2 Dec. 2009.

Wexler, Arnie, and Sheila Wexler. "The Hidden Addiction: Compulsive Gambling." *Legalized Gambling*. Ed. Mary E. Williams. San Diego: Greenhaven P, 1999. N. pag. Contemporary Issues Companion Ser. Rept. of "The Hidden Addiction." Professional Counselor June 1997: n.pag. Opposing Viewpoints Resource Center. Web. 1 Dec. 2009.

Chris McCandless: His Supporters and Critics

Eve Lee

University of California, Riverside
Riverside, California

In April 1992, adventurer Chris McCandless struck out alone into the Alaskan wilderness. According to his own diary and the accounts of those who met him on his journey, he packed few supplies and planned to rely only on his physical strength and foraging skills. He found an abandoned van near Denali National Park and Preserve and used it for shelter; he survived for 113 days by hunting and foraging. Author Jon Krakauer based *Into the Wild* on Chris McCandless's story; the book was made into a film in 2007.

After the publication of *Into the Wild,* McCandless became a nationally known figure. While some have painted him as a fearless, independent spirit whose only crime was too much faith in his abilities, others see him as a fool, and a bad example to those who would try to follow in his footsteps. Eve Lee takes on this polarizing figure through the opinions of Jon Krakauer himself, along with those of Terry Tomalin, a journalist. As you read, notice how Lee smoothly integrates quotations into her sentences and paragraphs, to scaffold her own ideas with her sources.

Chris McCandless's journey to Alaska has been a controversial topic 1
ever since writer Jon Krakauer first reported on it in *Outside* magazine in 1993. People have differing opinions about Chris McCandless and his adventure. While Krakauer, a defender of McCandless, believes that he was just a determined adventurer, critics such as Terry Tomalin, a journalist, believe that McCandless was an overeager and foolish man. Krakauer seems to respect McCandless's actions, comparing him to a monk and stating, "one is moved by [his] courage, [his] reckless innocence, and the urgency of [his] desire"

(97). McCandless's critics argue that McCandless was a "kook" and that "[he] had already gone over the edge and just happened to hit bottom in Alaska" (Krakauer 71). Although both sides disagree on many points, they acknowledge that Chris McCandless was an intelligent man, that his solitary journey to Alaska intentionally lacked thorough plans, and that he did not go to Alaska to commit suicide.

Critics and supporters alike agree that McCandless was deliber- 2 ately journeying with minimal supplies, although they do not agree with that decision. McCandless's critics do not understand or support his decision to journey without proper equipment and backup plans. Terry Tomalin, for example, the outdoors and fitness editor of the *St. Petersburg Times,* wonders why McCandless didn't use the $24,000 his parents had given him for college to get "the best outdoors gear money could buy." In addition, he argues "[had McCandless] brought a map, he would have seen there was an avenue of escape within a day's walk. Had he told a friend or relative where he was going and when he planned to return, he might have been rescued." Critics deem McCandless's actions to be arrogant, and they believe he was "lucky" to have survived for as long as he did (Krakauer 71–72). This is evident when Krakauer states that "[b]y design McCandless came into the country with insufficient provisions, and he lacked certain pieces of equipment deemed essential" (180). Krakauer even cites a critic who thinks McCandless was "purposely ill-prepared" (Krakauer 71).

Krakauer, on the other hand, seems able to relate to and under- 3 stand McCandless's need to forsake everyone and everything during his great experiment in the wild. He suggests that his ability to empathize with McCandless may be because he had problems with his father, as McCandless did. Krakauer seems to see himself mirrored in McCandless: "we had a similar intensity, a similar heedlessness, a similar agitation of the soul" (155). He understands that McCandless thought if he got down to basics, like Thoreau, he could "fix all that was wrong with [his] life."

While critics assume that McCandless's lack of planning was ig- 4 norance, arrogance, or carelessness, Krakauer argues that McCandless "knew precisely what was at stake" (181). According to him, "McCandless, in his fashion, merely took risk-taking to its logical extreme." Because he thinks McCandless just wanted to see how far he could push himself, while trying his best to come out unscathed, Krakauer is convinced McCandless did not intend to kill himself (156).

He claims "McCandless's death was unplanned, that it was a terrible accident" (134). Tomalin agrees. He interprets McCandless's "forag[ing] for wild plants" as evidence that he was fighting for his life.

Nevertheless, the two sides disagree on the cause of McCandless's death. Tomalin believes that the desperation and "panic" of starving, coupled with eating the "wrong" seeds, led to McCandless's death. He explains: "It is that critical moment that panic rears its ugly head. Give in to it, you die. Resist, you live." Krakauer believes that McCandless did not eat naturally poisonous seeds. Instead he argues that McCandless made an error, and put nontoxic wild potato seeds in a damp plastic bag, causing them to rot, and making them poisonous and fatal (194).

Chris McCandless's death garnered much attention because of the strange circumstances in which it occurred. It is not unexpected that an unprepared person would die in the wilderness, but it is strange that someone would go into the wilderness unprepared. Like in every mystery, there are many factors to consider. At first, critics and supporters of McCandless appear to view his story in drastically opposing ways—critics think he was foolish, but supporters see something in him to admire. However, both proponents and opponents of McCandless agree that he was an intelligent young man seeking adventure. A critic named Nick Jans states that McCandless "overestimated [himself]" and "underestimated the country" (Krakauer 71). Krakauer asserts that "[McCandless] wasn't incompetent—he wouldn't have lasted 113 days if he were" (85). They also believe that Chris McCandless made some regrettable decisions that could have saved his life. Krakauer states that there were "avoidable blunders" (Krakauer 185). Unfortunately, since it is impossible for McCandless to change his actions, the most people can do is "learn from his mistakes," according to Tomalin, and hope that he died peacefully.

WORKS CITED

Krakauer, Jon. *Into the Wild*. 1996. New York: Random House/Anchor Books, 1997. Print.

Tomalin, Terry. "Mistakes Can Be Deadly in the Wild." *St. Petersburg Times* 16 Nov. 2007, South Pinellas ed., sports: 2C. *Academic via LexisNexis*. Web. 3 Dec. 2009.

Virtual Reality?
Chris Sexton

University of California, Riverside
Riverside, California

In the past three decades, video games have evolved from simple side-scrolling, two-dimensional, eight-bit entertainment for children into cinematic, realistic, completely engaging environments for players young and old. As the quality of the technology has increased, so have the violence level and emotional intensity of many popular games. Parents and critics have been left to wonder whether this increased realism will blur the line for children between fiction and reality, and whether it could lead to real-world violence. And, although psychologists have studied the effects of video games on children, their results have been inconclusive.

In his essay, Chris Sexton presents the opposing viewpoints about video game violence, and particularly about the Grand Theft Auto franchise. He outlines the history of the controversy, and the range of opinions about violent video games. Although the sides disagree, he finds that they all support increased parental awareness of the content of video games. As you read, notice the variety of stakeholders that Sexton cites, and think about what their motivations might be.

A car whizzes through rush hour traffic with the ferocity of an un- 1
caged lion, barreling over pedestrians like a student driver knocks around traffic cones. Following this car is a steadily growing armada of police cars. The driver of the car makes a series of sharp turns at a pace that would make a NASCAR racer jealous, knocking cars aside like tumbleweeds in the road. More and more police are joining the fray, and on the horizon, they have set up a roadblock to put an end to this rampage. The driver of the car tries to double back, but he is soon caught in a storm of twisted metal. He takes off in any direc-

tion he can go at lightning speed, and hits an oncoming car with an extreme force. The police surround the car, and it is not long before the game ends and the perpetrator is shot dead.

This is not a scene from a car chase on the news, but from a video game. Depending on your perspective, this is either compelling entertainment or a frightening depiction of murder and crime. A debate has raged on for over a decade now, with some claiming that video games like this have a detrimental effect on the development of children. Others believe that games are not behavior-altering, and are an acceptable form of entertainment. While they have different perspectives on how violent games affect people, both sides of this issue agree on the need for a strong ratings system and parental responsibility.

Video-game violence came to the forefront of the news after the shooting at Columbine High School in 1999. When the perpetrators of this horrible crime were discovered to have been fans of the first-person shooter *Doom,* a violent science-fiction game with blood and gore, many were concerned that this game was the cause of it all. While both shooters had a variety of psychological issues, the fact that they were avid video-game players stuck out in the minds of many. Concerned parents believed there had to be a correlation between playing violent games like *Doom* and committing real-life violence. When *Grand Theft Auto III* was released in 2001, the issue got even more attention. Set in a fictional New York City, the game allowed players the freedom to kill civilians and police officers. Taking video-game violence from a science-fiction setting like *Doom* into a reality-based setting like *Grand Theft Auto* made parents' concerns even stronger.

The idea that video games are dangerous and cause violence, however, may be a misconception. According to a study from Swinburne University of Technology in Melbourne, Australia, only children who were already more predisposed to aggression reacted in a negative manner to video games ("Most Kids 'Unaffected' by Violent Games"). The researchers studied the behavior of 120 children aged 11 to 15 after exposure to the violent game *Quake II,* and did not see adequate evidence that video games are a major factor in affecting behavior ("Most Kids"). In fact, as Professor Grant Devilly said, hyperactive children actually became less aggressive while playing violent games, and most children showed no negative or positive effects from the video games at all ("Most Kids"). In regard to the notion that video games cause violence, Devilly notes "It's the only message parents have ever received and it's just not accurate" ("Most Kids").

Other studies have conflicted with this one, though. Research 5 by Iowa State University psychologists showed that violence in the media, and specifically video games, had a behavioral effect on children ("ISU psychologists publish three new studies on violent video game effects on youths"). They tested 161 nine- to twelve-year-olds, as well as 354 college students, and found that even depictions of cartoon violence could cause negative effects on brain development ("ISU psychologists"). They concluded that the act of intentionally harming another character in a game could affect behavior in the real world as well ("ISU psychologists"). While movies have for a long time shown graphic violence, the participant role that video games give players can affect their behavior in a way that movies and music do not. This study supports the notion that young children can become more aggressive in real life due to excessive video-game playing. However, research has not completely proven yet whether or not video games make young people more violent.

The video game depicted in the introduction of this essay is 6 *Grand Theft Auto IV*, released in 2008 by Rockstar Games for the Xbox 360, Playstation 3, and PC. Games in the *Grand Theft Auto* series are "sandbox games," games that let players roam the virtual world and complete missions and objectives in any order they want. Players can do missions for a variety of people throughout the massive in-game city and do side quests (missions not essential to the main story) such as street races and vigilante hunts. Unfortunately, giving players this much freedom in a game where violence is necessary to complete missions also allows them to commit heinous crimes against innocent in-game bystanders.. The series is acclaimed by video game players and critics, but this acclaim has not come without controversy.

The *Grand Theft Auto* series has for a long time been the target 7 of scorn from a range of critics, from concerned parents to current Secretary of State Hillary Clinton. In Clinton's 2005 speech to the Kaiser Family Foundation, she bemoaned the "demeaning messages about women" in games like *Grand Theft Auto,* and said that the game "encourages violent imagination and activities." Clinton was concerned that the omnipresence of the media is detrimentally affecting children. Their "steady diet" of violent material is desensitizing them to violence. She does not single out video games, however, also criticizing the Internet for giving children easy access to violent and pornographic material. She acknowledges that parental responsibility is an important solution to this problem, but claims that parents cannot do everything by themselves: "Parental responsibility is crucial but we also need to be sure that parents have the tools that they need to keep up with this multi-dimensional problem" (Clinton).

David Trend, a professor at the University of California, Irvine, 8 does not see the correlation between fictional and real-life violence. Trend, author of *The Myth of Media Violence*, explains that exposure to violence is nothing new. Violence is "deeply ingrained in our culture," and is an important part of storytelling in anything from television shows to religious texts like the Bible and the Koran (Trend 3). Video-game violence is no different from the violence that is a central part of human history. Trend believes that eliminating forms of violent entertainment is not a feasible plan: "Getting rid of offerings like *Fear Factor* and *The Amityville Horror* on the basis of violence alone would also rule out important films like *Saving Private Ryan, Schindler's List,* or *Hotel Rwanda*" (4). While *Saving Private Ryan* is a movie that shows intense violence, it is also mostly historically accurate and conveys an important message about war and sacrifice. Would it be right to shield people from a movie that many agree is a classic, just because it shows us the unfortunate truth of war?

This argument can be applied to video games as well. *The Call* 9 *of Duty* series is a good example of this. The series explores conflicts from World War II all the way up to the current unrest in the Middle East. It shows players an in-depth look at the horrors of war, and that includes graphic violence. Although violent, games like this are often surprisingly historically accurate and can be a learning experience for the player.

Although both sides of this issue seem to be set in their opin- 10 ions, they both see the need for parents to be informed about the video games their children play. Both sides support the ESRB, the Entertainment Software Ratings Board, which provides ratings for video games that are much like the ratings for movies. Retailers like Target and Wal-Mart, who are on the ESRB Retail Council, have a strict policy against selling Mature-rated games (the equivalent to an R-rated movie) to people under seventeen years old without a parent present ("ESRB Retail Council"). While this policy is not required by law, it is widely supported because it gives parents a way to monitor the games that their children are playing at home.

Parental responsibility is an important part of the issue of video   11
game violence. While some people act like violent games like *Grand Theft Auto* and *Halo* just fall out of the sky into the hands of children, it is ultimately up to parents to decide what is and is not allowed. If parents believe that their child is not mature enough to play violent games, it should not be the game developer or government's job to keep the game out of the house. Instead, the parents should closely monitor the games they are buying for their family. Every game has a rating on the front and back of the box, as well as descriptions of exactly why the game got this rating. For example, the Mature-rated game *Gears of War 2* is rated M for "Blood and Gore, Intense Violence, and Strong Language." Parents can see this just by looking at the box, allowing them to easily decide if the game is right for their family.

Both sides of this contentious issue acknowledge that parental   12
responsibility is extremely important, and the ESRB ratings system makes things easier on parents. Since research has not proven either way whether video games are harmful to children or not, it is still a judgment call for parents. The more information is readily available about video games, the fewer misconceptions there will be about their effects. More resources for parents will hopefully make video games less of a scapegoat in the future, and satisfy people on both sides of this issue.

WORKS CITED

Clinton, Hillary. "Speech to Kaiser Family Foundation Upon Release of Generation M: Media in the Lives of Kids 8 to 18." Kaiser Family Foundation, Washington, DC. 8 Mar. 2005. Address.

"ESRB Retail Council." *Entertainment Software Ratings Board*. Entertainment Software Ratings Board, n.d. Web. 17 Nov. 2009.

"ISU psychologists publish three new studies on violent video game effects on youths." Iowa State University. 22 Mar. 2007. Web. 16 Nov. 2009.

"Most Kids 'Unaffected' by Violent Games." *Sydney Morning Herald*. Sydney Morning Herald, 1 Apr. 2007. Web. 16 Nov. 2009.

Trend, David. *The Myth of Media Violence: A Critical Introduction*. Hoboken: Wiley-Blackwell, 2007. Print.

Arguing a Position 6

When you think of an "argument," if you're like most people, you probably think first of a disagreeable squabble. *Reasoned* argument, however, is something else altogether. Reasoned argument is more thoughtful and less dramatic than the heated exchanges people have when they are upset; and constructing such an argument can be both challenging and enjoyable.

In writing a reasoned argument, you must first examine all sides of the issue you're discussing: As you gain knowledge of your issue, you will move beyond what you have always thought about it, expanding your perspective in order to understand its advantages, drawbacks, and ambiguities. When you feel confident that you understand what's at stake, you will define and support a particular position. In order to do so effectively, you will have to anticipate other positions, accommodating those you find plausible, and refuting those you find flawed or weak.

When you have strong feelings about an issue, it is easy to overlook or dismiss positions different from your own. In reasoned argument, however, you demonstrate that it is possible to respect those who hold different views, even if you long to convert them to your way of thinking. In using well-supported reasons to justify your position and in thoughtfully considering opposing positions and your readers' likely objections, you present yourself as an informed and responsible citizen. In fact, inserting your views into the debates that swirl around contested issues is one of the most valuable and satisfying contributions to American life and culture that an educated person can make. Taking part in the conversation that sustains our diverse, contentious democracy is your fundamental right and opportunity and can foster productive change.

Reasoned argument is always addressed to particular readers—in the argument essays presented here, for example, Thomas Beckfield addresses drivers, appealing especially to those who encounter preoccupied cell-phone users in heavy traffic, while Jaclyn Melicharek addresses school administrators who might consider switching from a five- to a four-day school week. Your goal in addressing your audience is to challenge their thinking without ridiculing their values or beliefs. Whomever you address in a written argument, you should assume, as our student writers do, that they are an audience of informed, intelligent readers who can understand and empathize with a reasonable, informed argument.

The student writers in this chapter use facts, statistics, and expert testimony, in addition to writing strategies such as narration, description, exemplification, and comparison and contrast to present their arguments. Mary Hake, for example, calls attention to the unseen hardships of migrant farm workers by citing facts and statistics, but she puts this data in context by narrating the history of migrants' presence in the United States and by comparing their population to the population of several states. Tan-Li Hsu uses facts, statistics, and abundant examples to show how marketers are selling potentially dangerous energy drinks directly to teenagers. Courtney Anttila cites numerous research studies, as well as credible firsthand observations, in her argument that "TXTing" is part of the natural evolution of language.

Writing an argument like the ones these student writers produced may surprise you by making you question your own beliefs and assumptions, but this uncomfortable confrontation will expand the boundaries of your thinking and communicating. Stepping out of the status quo, you gain a productive, public voice and a larger role in our complicated and shifting world. So take a position. Study the issue. Consider likely differences between you and your readers. Speak out reasonably. Your fellow citizens are waiting to hear from you.

TXTing: h8 it or luv it
Courtney Anttila
Southwest Minnesota State University
Marshall, Minnesota

Many adults—instructors, journalists, and cultural commentators of all varieties—have begun to complain that, with the proliferation of instant messages and texting, students are losing the ability to write correctly. Courtney Anttila defends texting, arguing that it is simply another phase in the evolution of the constantly changing English language. Anttila cites linguistic research to show that misuse of texting slang is less common in formal contexts than alarmists might think. Anttila argues further that most students can "code-switch" between the language they use when sending casual text messages and the more formal language that is appropriate when writing for school. As you read her essay, think about how you decide which conventions of language use—vocabulary, style, voice, and the like—are appropriate in your own academic writing.

In 2005, about 7.3 billion text messages were sent within the United States every month, up from 2.9 billion a month the previous year (Noguchi). In August 2007, there were 92.5 million (or 43 percent) of mobile users actively using short-message-service (SMS), also known as text messages, and 41 million subscribers sent texts nearly every day ("M:Metrics Study"). Just imagine how many thumbs are typing messages at this moment. Human beings have been communicating in shorthand languages for years using different techniques such as Morse code, smoke signals, and other encrypted codes (Barker). Texting has created a "code" that people can decipher because most abbreviations are spelled phonetically; the slang is used in everyday life, and it is an extremely convenient way to communicate (Barker). Some see texting slang as butchering the English language. However, texting demonstrates the constant

1

developmental change and manipulation of language that happens over time and creates a new literacy for people to communicate with (O'Connor).

During the 1990s, instant messaging on a computer was the craze. A type of slang developed to communicate quickly while typing—"LOL" instead of "laughing out loud," "gr8" instead of "great," and other abbreviations and letter replacements. But using this shorthand form of communication just on the computer was not enough. Now, texting has become more popular than ever, and people can send 160-character messages from their phone to anyone who can receive them—allowing them to communicate with practically anyone at any time. Most texters don't even need to blink when deciphering the texting and instant messaging (IM) language used today.

Students and other text-message users have made the new language increasingly detailed over the years, letting people send more information in a smaller amount of space. This "texting language" can become so encoded into the minds of the users that they don't even have to change how they read or think to understand the message. But it is not appropriate all the time. Imagine a 15-year-old boy applying for a summer job and writing this: "I want 2 b a counselor because I love 2 work with kids" (O'Connor). It is clear what he is saying, but most people would be appalled at this language on an application because it isn't Standard English. Fortunately, people change their type of language depending on their situation daily; children rarely talk to their parents the same way they talk to their friends, and parents do not speak to their children the way they speak to their coworkers. Students' academic writing is not being as negatively impacted by texting as some people think. In the article "Txts r gr8 but not in exams," Ian McNeilly, a twelve-year secondary English teacher and director of the National Association for the Teaching of English, states, "I don't think text message and MSN messenger styles are a sign of declining standards, but changing literacies. Children are usually capable of differentiating between the two" (Barker). Texting slang is not a threat to students' writing for school or for work.

People may assume that texting replaces or damages Standard English because adolescents who text are not writing grammatically correct messages. Although there have been some instances where the "texting slang" has been used in inappropriate places, there is no direct correlation between people who text and poor scores on standardized English texts. In fact, the use of text-message abbreviations is connected positively with literacy achievements (Smith). There has been research suggesting that using text abbreviations might have a correlation to children's reading and writing skills. Researchers at Coventry University studied thirty-five eleven-year-olds and related their use of cell phones to their English reading, writing, and spelling skills. The researchers found that the children who were better at spelling and writing were the ones who texted the most (Smith). They found no evidence linking children who texted and a poor ability to use Standard English. Researcher Beverly Plester is "interested in discovering whether texting could be used positively to increase phonetic awareness in less able children, and perhaps increase their language skills, in a fun yet educational way" (Smith).

Texting slang is also considered to be much more common than it actually is. A researcher in language and communication at the University of Washington, Crispin Thurlow, studied 135 nineteen-year-old students at Cardiff University and analyzed 544 of their text messages (Barker). Thurlow found only 20 percent who used abbreviations, and 35 percent who used apostrophes correctly in their messages (Barker). Tim Shortis, who is carrying out a PhD in text messaging as a vernacular language at London University's Institute of Education, said "You get initialisms such as LOL for laugh out loud and letter and number homophones such as r and 2, but they are not as widespread as you think. There are also remarkably few casual misspellings" (Barker). 5

Not only do people make the wrong assumption that using texts is automatically a burden to the English language, but they also worry that texting has brought more cheating into classrooms. Now instead of passing notes, there is the option of sending electronic messages with cellular phones. It is true that phones allow their users to send and receive messages relatively quickly and secretly; however, students who cheat will find a way regardless of texting. And although some students text during class, teachers are getting better at detecting when students are using their cell phones. Cheating is not a new phenomenon; it has always been an issue in school, and it will continue to be. But it is not a problem solely because of texting. 6

Texting technology has not only made communication easier, but has also allowed young people to become more comfortable 7 with writing daily. Although students have always had to write in school, they previously talked mostly to their friends on the telephone. E-mail and instant messaging have made writing to people less intimidating—and hassle-free. Now, with texting, this generation has shown improvement in writing ability. Today's students write more and are better able to explain their thoughts and feelings with words (O'Connor). Even though they might not use the best grammar, kids are getting practice with their writing, and it shows. Adolescents have now surrounded themselves with less formal writing, and they are familiarizing themselves with the strategies that are important for written communication.

Until the next communication innovation comes along, texting   8
and its language are not going to go away. Texting is a part of the continual development of English and has a large impact on today's world. Though texting is a distraction when abused, it has helped put the written word back into our lives, making people more comfortable with the skill of writing. Texting has shown students a way to practice their writing skills outside of class. It is a convenient way for many people to get in touch . . . & it's a fast, EZ way 2 communic8.

WORKS CITED

Barker, Irena. "Txts R Gr8 But Not in Exams." *The TES*. TES Connect, 9 Feb. 2007. Web. 7 Feb. 2008.

"M:Metrics Study: 92.5 Million Active SMS Users Make Short Code-Based Mobile Marketing the Most Effective Platform for Mobile Advertisers." Blog posting. *Club Texting*. Club Texting Wireless Promotions, 25 Oct. 2007. Web. 2 Nov. 2007.

Noguchi, Yuki. "Life and Romance in 160 Characters or Less." Washington Post. *Washington Post*, 29 Dec. 2005. Web. 22 Oct. 2007.

O'Connor, Amanda. "Instant Messaging: Friend or Foe of Student Writing?" *New Horizons for Learning Online Journal* 11.2 (2005): n. pag. Web. 22 Oct. 2007.

Smith, Alexandra. "Texting Slang Aiding Children's Language Skills." *The Guardian*. The Guardian, 11 Sept. 2006. Web. 7 Feb. 2007.

Four-Day School Weeks: The Rule to Skip School

Jaclyn Melicharek

Brown University
Providence, Rhode Island

To most high school students, a four-day school week sounds like a dream come true. To Jaclyn Melicharek, however, it seems more like a nightmare. She explores the idea of a four-day school week, which some school districts have tried in order to cut costs, and finds evidence of severe negative consequences of the plan. Her essay expresses her urgent hope that, despite the economic woes of schools across the country, the four-day school week will not take root. As you read, notice how, toward the end of the essay, Melicharek brings up arguments in favor of four-day school weeks, then refutes them using points from earlier in her essay.

Alarm clock screens read six o'clock on a dreaded Monday morning as dawn breaks and alarms piercingly blare in unison from household to household. Groggy and worn down after the weekend's festivities, sleepy students awaken unwillingly, unprepared for the looming school day. Surprisingly, not every secondary school student experiences such a painful awakening so early in the week. Across the country, other students sleep soundly, planning to get up sometime in the next four hours and spend the day playing video games, watching television, or competing outdoors. Some people would call this playing hooky. However, these students aren't collectively ditching their daily classes—this extra day of the weekend is their school district's idea. In an effort to reduce secondary schools' soaring annual budget costs, policymakers have recently tried adopting a four-day school week. However, switching to four-day school weeks has caused controversy among students, parents, teachers, and school

95

administrators. Changing to a four-day secondary school week is not beneficial, because it lowers academic performance, hinders the quality of education for young students, and disrupts the lives of school faculty and staff.

The transition from five days of school per week to four is happening in many counties throughout the United States owing to economic problems affecting educational institutions. With four-day school weeks, students attend classes Tuesday through Friday, each day lasting approximately ninety minutes longer to account for the shortened week. The radical change to four-day school weeks was last employed in the 1970s as a way to reduce high transportation costs. During the 1970s oil crisis, only a few school districts switched to four-day school weeks and many reverted back to five-day weeks after the economic issue subsided. However, according to a recent survey by the American Association of School Administrators, about one in seven school boards across the nation is currently considering dropping a school day each week (Kingsbury par. 3). As early as 2003, ten states contained school districts operating on the four-day school week, most located in the Midwest (Durr par. 15). This number has grown in the past six years to about seventeen states, or a total of one hundred school districts shifting to four-day school weeks. With the four-day school week trend only continuing to grow, it is vital that policymakers be fully aware of the detrimental effects this plan has on educational quality.

One of the main consequences of four-day school weeks is less time spent in school. Compared to other developed nations across the world, in terms of weekly instructional hours, the United States ranks astonishingly low. In China and Korea, students attend classes for more than 220 days per year, while most American youth are in session the mandated minimum 180 school days per year (Kingsbury par. 8). The transition to four-day school weeks would lower this minimum value tremendously. Although the number of hours students engaged in classroom activities per day would increase, overall, students would potentially only be at school 150 days per academic year. More than half of a calendar year would be spent outside of a structured learning environment.

In regard to time spent in school, quantity does overpower quality. A recent study in *Time* magazine shows that students in Europe and Asia who engage in more instructional learning time per year regularly outperform American students in math, science, and reading (Kingsbury par. 8). With more hours per week spent in the classroom, foreign students are given more educational opportunities and it is not surprising their intelligence ranks supreme. It is frightening to consider how a four-day school week would impact United States students' levels of academic achievement, for they are given even fewer days per week to learn directly from teachers, interact with peers, and study attentively in the classroom.

Closer to home, according to *Time*'s "Four-Day School Weeks," a network of charter schools in San Francisco, also known as the Knowledge Is Power program, aims to keep students in class 60 percent longer than typical public school children (Kingsbury par. 9). Compared to students in regular district schools, 100 percent of the students involved in the charter schools program ranked higher in academic gains in English, math, and other secondary school subjects. The test results from these students who are engaged in more instructional time per week further strengthen the argument against four-day school weeks. Likewise, an article from *USA Today* titled "Four Is Not Enough" reports that all the way across the continental United States similar results were found (in a Massachusetts school district). Ten schools extended their instructional time by only twenty five percent, which served to raise state testing scores in math, English, and science for all grade levels ("Four Is Not Enough" par. 7). These studies demonstrate the strong positive correlation between time spent in school and academic excellence. Boosting learning time has been shown to significantly pay off in the classroom, and transitions to four-day school weeks take away any chance of increasing instructional hours. Four-day school weeks would hinder learning gains, leaving students under this policy unable to attain the high level of education received by those students under a five-day week.

If lower academic test scores are not enough evidence for opposing four-day school weeks, the emotional toll this policy places on students should be. As previously stated, four-day school weeks require Tuesday through Friday to be extended days—almost two hours longer than a normal school day. This is a serious issue, especially for elementary and middle school students. Many parents and teachers rightly worry about their children being too tired in class as they attempt to cope with the lengthened day. It is likely students would lose focus during the last two hours of each day. Without sharp attention spans, students will not retain the proper information and risk failing courses due to a schedule change that is truly out of their control. Four-day school weeks will continually wear down young students to the point where their concentration will be too low to receive a quality education.

Although older students may be able to mentally handle the longer school day, for high school students, four-day school weeks complicate participation in extracurricular activities. With extended school days, most students would not be done with classes until approximately four-thirty in the afternoon. According to Kingsbury, ending school this late creates a serious problem because students simply "won't have the time—or the energy—for after-school activities" (par. 11). Extracurricular activities are fundamental for older students' success and happiness in high school. Four-day school weeks potentially eliminate this source of release and fun for students. Many kids could not handle three hours of practice after slogging through an eight- to nine-hour school day.   7

Additionally, four-day school weeks affect high school students by placing more stress on students if they are absent. If a student is sick or unwillingly absent one of the four days, what type of "stiff penalty" would he or she face ("Four Is Not Enough" par. 8)? Students who are absent would miss a significant amount of material in one day alone and would have less turnaround time to deal with the makeup work, since their homework time would also be cut short by the longer school day. The policy would harm students emotionally and academically.   8

Despite evaluating the negative effects a four-day school week has on students, some educational officials believe a shortened school week would help cut a school district's budget during this economic crisis. It is true that under the four-day school week plan, transportation costs would be cut as there would be no need for buses one day of the week. However, teachers' salaries, not transportation costs, comprise most of a school district's budget ("Four Is Not Enough" par. 8). Teachers' salaries would not be influenced by the transition to a four-day school week. A recent study by the Southern Regional Education Board found "the savings from a shift to four days may be as little as two percent" ("Four Is Not Enough" par. 10). This small savings is not worth damaging the education of young children.   9

According to an article published in *State Legislatures* magazine, a school in Utah had to terminate its four-day school week policy   10 early because not only were no savings actually reported, but scheduling complications had severe effects on the student body (Durr par. 4). Transitioning to four-day school weeks, as this Utah school shows, creates unnecessary disruptions for students—along with further monetary setbacks to reverse the program.

The four-day school week also hurts teachers and other secondary school employees. Under the four-day school week policy, cafeteria workers, bus drivers, and custodians find themselves without jobs one extra day of the week. As a result, these hard workers would lose significant wages. Without a stable income, these employees could have to leave for other jobs, resulting in more complications in staffing for both primary and secondary schools. Four-day school weeks also make it difficult for staff employees who balance two jobs on a daily basis. Longer school days force these workers to quit one job—an impossibility when one job alone cannot support a decent standard of living. By severely affecting employees, implementing the four-day school week plan could have serious consequences both within individual schools and on a national economic scale. 11

Teachers as well report feeling the burden from switching to four-day school weeks. Although they work one day less each week, Tuesdays through Fridays are extremely long, not to mention physically and mentally exhausting. These teachers have to fight for their tired students' attention, and be actively educating for an extra two hours each day. This time requirement does not include the additional hours teachers put in creating lesson plans and attending mandatory staff meetings. An article from *School Board News,* "Four-Day School Weeks? Only If They Fit" analyzes the effect that four-day school weeks have on a teaching staff and directly reports, "The teachers are tired. They're not as flexible as students are with the longer day" (61). Tired teachers cannot be expected to successfully motivate students to learn. In a four-day school system, teachers have one less day to reach out to their students, which is why it is vital they be fully engaged in the classroom for the four days they are actually working. 12

Even if educators are not exhausted, it is "hard for some teachers to get five days of instruction into four days" (Yarbrough and Gilman 84). Cramming five days of teaching into four overwhelms students, and makes them unable to put their full effort into each individual assignment. Karen Hoffman, an interventionist at Central 13

Five School in Union Township, New Jersey, worries that four-day school weeks block core curriculum standards from being met. She states, "four-day school weeks burn out students too quickly, restricting teachers from assigning too much reinforcement work at home." Without enough reinforcement time at home, students fail to acquire the material or sense of satisfaction from completing homework on their own. Once the school day is complete, Hoffman fears teachers will not have the extra time to create appropriate lesson plans for the next day that follow the proper standards for academic enrichment. Each day, teachers are required to bring new ideas and a fresh perspective to the classroom in order to stimulate learning for their students. Fatigued teachers are simply unacceptable. If school district administrators endorse a schedule change like a four-day school week they are risking a weaker teaching staff, leading to poorer academic performance from students.

Four-day school weeks also put numberous burdens on students' parents, especially those in the workforce. Most parents work five days a week, a serious problem when one of those days their children are out of school. For parents with younger children, day care may be the only option. However, with numerous U.S. households suffering from the economic crisis, "many families can't afford to hire outside help" (Kingsbury p. 10). In "Four-Day School Weeks? Only If They Fit," superintendent Wes Hooper notes, in areas of the country "where students might use the extra day for the purpose of watching TV, playing video games, or roaming the streets—a four-day school week wouldn't work as well" (60). Even families that can afford day care services or babysitters must leave their kids alone all day in an environment that does not foster learning as an academic classroom does. Students of all ages would be sitting at home, wasting a day of the week that could have been a day full of learning. Without four-day school weeks, parents would not have to disrupt their working schedules and be concerned with the extra day of freedom granted to their children.

The administration of four-day school weeks first occurred in rural areas. When initially being tested, four-day school weeks seemed like "a creative option for rural areas" and were deemed beneficial because they "allow children to be able to work on their family farms" on their day off (Durr par. 1; Chmelynski 59). A few rural school districts showed no negative impacts from four-day school weeks, and therefore it was assumed that the policy could

14

15

work for all school districts, rural or urban. However, just because no negative influences were observed, this does not mean positive effects occurred. Although some rural districts have survived adequately under four-day school weeks, adopting this policy in urban areas proves downright illogical. In cities, countless opportunities for trouble are available to kids on their day off. Family issues would arise in urban communities as four-day school weeks are not "family friendly"; younger students would be dumped in day care on most Mondays (Chmelynski 60). Students may not be in school, but that does not mean they are spending quality time with their families, an idea some policymakers may use as a rationale for the four-day school week. Instead, four-day school weeks cause communities to adjust to more students roaming the streets, school employees earning less, and parents constantly worrying. Four-day school weeks disrupt the normal everyday routines of families and entire communities, breaking the cohesion found in areas with regular five-day weeks.

Despite the drawbacks of four-day school weeks, there are some supporters of the policy. Those in favor of four-day school weeks state the shortened schedules result in "a decline in dropout rates, decreased disciplinary referrals, improved attendance, fewer class interruptions, and a more positive attitude about school" (Yarbrough and Gilman 81). Even if these ideas are all true, the studies were mostly performed in rural areas—the only place where there has been any success using four-day weeks. Student attitude may improve slightly, but with four-day school weeks districts encounter problems "keeping primary students engaged during the longer school day, accommodating the needs of at-risk students, meeting national and state reform mandates, and gaining the commitment of the local community" (Yarbrough and Gilman 81). These consequences are much more important, and even hazardous to the well-being of school districts and communities.   16

In addition to lowering dropout rates and improving attendance, four-day school weeks can free up Mondays for professional development for teachers, supporters argue. These "professional development" days seem like a way to make four-day school weeks look practical, but are just a burden to teachers who are already working very hard. It has also been argued that four-day school weeks do not negatively affect student achievement. Nevertheless, they certainly do not improve academic performance. Proponents also claim that four-day school weeks save money for the school   17 district in times of economic trouble. However, hardly any reports show worthwhile savings under a four-day school week policy.

In the long run, the negative consequences of such a policy 18 strongly outnumber the advantages. Five-day school weeks have been the norm for decades, and to disrupt such a smooth schedule and lifestyle for an entire district is unwise. Understandably, the economy requires changes and budget cuts. These changes, however, should not come from education. Four-day school weeks are a desperate attempt to lower costs, and do not help raise the educational standard of the United States. Policymakers must seek ways to stimulate local budgets without affecting school systems. Four-day school weeks are impractical, create more problems than solutions, and contradict the beliefs and teachings of so many people who encourage young adults to receive as high a level of education as possible.

WORKS CITED

Chmelynski, Carol. "Four-Day School Weeks? Only If They Fit." *Education Digest* 68.5 (2003): 58. Print.

Durr, Greta. "Four-Day School Week?" *State Legislatures* 29.5 (2003): 21. Print.

"Four Is Not Enough." Editorial. *USA Today* 17 Nov. 2008: 14A. Print.

Hoffman, Karen. Personal interview. 1 Apr. 2009.

Kingsbury, Kathleen. "Four-Day School Weeks." *Time* 14 Aug. 2008: 49–50. Print.

Yarbrough, Rachel, and David Alan Gilman. "From Five Days to Four." *Educational Leadership* 64.2 (2006): 80–85. Print.

Banning Cell Phone Use While Driving

Thomas Beckfield

Mt. San Jacinto College, Menifee Valley
Menifee, California

"Study after study concludes similarly: it is the talking, the cognitive distraction of conversation, that leads to accidents, not the dialing," writes Thomas Beckfield, challenging the cellular industry's claim that more public safety training, not a ban on cell phone use while driving, will resolve the problem of cell-phone-related accidents.

With supporting evidence that demonstrates that talking on the phone while driving limits field of vision and affects focus—whether or not a hands-free device is used—Beckfield argues for turning cell phones off before turning vehicles on. After reading this essay, you may think twice about heading out of the garage or parking lot while talking on your own cellular device or about riding with a friend who uses the phone while driving.

On February 4, 2002, a driver of a Ford Explorer lost control of his 1 vehicle while commuting on a Washington highway and hurtled over a guardrail into oncoming traffic. The driver of the SUV and four unsuspecting passengers in the minivan with which it collided were killed ("Car Accident"). Until this accident, federal investigators with the National Transportation Safety Board (NTSB) had never "identified use of a cell phone as a possible factor" in a fatal automobile crash ("Car Accident").

Most of us, as either a driver or a passenger, have been behind 2 someone who is driving erratically as he or she tries to use a cell phone. Living in Los Angeles, I have seen countless drivers dangerously weave and zigzag in and out of traffic, fight to stay in their lane, and almost lose control of their vehicles as they talk on their cell phones. Such recklessness can be terribly scary, made all the more sobering by the sight of a young child or infant seated in the back of the wayward vehicle. With many lives put at risk each day by drivers who disregard their own safety and the safety of others, cell phone use while driving a vehicle should be banned.

Exactly how dangerous is it to use a cell phone while driving?   3
Opinions differ. On the one hand, safety advocates insist that cell phone use in cars should be banned completely. A California Highway Patrol report found that "[s]ome 4,700 accidents in 2001 could be traced to cell phone use while driving. . . . Of those accidents, 31 people died and nearly 2,800 people were hurt" (Bell). Federal investigator Dave Rayburn, the NTSB agent in charge of the February 4, 2002, case, reported, "Some of the issues we are looking at are the fact that the (Explorer) crossed the median and overrode the barrier. The other is cell phone use. Witnesses said the victim was on a phone conversation two or three minutes at the time of the crash" ("Car Accident").

Ever since cell phones became a part of our national culture in   4
the 1990s, scientists and researchers have debated their impact on driving. The most notable research to date was a 1997 study published in the *New England Journal of Medicine*. The study found, in part, that cell phone users were four times more likely to have an accident than those same drivers when they were not using their phones. To clearly convey the findings' seriousness, Redelmeier and Tibshirani, the study's authors, equated the increase to "driving with a blood alcohol level at the legal limit" (456).[1] Redelmeier and Tibshirani also noted that personal characteristics, such as age and driving experience, did not have a significant "protective effect" against the dangers of cell phone use while driving (455). In short, the study provided significant evidence that the driving skills of different groups of people are seriously affected when using a cell phone while behind the wheel of a car.

Other studies have also linked cell phone use to poor driving   5
or increased accident rates. Researchers at the University of Rhode Island (URI)—Manbir Sodhi, professor of industrial engineering, and Jerry Cohen, professor of psychology—demonstrated a correlation between cell phone use while driving and reduced field of view. Funded in part by the URI Transportation Center, the researchers

chose to concentrate on a specific attribute to measure one's driving skill: the breadth of the visual field to which the driver is paying attention. The subjects in Sodhi and Cohen's experiment wore a head-mounted tracking device that recorded—approximately fifty times per second—where the drivers' eyes were focused (McLeish).

Sodhi and Cohen concluded that a considerable decrease in driver alertness occurred when the participants conducted cognitive tasks, such as remembering a list of items, calculating math in one's head, or using a cell phone, while driving (McLeish). The URI researchers discovered another interesting finding: tunnel vision caused by cell phone use continues well after the conversation ends. This dangerous occurrence while driving probably occurs because drivers are still thinking about the conversation they just completed on their cell phone (McLeish). Their minds are simply not focused on their driving environment. 6

While proponents for the cellular industry recognize and acknowledge the relationship between cell phone use and accidents, they believe banning cell phone use while driving to be zealous, that problems associated with driving and cell phone use may be easily corrected with education and training. In 1997, the Cellular Telecommunications Industry Association committed nearly $15 million to educate their customers on using cell phones safely while driving (Koffler). With public service announcements, television commercials, and radio spots, the campaign advocated the use of hands-free devices, such as headphones, earpieces, and voice-activated dialers, as well as common sense when using a cell phone while driving (Koffler). Yet study after study concludes similarly: it is the talking, the cognitive distraction of conversation, that leads to accidents, not the dialing. 7

If we do not change the laws regarding the use of cell phones while driving, countless lives will inevitably be put at risk. In an interview with the *Washington Post*, NTSB spokesman Ted Lopatkiewicz commented, "We expect down the road to investigate more crashes involving cell phones as they come up" (qtd. in "Car Accident"). And while the cellular industry lobby is still advocating the freedom to use a cell phone as an American right, when one's cell phone call made while driving causes another's injury, some restrictions on freedom are warranted. 8

NOTE

1. In a survey conducted by InsightExpress, 23 percent of respondents believed that using a cell phone while driving was as dangerous as driving drunk. While 70 percent believed that using a cell phone while driving was dangerous, 61 percent disagreed with proposed legislation to ban cell phone use while driving, and 54 percent disagreed with the idea that cell phone use while driving should be regulated by the government ("Don't Ban").

WORKS CITED

Bell, Rick. "Time for Drivers with Cell Phones to Hang Up." *San Diego Business Journal* 18 Nov. 2002: 38. Print.

"Car Accident May Be Blamed on Phone." *CBS News.* CBS, 4 Feb. 2002. Web. 24 Mar. 2003.

"Don't Ban Dialing Drivers." *Fairfield Country Business Journal* 16 Oct. 2000: 11. *EBSCOhost.* Web. 24 Mar. 2003.

Koffler, Keith. "Outside Influences: Speed Bumps for Cell Phones." *Congress-Daily* 21 June 2000: 12. *EBSCOhost.* Web. 24 Mar. 2003.

McLeish, Todd. "URI Study on Cell Phone Use Attracts National Attention." *The University Pacer.* U Rhode Island, Sept. 2002. Web. 24 Mar. 2003.

Redelmeier, Donald A., and Robert J. Tibshirani. "Association between Cellular-Telephone Calls and Motor Vehicle Collisions." *New England Journal of Medicine* 336.7 (1997): 453–58. Print.

Energy Drinks

Tan-Li Hsu

University of California, Riverside
Riverside, California

In this essay Tan-Li Hsu takes on energy drinks for their high levels of caffeine (which aren't mentioned on the labels) and their marketing campaigns aimed at teenagers. Although energy drinks can certainly help teens pull all-nighters, they can also lead to serious health problems. Hsu cites news articles reporting studies about caffeine abuse in teenagers; he also cites the American Beverage Association, which defends its labeling practices. By bringing his opposition into the debate and refuting their claims, Hsu strengthens his own position.

Like many of Hsu's other readers, you may never have thought before about caffeine levels in energy drinks or the dangers of caffeine. As you read, think about how Hsu presents the issue to his readers, and consider his strategies for convincing them of his argument.

Ever since Red Bull energy drink was introduced in the United 1
States in 1997, the market for energy drinks has been continually expanding. Roland Griffiths, a professor of psychiatry and neuroscience at Johns Hopkins University School of Medicine and author of a study published in the journal *Drug and Alcohol Dependence*, estimates that the market for energy drinks now totals at least $5.4 billion a year (Doheny). These popular drinks are packed with caffeine, a stimulant that is able to freely diffuse into the brain and temporarily increase alertness. Although the Food and Drug Administration places a limit on how much caffeine food products can contain—71

milligrams for each 12-ounce can—energy drinks are considered to
be dietary supplements and not food products, allowing the caffeine
content of these drinks to remain unregulated (Roan). As a result,
hundreds of brands of energy drinks with ridiculous amounts of caffeine not specified on labels flourish in the market.

Furthermore, marketers intentionally target teenagers who are   2
more susceptible to drinking multiple cans because they tend to live
active lifestyles that leave them sleep deprived. It's no wonder that
"[t]hirty-one percent of U.S. teenagers say they drink energy drinks,
according to Simmons Research. That represents 7.6 million teens"
("Teens"). With the increased usage of energy drinks combined
with the lack of caffeine content and warning labels on cans, emergency room doctors and poison control centers are reporting more
cases of caffeine intoxication (Seltzer). Energy drink manufacturers
are putting teenagers in danger by not clearly indicating the amount
of caffeine on labels and by marketing highly caffeinated energy
drinks to teenagers.

All energy drinks list caffeine as an ingredient on labels, but   3
many don't specify how many milligrams of caffeine are in the drink.
Some brands, like "Wired" and "Fixx," have 500 mg of caffeine per
20-ounce serving, about ten times the caffeine found in cans of soda
(Doheny). Another ingredient, guarana, is a source of caffeine that
adds to the drinks' already high caffeine content. Unsuspecting
teens who crave a buzz by drinking several cans of energy drinks are
unknowingly putting themselves at risk for the irregular heartbeat
and nausea associated with caffeine intoxication. In rare cases, such
as that of nineteen-year-old James Stone, who took "two dozen caffeine pills for putting in long hours on a job search," intoxication
may even lead to death by cardiac arrest (Shute).

It is possible to promote responsible consumption of energy   4
drinks by including possible health hazards along with caffeine content on can labels that encourage drinking in moderation. The reason why such warning labels don't already exist is because marketers
are more concerned with money than the health of consumers.
"Vying for the dollars of teenagers with promises of weight loss, increased endurance and legal highs . . . top-sellers Red Bull, Monster
and Rockstar . . . make up a $3.4 billion-a-year industry that grew
by 80 percent last year" ("Teens"). By warning about the possible
health hazards of drinking too much caffeine, manufacturers of en-

ergy drinks risk a decrease in purchases. Maureen Storey, a spokes-woman for the American Beverage Association, argues that "most mainstream energy drinks contain the same amount of caffeine, or even less, than you'd get in a cup of brewed coffee. If labels listing caffeine content are required on energy drinks, they should also be required on coffeehouse coffee" (Doheny). This argument has some validity, but it fails to include ingredients in energy drinks that func-tions as a hidden source of caffeine, such as guarana. Guarana is a berry that grows in Venezuela that contains a high amount of guara-nine, a name for caffeine derived from the guarana plant. Assuming that energy drinks and coffee have the same amount of caffeine, the risk of caffeine intoxication from energy drinks is much higher be-cause of the guaranine.

It is obvious that marketers are taking advantage of teens and 5 encouraging them to drink more with attractive brand names such as Rockstar, Monster, and Cocaine Energy Drink that promise to enhance performance. There are many reasons why marketers target teenagers instead of a more mature age group. The first is that teens are more easily tricked by claims that energy drinks will increase en-durance and mental awareness. Also, teens are out partying late at night more often than adults who recognize the importance of a good night's sleep. It's no surprise that marketers are targeting ex-hausted teenagers who are more likely to purchase these drinks than an adult who makes sure he is in bed by 10 p.m. However, marketers fail to realize the consequences of such marketing techniques. A study led by Danielle McCarthy of Northwestern University showed "a surprising number of caffeine overdose reports to a Chicago poi-son control center" ("Teens"). "Although adults of all ages are known to use caffeine, it is mainly abused by young adults who want to stay awake or even get high, McCarthy said" ("Study").

Another reason why marketers shouldn't incite teens to buy 6 energy drinks is that the half-life of caffeine in a young body is signif-icantly longer than in an adult's body (Shute). Half-life is the time required to remove half the amount of a substance to prevent accu-mulation in the body. With a longer half-life in teens, caffeine can ac-cumulate more easily and increase the risk of caffeine intoxication. Preteens are getting hooked on caffeine as well: "A 2003 study of Columbus, Ohio, middle schoolers found some taking in 800 milli-grams of caffeine a day—more than twice the recommended maxi-

mum for adults of 300 milligrams" (Shute). The problem for pre-
teens is especially dire because "their body weight is low," as Wahida
Karmally, the director of nutrition for the Irving Center for Clinical
Research at Columbia University Medical Center, explains (Shute).
Moreover, researchers do not know how such high levels of caffeine
consumption affect the child's developing body.

Manufacturers argue that marketing to teenagers and preteens is   7
acceptable because energy drinks can be part of a balanced lifestyle
when consumed sensibly. While convincing, this argument does not
demonstrate a clear understanding of the scope of the problem. If a
student drinks an energy drink while studying at night and can't
sleep because of it, he might drink another in the morning to help
wake up. According to Richard Levine, a professor of pediatrics and
psychiatry at Penn State University College of Medicine and chief of
the division of adolescent medicine and eating disorders at Penn
State Milton S. Hershey Medical Center, "too much caffeine can
make it harder to nod off, even when you're tired. Then you risk
falling into a vicious cycle of insomnia caused by energy drinks followed by more caffeine to wake up" (Seltzer). Those who fall into
this cycle become addicted to energy drinks and this addiction
threatens the very idea of sensible consumption. For example, 15-
year-old Eric Williams explained that "he used to drink two to four
energy drinks a day, and sometimes used them to stay awake to finish
a big homework project (Seltzer). The headaches he got when he
didn't drink them convinced him to quit "although it took him two
weeks" to break the habit (Seltzer). Teens shouldn't rely on energy
boosters to achieve a balanced lifestyle; they should learn time management and get into the habit of a good night's sleep every day.

Exciting brand names, appealing promises of enhanced perfor-   8
mance, and lack of clear warning labels have allowed energy drink
manufacturers to intentionally target a younger audience. With
these tactics, the energy drink market has grown into a billion dollar
industry. Although manufacturers are enjoying profits, consumers
are placing themselves at risk for serious health problem associated
with caffeine intoxication. The most susceptible to intoxication are
teenagers who drink either to delay exhaustion or to get a buzz.
Caffeine content and overdose warnings must be placed on energy
drinks in order to make teens aware of the potential dangers of
drinking too much.

WORKS CITED

Doheny, Kathleen. "Energy Drinks: Hazardous to Your Health?" *WebMD Health* News. WebMD, 24 Sept. 2008. Web. 18 Jan. 2009.

Roan, Shari. "Energy Drinks Can Cause Caffeine Intoxication." *Booster Shots.* Los Angeles Times, 28 Sept. 2008. Web. 16 Jan. 2009.

Seltzer, Rick. "Heavy Use of Energy Drinks Can Threaten Teens' Health." *Atlanta Journal-Constitution.* Atlanta Journal-Constitution, 27 Aug. 2008. Web. 16 Jan. 2009.

Shute, Nancy. "Over the Limit?" *U.S. News.* U.S. News & World Report, 15 Apr. 2007. Web. 12 Jan. 2009.

"Study: More People Abusing, Getting 'High' on Caffeine." *Fox News.* Fox News, 24 Feb. 2009. Web. 24 Feb. 2009.

"Teens Abusing Energy Boosting Drinks, Doctors Fear." *Fox News.* Fox News, 31 Oct. 2006. Web. 24 Feb. 2009.

With Each Seed a Farmer Plants

Mary Hake

Pierce College
Lakewood, Washington

Farms are an important part of the United States' national self-image—we take for granted the "amber waves of grain" that provide food for us and for the world. Mary Hake writes about a grimmer side of this story: the plight of migrant farm workers. By citing statistics and by evoking reader sympathy for the migrant workers, she eloquently argues for rights for these workers. Hake claims that United States agriculture is a "broken system," which cannot survive without abusing the labor force it depends on. As you read, think about Hake's purpose in writing this essay, and what kinds of audiences she might have written it for.

When we sit to eat our meals and join in the family chatter this Thanksgiving Day, many of us will have tables laden with food. Americans live in one of the richest nations on earth. We have fertile farmland, agricultural techniques that are modern and efficient, agreeable rainfall in many areas and irrigation provided by flowing rivers in others. Seeds are plentiful, orchards bloom and flourish, grains ripen each year. Yet, within this framework are the harvesters of our bounty: the migrants who have fought for decades for a decent wage, livable housing, clean water, and enough food to feed their own children even as they pick our celebratory feast. As Edward R. Murrow referred to these people on Thanksgiving Day, 1960: "The under-educated, unprotected, under-fed and unclothed. The forgotten ones" ("Harvest of Shame"). How is it, then, that they can still be "forgotten" forty-six years later?

Living in a country that prides itself on its heritage of personal   2
freedom and individual rights, we have neglected an entire group of
people who are without the strength, or the voice, to demand otherwise from us. The same science that tells us that unclean water and
overcrowded living conditions breed disease, that great fatigue can
cause dangerous accidents in the field, and that poverty is a reason
why those who are sick or injured do not seek the medical care they
need to stop its spread, also tells us how to grow even more food in
less time, necessitating many more harvesters to do this dirty work
each growing season. With each seed a farmer plants, he grows two
things. One is a valuable crop; the other is poverty. Seen in this
light, every migrant farm worker who harvests food in the United
States should have equal access to the health care and basic human
services we deem as our right as Americans, for to do anything less is
to put the nation's food supply in danger.

Our current use of a migrant workforce has its roots in the   3
1940s, when the United States government instituted a program to
provide cheap labor for the fruit and vegetable farmers (Reynolds).
These farmers needed help picking their produce in the limited
amount of time they had before it began to rot in the fields. Many
of their previous helpers had been lost in World War II. The cheap-
est and fastest way to provide these replacement laborers was to
go into Mexico and hire more than three million Mexican Nationals
between 1942 and 1964 (Reynolds). This plan, named the Bracero
Program, brought these workers across the border by bus for the
length of the harvest season. Then, without ceremony, these
farmhands were sent home again. For almost twenty years, American
agriculture sent for foreign help to harvest our food in this revolv-
ing-door fashion and in relative secrecy.

By the 1960s, however, that began to change, largely through   4
the efforts of one man, Cesar Chavez. A farm laborer from the age
of ten, Chavez realized that American farm hands were being denied
a fair wage and safe working conditions (Wheeler 33). As business-
men, the field owners wanted to increase their profits, a goal they
accomplished by paying the lowest possible wage to the braceros.
Some farm workers, like Chavez, were born in America of Mexican
heritage, while others were Mexican citizens who were bused across
the border each growing season directly to the fields. Through a
philosophy of nonviolence and the action of "organized sit-down
strikes in the fields," Chavez worked to protest this situation (Wheeler

33). When the braceros returned the next season, Chavez became convinced of the need to organize the farm workers into a Union that would eventually become known as the N.F.W.A, or the National Farm Workers Association (Wheeler 36). In 1965, after much struggle, the N.F.W.A. reached its goal of a national boycott to call attention to the plight of the American migrant.

Migrant workers, as they will be defined for this essay, are farm   5
laborers who travel more than one day to reach their places of employment. Men, women and children have historically performed this role, often from a very young age and for very little money. Some have been born into it, some forced by financial need to take any work they could find. An anonymous farmer speaking of his workers more than forty years ago said: "We used to own our slaves, now we just rent them" ("Harvest"). It is within this context that the modern American must examine how we pay for the food that we eat.

Most migrants have an income far below the poverty line and   6
are rarely in one place long enough to acquire the legal residence necessary to apply for aid. As writer Eric Schlosser states, "Migrants are among the poorest workers in the United States. The average migrant is a twenty-nine year old male, born in Mexico, who earns less than $7,500 a year for twenty-five weeks of farm work" (*Reefer Madness* 79). Many have no money at all and work only to feed themselves.

This transient life has a direct impact not only on the adult labor-   7
ers but on the entire family as well. Some have argued that migrants are culturally unable to sustain permanent residence, and that they actually enjoy moving with the seasons and would feel limited otherwise. There is absolutely no evidence to support this point of view. Moving as they must, the children are malnourished owing to the lack of money to feed them and the lack of time to prepare their meals. They have little or no warm clothing and lasting friendships are unheard of. Educational needs cannot be met because no single teacher is in control of what is taught, thus completing a generational cycle of illiteracy. It is true, also, that small hands may be needed in the fields. Legally, children as young as ten years old may work as harvesters, side by side with adults. Molestation and sexual assault are very real threats and when they occur are often unreported crimes (*Reefer Madness* 85).

Jill Wheeler's book *Cesar Chavez* recounts one migrant child's   8
difficulty attending school: "It was hard for the children of the farm

workers to get an education because they were working to help their families. They constantly moved from one job to the next. As a child, Cesar attended nearly forty different schools" (Wheeler 14). The bright migrant child, under this burden of transience and without the continuity of curriculum, has little hope of academic success. He or she will never fully advance with the class and indeed most migrant children do not continue their schooling beyond the sixth grade. With no high school diploma and no formal training, many barely able to speak English, they are ill-equipped for any work other than the fields. They cannot escape the patterns of the harvest, the same necessary and seasonal migration that trapped their parents before them. Similarly, without a decent wage earned, or credit history established, many farm workers are without the means to live in private quarters. At the mercy of their employers, they are often left with no choice but to sleep outside or in communal tents with strangers.

Journalist Carole Pearson notes: "A lack of adequate, affordable housing forces many seasonal migrant workers to live in deplorable conditions. Because growers are not required to provide accommodations for their employees, it's not uncommon to see workers camped along the river banks or in the orchards, living in shelters of discarded cardboard and plastic tarps" (Pearson 4). Migrants are expected to work long hours, always outdoors, whether in pouring rain or blazing sunshine; they are also expected to sleep wherever they can. Some have roofs, but not all. Some have floors, but many do not. Most are in the midst of shanty towns where clean running water is not guaranteed, bathroom facilities may not be available, and nothing stops the spread of contagious diseases (Pearson 6). 9

The possibility of a spreading epidemic, created by ignorance and poor hygiene among a mostly transient population, has frightening consequences for the general public. Estimates of the number of migrants working in the United States during any one harvest period vary, but all studies agree there are at least 1.5 million people who work the fields under these circumstances. Some studies state that number may be as high as 5 million individuals; 5 million chances for a disease to move (Carrasco-Mendoza 2). 10

By contrast, according to a recent census more than half of these United States have less than 5 million residents (Factmonster .com). Colorado ranks as our twenty-second most populated state with a mere 4,700,000. Arkansas drops down to under 3 million. When added together the population of the states of Maine, Idaho, 11 and Hawaii does not equal the estimated number of migrant workers. Even taking the more conservative estimate of 1.5 million leaves us with a migrant group larger than the populations of Delaware, Hawaii, Idaho, Maine, Montana, New Hampshire, Rhode Island, Vermont and Wyoming (Factmonster.com).

Separated, unnoticed, and uncared for, this undeniably large   12
group of people is spread across every state's farm land. Touching every agricultural community, they bring their own risk factors with them. As Pat Hanson points out in the article "Migrant Farmers 'Suffering in Silence'": "Close to one third had never been to a doctor in their lives. Seventy-five percent had no health insurance" (Hanson 3). Without health insurance, money becomes the most important obstacle to healing. Very few doctors will treat undocumented workers unless they are able to pay cash or provide a billing address. Additionally, cultural, educational and language differences, as well as prejudice and discrimination, are cited barriers to obtaining health care (Carrasco-Mendoza 2). Without money, the ability to understand what care is needed, or the ability to speak English fluently, many migrants are treated as undesirable aliens who must be turned away.

Many would argue that doctors who will not treat indigent tran-   13
sient workers are simply protecting themselves and the entire health care industry from potentially hundreds of thousands of dollars or more in health care costs. For a system that is already overwhelmed by rising fees and an uncontrolled number of patients, adding the additional migrant population might cause a final catastrophic collapse, in effect leaving all Americans without proper care. Additionally, this argument holds, for an individual farmer to insure each of his migrant workers would nearly bankrupt an already fragile agricultural system.

Both of these points, while valid, are solely based on economic   14
payout and overlook the need for each system as it currently stands to be overhauled. In essence, they state that we cannot afford to help the migrant living in poverty because it would break an already broken system. According to Wikipedia, "the generally high cost of treatment has led to the concept of doctors completing their *pro bono* work, although in practice even serious conditions are left untreated. Health insurance is expensive and medical bills are overwhelmingly the most common reason for personal bankruptcy in the United States" ("Health Care in the United States"). By contrast,

government funded health care systems such as Canada's can provide an equal opportunity for treatment regardless of the patient's ability to pay. In America, however, it is still possible to die of an expensive disease.

Similarly, American agriculture is changing under severe pressure   15
from large corporations. Those who still own a small family farm have difficulty raising and selling enough crops to stay competitive. Aggressive techniques are used to raise crop yields—bioengineering more hardy and weather-resistant varieties combined with multiple pesticide usage. In the center of this David-and-Goliath battle is the migrant farm worker. With a larger crop to harvest, smaller farms must turn to outside help or lose their investment. Eric Schlosser addresses this issue extensively in his book, *Fast Food Nation*: "Family farms are giving way to corporate farms that stretch for thousands of acres. These immense corporate farms are divided into smaller holdings for administrative purposes, and farmers who are driven off the land are often hired to manage them" (118).

The argument, then, that the paying for health care and the   16
providing for the basic living needs of the harvesters would harm the individual farmer, doesn't apply if the real wealth behind agriculture belongs to large and often multinational corporations whose profits can be measured in the billions of dollars. While it may hurt the smallest, independent farmer financially, it also follows that the least amount of acreage would require the least help to manage it. If five men can pick one hundred laden apple trees, only the largest orchard would find this requirement unduly burdensome.

Another argument raised against providing for the migrants   17
simply states that this kind of care and benefit should be reserved for United States citizens alone, and that to treat those who are illegal immigrants as equals is unjust to the American fieldhand. This point of view refuses to acknowledge the migrants' contribution to the American economy. The United States fruit and vegetable industry, worth 28 billion dollars annually, would lose both its function and its profitability without the work of the migrant harvester (Schlosser, *Fast Food Nation* 230). The Thanksgiving table itself would have no harvest to celebrate; it would be empty of both food and spirit. Indeed, the migrants' contribution to America cannot be separated from the United States economy. Every day that is spent in the field supports this country and its citizens. It seems only fair, then, that migrant workers should receive something back.

Some writers state that to aid undocumented workers is to 18
reward them for breaking the law. This quote from William Triplett
puts forth that idea quite plainly: "Some farm bosses even have been
convicted in recent years of enslaving workers, most of whom are illegal aliens afraid to speak out for fear of deportation. Human rights
advocates say the only way to improve conditions is to give undocumented workers legal residency, but opponents say that would reward
illegals for breaking U.S. immigration laws and ultimately spark more
illegal immigration" (829).

This position implies that the United States is undeniably a bet- 19
ter place to live than anywhere else, and that given any reason to do
so many more immigrants would come here to live illegally. It does
not specifically address how that would be easier to do, or why many
more people would wish to do so. At its heart, this argument is a
form of national arrogance, but more than that, it too, seems to miss
the most obvious point. Namely, the illegal immigrant as migrant
worker has toiled and bled as little more than slave labor for over
sixty years and should, indeed, be rewarded. It was the United
States, after all, that created the Bracero Program and in so doing
created an artificial reliance in both cultures, Mexican and American,
on transient and low-paid work. It is in the interest of international
justice to acknowledge our role in the creation and proliferation of
our immigrant workforce, legal or otherwise.

As Americans, many of us are far removed from our own food 20
chain. Most cannot grow enough to survive. Many have no idea
how to pick different kinds of produce when they are ready to harvest and some do not even know how to prepare them. It cannot be
wise, then, to treat those who do have that knowledge so poorly.
The migrant workers among us are the silent, movable backbone of
our agriculture. Intricately tied to our ability to feed ourselves and
by extension the world, they play an irreplaceable role in our economy. Even so, their lives are endangered daily by ignorance, prejudice, poverty, and disease. If the state population of Colorado cried
out in one tormented voice of great distress, thousands across the
nation would hasten to answer. It cannot be, and must not be, any
different when the voices come from the farms, in every direction,
and speak in Spanish.

But ours is a land of nomad harvesters. 21
They till no ground, take no rest, are homed nowhere.

Travel with the warmth, rest in the warmth never;
Pick lettuce in the green season in the flats by the sea.
Lean, follow the ripening, homeless, send the harvest home;
Pick cherries in the amber valleys in tenderest summer.
Rest nowhere, share in no harvest;
Pick grapes in the red vineyards in the low blue hills.
Camp in the ditches at the edge of beauty.

> —from "The Nomad Harvesters"
> by Marie De L. Welch (Sackman, xii)

WORKS CITED

Carrasco-Mendoza, Rachel. "Migrant Farm Workers Significant to America's Way of Life." *La Voz* 27 Aug. 1997: 3. *ProQuest*. Web. 8 Nov. 2006.

"Facts and Figures, United States Populations by State." *FactMonster.com*. Fact Monster/Information Please Database, 2005. Web. 15 Nov. 2006.

Hanson, Pat. "Migrant Farmers 'Suffering in Silence': California Groups Look at Problems and Solutions." *The Hispanic Outlook in Higher Education* 12.17 (2002): 28–32. ProQuest. Web. 9 Nov. 2006.

"Harvest of Shame." Narr. Edward R. Murrow. *CBS Reports*. CBS. WCBS, 25 Nov. 1960. Fox Video, 1992. Videocassette.

"Health Care in the United States." *Wikipedia*. Wikipedia Foundation, Inc., 14 Nov. 2006. Web. 16 Nov. 2006.

Pearson, Carole. "A Case of Apples: Mexican Farm Workers in Washington." *Our Times* 20.6 (2002): 21. ProQuest. Web. 10 Nov. 2006.

Reynolds, Kathleen, and George Kourous. "Legislation and Regulation Favor Agribusiness: An Overview of Health, Safety and Wage Issues." *Border Lines* 6.8 (1998): n. pag. *ProQuest*. Web. 9 Nov. 2006.

Sackman, Douglas C. Foreword. *Factories in the Fields*. By Carey McWilliams. Archon: North Haven, 1969. Print.

Schlosser, Eric. *Fast Food Nation*. New York: Houghton, 2002. Print.

———. *Reefer Madness*. New York: Houghton, 2003. Print.

Triplett, William. "Migrant Farmworkers." *CQ Researcher* 14.35 (2004): 829–52. *CQ Researcher*. Web. 9 Nov. 2006.

Wheeler, Jill C. *Cesar Chavez*. ABDO & Daughters, 2003. Print.

7 *Proposing a Solution*

Problem solving requires a questioning attitude—a refusal to accept things as they are simply because they've always been that way. It invites creative effort—time spent imagining how things might be improved. When you identify a problem that has long existed or notice that old solutions are failing because they're outdated, you take a step toward positive change. As a student, you are in an enviable position to identify and solve problems. Studying and writing, you have been practicing a stance that problem solving requires—thinking skeptically and creatively. And you have the luxury of time to notice problems and think hard about solutions.

Don't be afraid to research problems that are new to you—an outsider's fresh, unbiased point of view is often very valuable. But remember to consider problems from an insider's perspective, too: problems of your town and city, neighborhood and dormitory, athletic team and booster club. If you volunteer time and effort on behalf of political parties, religious and cultural groups, or gender and environmental organizations, this experience with specific groups uniquely qualifies you to examine their limitations. What's more, a proposal to solve a local problem may well have national implications. For example, Jeff Varley's essay about later high school starting times grew from his struggle with early classes as a high school teen, yet his proposal applies to every high school in the nation.

In addition to giving you a say in your community, practice in presenting problems and proposing solutions will expand your professional-writing repertoire. If student writer Bonnie Lapwood pursues a career in management, applies for a job directing a nonprofit, or volunteers to work for a local political organization, she will have demonstrated her ability to notice and analyze problems and suggest ways to fix them, while acknowledging the concerns of the people who would have to carry them out—in this case, school administrators who create cafeteria policy and the cafeteria employees who would have to learn new rules and techniques if existing policies were changed.

It can be frustrating to work diligently on a proposal for a problem that you know you have little power to solve; no matter how well argued, many proposals are never carried out. People who are quite insightful about solving problems may be hampered or thwarted by economic constraints or aggressive opposition from prominent stakeholders. But this shouldn't deter you from proposing a solution to a problem, especially when you choose a local problem in which you have a personal interest. For example, a friend's account of her experience as a long-term-care nurse inspired Kim Spencer Kline and Dana Jordan to tackle the problem of poorly regulated nursing homes in their state. The students interviewed their friend, reviewed newspaper accounts of nursing home violations in Iowa, researched the laws regulating nursing homes in their state and in others, and set out to write "a real proposal, not just an assignment." Their hard work paid off. Kline reports: "Through a friend, we were able to share this paper with a candidate for governor in our state, who was quite impressed with our work and asked to keep a copy of it."

Don't underestimate the power of interviewing people affected by the problem you intend to solve and of approaching others who have the power to change it. Interviews with those who have first-hand experience with the problem can help you anticipate objections to your solution and will allow you to test it with an audience directly involved. Scheduling an interview with someone who has the power to solve the problem may help you anticipate and counter resistance to your proposal.

You are ready to add your voice to the conversations about problems on your campus; in your town; at your job; or with college, government, or corporate officials, whose policies affect your life and the lives of your family and friends. If your proposal can convince readers to consider and perhaps implement your solution, you will have succeeded in altering the conditions of your world.

High School Starting Time

Jeff Varley

Western Wyoming Community College
Rock Springs, Wyoming

It is the rare student who doesn't find it difficult to get out of bed in the morning. Recent high school grad Jeff Varley strategically directs the following essay proposing later high school starting times to an audience of his peers—fellow late risers—while also offering sound evidence to sway adult readers who make school-scheduling decisions. Varley even shows how taxpayers in communities where high school students live would benefit from later starting times—no one can accuse him of ignoring the greater good! With an attention-getting introduction, an alarmingly long list of the problems caused by sleepiness among high school students, and a solution that's unexpectedly simple—and even accounts for the several obstacles that might stand in its way—Varley's proposal is unlikely to put you to sleep, whether you're an early bird or not.

Ah, sweet memories of high school: waking up at 6:30 in the morning, stumbling into the bathroom to get ready for the day, dressing while still half asleep, munching a piece of toast while listening to our parents tell us that if we just went to bed earlier we wouldn't be so sleepy in the morning (or worse, listening to our parents call us lazy), catching the bus as the sun began to top the trees, and wandering into our first-period classes merely to lay our head down on our desks to doze off for the next fifty-five minutes. 1

We could never seem to catch up on our sleep, especially during the week. And even if we followed our parents' advice and tried going to bed earlier, the earlier bedtime did not make much, if any, difference in how awake we were the next morning. In fact, for those of us who tried going to bed earlier, we generally just lay there until 10:30 or 11:00 before finally going to sleep. The next school morning, we were still as tired as when we had gone to bed later. 2

122

Yet recent studies provide evidence that the sleep patterns for 3
adolescents are significantly different from those of both young children and adults. Studies of sleep patterns by Mary Carskadon, a professor of psychiatry and human behavior at the Brown University
School of Medicine and Director of Sleep and Chronobiology Research at E. P. Bradley Hospital in East Providence, Rhode Island,
revealed that adolescents, as opposed to younger children or adults,
actually function better when they go to bed later and awake later.
Professor Carskadon's research demonstrates that most adolescents'
biological clocks are naturally set to a different pattern from the
clocks of most children and adults.

The timing of the need for sleep also shows biological changes as 4
children reach puberty. Melatonin, a hormone produced in the
pineal gland, is an indicator for the biological clock that influences
wake/sleep cycles. Carefully controlled studies found that "more mature adolescents had a later timing of the termination of melatonin
secretion" (Carskadon 351). This indicates that post-pubescent teens
have a biological need to sleep later in the morning. The impact of
forcing people to try to be alert when every nerve in their body is
begging for more sleep can only be negative. This discovery has a
major impact on high school students who are required to wake up
early in order to arrive at school early, for asking teens to learn a
complex subject, such as math, science, or English, before the brain
is awake is futile.

Tardiness, poor grades, depression, automobile accidents, after- 5
school on-the-job accidents, and general lethargy have all been identified as the consequences of insufficient sleep among high school
students. Yet school districts persist in retaining high school starting
times that begin early in the morning, usually around 7:30 a.m. But
such an early starting time does not benefit the students for whom
the educational system is supposedly structured. How do we resolve
the conflict of early high school starting times versus sleepy students?

An obvious solution would be to start high school classes later in 6
the morning. A later starting time for high schools can be a controversial proposal if all of the affected parties are not consulted and
kept informed. Kyla Wahlstrom of the Center for Applied Research
and Educational Improvement at the University of Minnesota
pointed out that "changing a school's starting time provokes the same
kind of emotional reaction from stakeholders as closing a school or
changing a school's attendance area" (Wahlstrom 346). Presumably,

if parents and other interested parties knew about Carskadon's research, they would be more willing to consider changing the start time for high school.

Some schools have recognized the benefits of later starting times and have implemented a new schedule. One such school is located in eastern Minnesota. In 1996, the Edina Public School District pushed back the start time for 1,400 high school students from 7:25 to 8:30 a.m. Edina Public School District Superintendent Kenneth Dragseth reports that the later schedule has led to better grades, fewer behavioral problems, and a better-rested student body (Dragseth). Dragseth's anecdotal evidence that better-rested students perform better is supported by research performed by psychologists at the College of the Holy Cross in Worcester, Massachusetts. Working with Carskadon, the psychologists "surveyed more than 3,120 Providence [Rhode Island] area high school students and found students who got A's and B's averaged about 35 minutes more sleep on both weeknights and weekends than students who received D's and F's" (Bettelheim 557). 7

In addition to better grades, other positive effects cited by researchers include better attendance, fewer tardies, far fewer students falling asleep at their desks, more alert students more engaged in the learning process, less depression, fewer problems at home and among friends, enhanced school atmosphere, and fewer illnesses (Lawton; Wahlstrom and Taylor). With so many benefits to starting high school classes later, why haven't more districts done so? 8

One of the most common concerns comes from participants in extracurricular activities. If practices currently often run until 8 or 9 p.m. with a school day that begins at 7:30 a.m., what will happen if school starts an hour later? This is a legitimate concern that would need to be addressed on a team-by-team or group-by-group basis. Some practice sessions could be held immediately after class in the early afternoon. Some activities could convene after a short dinner break. If these activities began earlier in the evening, they could be finished sooner in the evening. The one factor every coach or sponsor would have to consider is how important any extracurricular activity is in relation to the primary mission of the school, which, of course, is learning and education, not sports or clubs. 9

Availability of buses is another concern for many school districts when any discussion of changing schedules begins. School officials in Montgomery County, Maryland, estimate it would cost $31 million to 10 buy enough buses to accommodate later start times for high school without inconveniencing elementary and middle school students (Bettelheim 557). Minneapolis, which buses 90 percent of the 50,000 students in the school district, solved the transportation problems caused by starting high school classes later by starting the grade school classes earlier (Lawton). This has the added benefits of bringing younger children to school at a time when many of them are most alert and decreasing the need for before-school child care for these students (Reiss; Lawton). With careful planning and scheduling, the transportation tribulations can be addressed in cost-effective ways.

As the world we live in becomes ever more complex, education   11
becomes increasingly important. It is important that the time spent on education be spent as effectively as possible. James Maas, a psychologist at Cornell University, points out that "people are beginning to realize it doesn't make sense to pay heavy school taxes when the audience you're teaching is asleep" (qtd. in Bettelheim 556). It is time to consider school schedules that provide the best education at times that are most appropriate to the students.

WORKS CITED

Bettelheim, Adriel. "Sleep Deprivation." *CQ Researcher* 8.24 (1998): 555–62. Print.

Carskadon, Mary A. "When Worlds Collide: Adolescent Need for Sleep versus Societal Demands." *Phi Delta Kappan* Jan. 1999: 348–53. Print.

Dragseth, Kenneth A. "A Minneapolis Suburb Reaps Early Benefits from a Late Start." *School Administrator*. American Association of School Administrators, Mar. 1999. Web. 22 Mar. 2003.

Lawton, Millicent. "For Whom the Bell Tolls." *School Administrator*. American Association of School Administrators, Mar. 1999. Web. 22 Mar. 2003.

Reiss, Tammy. "Wake-up Call on Kids' Biological Clocks." *NEA Today* 6.6 (1998): 19. Print.

Wahlstrom, Kyla L. "The Prickly Politics of School Starting Times." *Phi Delta Kappan* 80 (1999): 345–47. Print.

Wahlstrom, Kyla L., and John S. Taylor. "Sleep Research Warns: Don't Start High School without the Kids." *Education Digest* 66 (2000): 15–20. *EBSCOhost*. Web. 22 Mar. 2003.

Cracking Down on Lighting Up

Monica Perez

The Catholic University of America
Washington, D.C.

Only people with their heads in a cloud of smoke could have missed the many public campaigns warning Americans about the dangers of tobacco. But in a proposal essay, even the most well-publicized problem bears repeating, and Monica Perez does this well by solidifying the risks of smoking and the benefits of quitting with statistics and expert testimony. Having readied readers for her proposal by refreshing their memories about the horrors of the "nasty habit," Perez outlines a three-part action plan to "help push smoking out of society," and successfully responds to possible objections to her proposal from tobacco companies, states, and bar and restaurant owners. As you read, pay attention to Perez's tone, which reveals both her disgust with smoking and her determination to "crack down" on it. How effective is that tone as a call to action? Does it anger you? Inspire you?

On September 29, 2002, more than a thousand young people converged on Louisville, Kentucky—the heart of tobacco country. They brought some cameras; the media brought some more . . . and for what? To drop dead. Where? In front of a major tobacco manufacturer. That's what it looked like, anyway, as the students—recruits from nearby colleges and universities—fell to the ground in unison for the filming of a commercial. The commercial, sponsored by the American Legacy Foundation, is part of an antismoking campaign called The Citizen's Commission to Protect the Truth, which joins a decades-long movement to educate the public about the dangers of smoking. 1

Smoking is a nasty habit that is the leading cause of many types of cancer; these include cancer of the kidney, cervix, bone marrow, 2 pancreas, and stomach, to name a few. Some of the more obvious diseases caused by smoking include lung, oral, and throat cancers, along with chronic lung disease. Studies have also linked smoking to heart disease, osteoporosis, and cataracts. Secondhand smoke is another side effect of smoking, but this affects not smokers but the bystanders who happen to be around smokers. According to the Environmental Protection Agency, secondhand smoke is a "Class A carcinogen," meaning that it causes cancer and that it is not safe to be exposed to at any level or for any amount of time. One estimate stated that environmental tobacco smoke kills "53,000 Americans every year" (Clark).

Thankfully, many of the harsh effects of smoking can be reversed. By quitting smoking, you can reap the healing benefits. According to About.com, after twenty-four hours of not smoking, blood pressure decreases, body temperature increases, carbon monoxide and oxygen levels return to normal, and the chance of a heart attack decreases. After two days, nerve endings begin to regrow, and there is an improvement in one's ability to taste and smell. Soon, former smokers may have a new lease on life: in as little as a month, there is significant improvement in coughing, fatigue, shortness of breath, and sinus congestion ("Quit Smoking Benefits"). The question isn't, however, why should someone quit smoking, but how do we get them to do so? How do we help change society's mentality on smoking? We should start with continuing prevention and treatment programs, implementing clean-air laws and smoke-free policies, and continuing to increase cigarette sales taxes.

The best way to get people to quit smoking is to make sure that they never start. "Prevention is a far better investment" than treatment simply because it is so much harder to rid people of an addiction than it is to keep them from falling victim to one ("Smoking Kills"). When it comes to prevention, education is key. We must continue to target younger audiences and teach them the risks of lighting up. If we start to educate children as soon as they enter the schooling system, there is a much better chance they will not be influenced later on. We must also focus our attention on teens. As a group, teenagers and young adults have one of the highest growth rates of new smokers, with three thousand young people beginning every day ("Smoking"). To reduce the number of teens who start smoking, we need to change smoking's image. It doesn't help that our society is bombarded by continuous advertisements and positive

images of smoking in movies and television shows. An internal tobacco company marketing report from 1989 said, "We believe that
most of the strong, positive images for cigarettes and smoking are
created by cinema and television" ("Facts"). We must teach the next
generations to filter out these false images. There are thousands of
different organizations, like The Truth, that can help. But it must be
a cooperative effort; parents must speak to their kids, and teachers
must act as role models and continue to stress the dangers of cigarette smoking. We also cannot forget that young smokers need extra
support and encouragement to quit.

Implementing or strengthening clean-indoor-air laws and smoke-   5
free policies state-by-state is another way to help reduce smoking
nationwide. These policies include prohibitions against smoking in
public places, such as bars, restaurants, and the workplace. It is important that the public know that clean-indoor-air laws "prompt
more smokers to try to quit; increase the number of successful quit
attempts; reduce the number of cigarettes that continuing smokers
consume," and have a strong, documented "positive impact . . . on
preventing children and adolescents from ever starting" to smoke
(Barry, "Clean Indoor Air"). *The American Journal of Public Health*
reviewed nineteen studies on smoke-free workplaces and found that
all reported either declines in daily cigarette consumption by continuing smokers or reductions in smoking prevalence after bans on
smoking in the workplace were introduced (Barry, "Clean Indoor
Air"). Smoke-free homes and workplaces also significantly lower
adolescent smoking rates. And smoke-free policies are also good for
nonsmokers. According to Charles S. Clark, "88% of Americans find
cigarette smoke annoying." Some people have even developed aller-
gies to smoke, especially those with asthma. Others just plain don't
like the smell and certainly don't want to taste the smoke in their
food. According to a report by the Campaign for Tobacco-Free
Kids, "People are speaking up for their right to breathe clean,
smoke-free air" ("Smoke-Free Laws"). Smoke-free policies will help
protect nonsmokers and smokers alike, although perhaps for different reasons.

Like implementing smoke-free policies, raising the sales tax on   6
cigarettes is another indirect way to encourage people to quit or to at
least cut down on smoking. If you are a smoker, then you know just
how expensive packs are becoming these days. As of 2003, the average price per pack, with all taxes, was about $4.12. And that average

is rising, with cigarette taxes in many states going up. Virginia raised its tax to 35 cents per pack from 2.5 cents in February 2004. Alabama followed Virginia's lead by increasing its tax by about 26 cents per pack in May 2004. Results from recent surveys conclude that teen smoking decreases by 7 percent and overall smoking goes down by 3–5 percent for every 10 percent increase in the price of cigarettes ("Update from the States").

Opposition can be seen from every corner. The tobacco companies, the states, and bar and restaurant owners all have something to say. Tobacco companies are upset for the obvious reason that if measures such as these are taken, sales will go down and the number of new smokers will decline—which really isn't such a bad thing. One of the biggest misconceptions about smoke-free laws is that they harm business for restaurants and bars. Not only will these laws "help protect restaurant and bar employees and patrons from the harms of secondhand smoke," but there is overwhelming evidence—dozens of studies and hard economic data—that smoke-free laws can do this without harming business (Barry, "Smoke-Free Laws"). In March 2003, New York passed a citywide comprehensive smoke-free law. A year later, the city reported that "business receipts for bars and restaurants have increased, employment has risen, and virtually all establishments are complying with the law." Moreover, the 2004 Zagat Survey found that while 4 percent of New Yorkers surveyed were eating out less often because of the smoke-free law, a whopping 23 percent were eating out *more* often because of the law (Barry, "Smoke-Free Laws"). There will be the occasional bar that hurts because they "relied on customers who spent a majority of their day there smoking and drinking," but overall the positive effects far outweigh the negative effects. States worry about the loss of cigarette revenues and the fate of the tobacco farmer. I say, in this day and age, a health-savvy trend is sweeping the nation and especially the younger generations. It is only a matter of time before the number of new smokers drops so significantly that they cannot support the tobacco industry. States that rely on tobacco revenues should start switching their areas of income now. Tobacco farmers can help this transition by growing soybeans or corn instead. For those wary states, why not at least pursue a trial period of passing smoke-free laws or flat out banning smoking to see the results for yourselves? There will hardly be a "negative economic impact, so there are no valid reasons for . . . states not to pass similar laws" ("Profile: New Study").

According to Terry Martin, "Smoking remains the leading pre- 8
ventable cause of death in this country." Thousands of lives will be
taken this year. Perhaps by implementing these suggested measures, a
few may be saved. I can't think of a logical reason not to do everything within states' power to help push smoking out of society. The
American community as a whole needs to join together in a collective
effort to rid our country of the maladies smoking brings. Neither one
person nor one state can do it alone.

WORKS CITED

Barry, Matt. "Clean Indoor Air Laws Encourage Smokers to Quit and Dis-
    courage Youth from Starting." *Campaign for Tobacco-Free Kids.* Cam-
    paign for Tobacco-Free Kids, 1 July 2004. Web. 10 Apr. 2005.
———. "Smoke-Free Laws Do Not Harm Business at Restaurants and Bars."
    Campaign for Tobacco-Free Kids. Campaign for Tobacco-Free Kids, 1 July
    2004. Web. 10 Apr. 2005.
Clark, Charles S. "Crackdown on Smoking." CQ Researcher Online. CQ
    Press, 1992. Web. 8 Apr. 2005.
"Facts." *truth.* Truth.com, n.d. Web. 8 Apr. 2005.
Martin, Terry. "The Health Consequences of Smoking." *Smoking Cessation.*
    About.com, 8 Sept. 2004. Web. 8 Apr. 2005.
———."Quit Smoking Benefits—One to Nine Months." *Smoking Cessation.*
    About.com, 8 Sept. 2004. Web. 8 Apr. 2005.
McMahon, Katie. "State Cigarette Tax Rates & Rank, Date of Last Increase,
    Annual Pack Sales & Revenues, and Related Data." *Campaign for Tobacco-
    Free Kids.* Campaign for Tobacco-Free Kids, 18 Mar. 2005. Web. 10 Apr.
    2005.
"Profile: New Study Shows Effect of Statewide Smoking Ban in Massachu-
    setts." Narr. Steve Inskeep. *Morning Edition.* National Public Radio, 5
    Apr. 2005. Transcript. *Proquest.* Web. 8 Apr. 2005.
"Smoke-Free Laws: Protecting Our Right to Breathe Clean Air." *Campaign
    for Tobacco-Free Kids.* Campaign for Tobacco-Free Kids, 5 July 2004.
    Web. 8 Apr. 2005.
"Smoking Kills Millions Each Year." *Australian Nursing Journal* 12.7 (2005):
    27. Proquest. Web. 8 Apr. 2005.
"Smoking: U.S. Won't Meet Smoking Goals." *Medical Letter on the CDC &
    FDA* 10 Jan. 2000: 11. Proquest. Web. 8 Apr. 2005.
"Update from the States: Tobacco Taxes and Smoke-Free Policies in Action."
    American Heart Association. American Heart Association, 28 Mar. 2005.
    Web. 8 Apr. 2005.

Quality Long-Term Care: Our Elderly Deserve It

Kim Spencer Kline and Dana Jordan

Des Moines Area Community College
Des Moines, Iowa

Kim Spencer Kline and Dana Jordan begin their essay by briefly recounting several sad and gruesome incidents, including the choking death of an elderly Des Moines woman. These stories get readers' attention and create a framework for the students' proposal, which aims to protect some of Iowa's most vulnerable citizens: men and women in nursing homes. But if stories interest and orient, it is often drier details—laws and regulations, for example—that tip interest into motivation. This is as true for writers as it is for readers: Kline's friend's experience as a long-term-care nurse got the cowriters interested in their topic, but it was the students' research into Iowa's laws and the laws of other states that motivated them to "write a real proposal, not just an assignment," and address not only their teacher and fellow students but also lawmakers and lobbyists. As you read, notice the range of interest- and motivation-generating strategies Kline and Jordan use to win their audience's ear—from asking rhetorical questions and telling stories to citing graphs and legislation.

During your lifetime, you or someone in your family will probably need to be placed in a nursing home. One of your grandparents or parents may already be in a long-term care facility. Does that facility neglect or abuse its patients? Are patients' lives in jeopardy simply because the facility is short on staff? Far too often, the answer is yes. For instance, between March and April 2004, the *Des Moines Register* printed more than seven articles advising the public of the numerous noncompliance issues at the Abbey Nursing Home (Kauffman; Kauffman and Leys). On April 4, 2004, the Department of Inspections and Appeals declared the forty-one residents of the Abbey in "immediate jeopardy." Indeed, the residents were in jeopardy. In one recorded incident, a female resident died from choking on food while unattended in the dining area. Former Abbey employee Joanie Grace, a long-term care nurse of fifteen years, recounted another incident in which the Abbey staff could not locate an oxygen tank to resuscitate a patient. Dangerous situations like these stem from inadequate staffing. To prevent similar problems at long-term care facilities across Iowa, we propose that the Iowa legislature implement specific nursing-staff requirements and implement laws to enforce penalties for noncompliant facilities.

Inadequate Staffing Issues

Incidents of abuse, neglect, and accidental death occur all too often in Iowa's care facilities. A shortage of qualified LPN and RN nurses and certified nursing assistants on each shift results in most of these tragedies. And the staffing problem is only getting worse: over the past three years, complaints to Iowa's ombudsman's office have increased (see Figure 1).

Many patients require extensive care from skilled nurses. Joanie Grace reflects, "If I am responsible for fifty-eight patients on a shift and some of them require G-tube feedings, trach care, and vent monitoring, a sick patient down the hall may not get assessed until he or she is acutely ill and needing hospitalization. We may have been able to treat the patient at the facility if he or she had been assessed sooner."

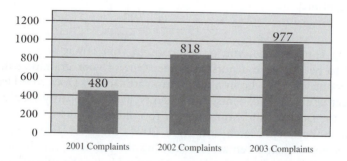

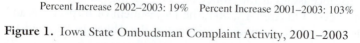

Percent Increase 2002–2003: 19%   Percent Increase 2001–2003: 103%

Figure 1. Iowa State Ombudsman Complaint Activity, 2001–2003

She continues, "This adds to the burden of financing health care. We need more staff. The inability to provide necessary care is scary for the patient and for the nurse whose license is on the line."

Unfortunately, Joanie's experience in the long-term care field is   4
not uncommon. Understaffing at many hospitals means that most nurses must cover three shifts, including holiday and weekend shifts. When a licensed practical nurse or CNA does not report for work, the staff must scramble to find someone to cover his or her shift, often requiring another nurse to pull a double shift.

Inadequate staffing poses risks for patients and nurses alike. Resi-   5
dents may be unattended at crucial times, which can result in falls or choking incidents. Calls for assistance to the bathroom or shower may go unanswered for long periods of time, leaving residents lying in their own waste for hours. Important information in medical charts may be overlooked or omitted by overburdened nurses, resulting in incorrect dosing of medications or improper diets that could lead to serious medical complications. The nurses are directly affected since they are held accountable for any mistakes or oversights in patient care. Proper staff-to-patient ratios could prevent many of these problems.

CURRENT LEGISLATION

The state of Iowa currently requires "adequate staffing" but does not   6
suggest actual minimums—based on facility size and resident acuity (care) levels—to fulfill this requirement (State of Iowa House File 2990). In fact, none of the regulations are well-defined. The ambiguity of the law's language makes appealing noncompliance fines all too easy. What's more, extended care facilities are excluded from the adequate staffing requirement:

> "1. A health facility, *other than an extended care facility,* shall ensure that it is staffed in a manner that provides sufficient, appropriately qualified direct-care nurses in each department or unit within the facility in order to meet the individualized care needs of its patients and to meet the requirements specified in this section." Bill: H.J.259.2, Sect. 4, 135M.4, 5:4–9.

This leaves the staffing requirements for long-term care facilities in the hands of individual facilities. Inadequate staffing has often been the result.

THE FLAWED PROCESS OF THE DEPARTMENT OF INSPECTIONS AND APPEALS

The Iowa Department of Inspections and Appeals annually inspects care facilities, issuing fines to those they find noncompliant. As stated above, facilities can appeal these fines and be exonerated. In addition to being fined, a facility that has been noncompliant for six months or more can lose its Medicaid/Medicare certification. This means the facility is unable to receive additional Medicare patients until the facility has reached the "reasonable assurance" period and is eligible to apply for recertification (Wood).   7

The use of fines and penalties has proven to be ineffective in most cases because, when faced with thousands of dollars in fines, many long-term care facility owners will voluntarily close their business and sell it to the highest bidder. Some reopen facilities under a new name or declare bankruptcy. Many facilities are owned by corporations or partnerships that, upon being closed down in one state, simply open another facility in another state and proceed to run that facility into the ground.   8

Though fines and penalties are aimed at punishing the owners and administrators of facilities, in the not-so-long run, staff and residents suffer the consequences. A facility that owes huge debts for noncompliance has less money to spend operating the facility efficiently. The result is inadequate staffing, poor wages, inadequate management, or lack of resources, all elements that directly affect patients. A reform in the law regulating long-term care facilities is desperately needed. The health, safety, and financial well-being of the people who live in these facilities are at stake.   9

GIVING OUR ELDERLY THE QUALITY CARE THEY DESERVE

First, we propose that the law clearly define staffing requirements for long-term care facilities, mandating specific staff-to-patient ratios that take into account the number of residents and level of acuity in a facility, just as staff-to-patient ratios are mandated for other health-care facilities. For example, a reasonable ratio for patients requiring intermediate care would be 7:1, seven patients to one staff member. In addition, each facility should be required to contract with a private nursing pool to provide staffing in emergency situations.   10

Furthermore, each facility must develop a state-mandated man- 11
agement team that includes not only the facility's administrator and
selected staff, but also a state administrator from the Iowa Department of Inspections and Appeals, who interacts with this management team monthly. A state administrator team member should
oversee no more than fifteen local facilities to ensure that he or she
devotes an adequate amount of time to problem solving in any one
facility. The management team would be responsible for overseeing
and maintaining proper staffing ratios, ensuring efficient resource
management, problem solving for quality-care issues, and implementing incentive programs to encourage good employee attendance
and quality work. The state administrator would be responsible for
offering alternative solutions to specific problems, such as finding reliable staff.

Next, we propose that the Iowa state legislature implement laws 12
to enforce penalties for noncompliant facilities. Our proposal requires
that any long-term care facility that does not meet 90 percent compliance following two consecutive inspections loses its Medicaid/
Medicare certification as well as its license to own and operate a long-
term care facility in the state of Iowa. Fines based on level of noncompliance would be issued, and the facility would have thirty days
to transfer its residents and close its doors.

To prevent chronically noncompliant owners from reopening 13
elsewhere, the existing public registry needs to provide state licensing
agencies with a detailed history of all owners/corporations of long-
term care facilities, complete with each company's noncompliance issues, penalties, and fines. Serious complaints should be noted in this
registry. This registry needs to be accessible on a national scale and
should make use of a grading scale for easier deciphering of information. Information should be graded on a scale of 1–4, mirroring the
grading scale of the inspections department. Implementation of a
complete public registry will help prevent other long-term care facilities from being opened by the same people who ran shoddy, unsafe
operations elsewhere.

THE OTHER SIDE

Some may argue that current Iowa regulations as stated in House File 14
2290 are sufficient. But the current regulations leave the responsibility

for maintaining adequate staffing in the hands of the individual facilities; there is no accountability. The management teams we suggest would provide the accountability and the resources necessary to provide quality care in a safe and positive environment.

Other options have been suggested, such as cameras in residents' 15 rooms to monitor the level of care (Huggins). Not only are cameras an infringement of a citizen's right to privacy, but they also "institutionalize" the atmosphere of long-term care facilities.

The state has considered incentive programs to hire better qual- 16 ity nurses, but this does not solve inadequate staffing problems.

Facility administrators may argue that they cannot afford more 17 nurses, but the management team we have proposed would look at time-management issues within the existing staff to better allocate responsibilities. Also, funds that are currently spent on the lengthy inspection and appeals process could be used in the management of facilities.

THE BOTTOM LINE

With the increase in complaints about elder care in Iowa, the time has 18 come for Iowa lawmakers and citizens to set a higher standard for quality of life for our elderly generation. Iowa standards in long-term care should set the example for the rest of the nation. Our proposal eliminates staffing problems, distributes funds more efficiently, and encourages quality health care in a positive environment. Happy, healthy residents are the best advertisers for long-term care facilities, and a positive work environment promotes loyal and competent employees. The focus in long-term care facilities needs to be directed back to the residents, where it belongs.

WORKS CITED

Grace, Joanie. Personal interview. 17 Mar. 2005.
Huggins, Charnicia E. "States Consider Allowing Cameras in Nursing Homes." *Global Action on Aging.* N.p., 23 Aug. 2004. Web. 1 Apr. 2005.
Kauffman, Clark. "Care Center Investigated Again." *Des Moines Register.* Des Moines Register, 19 Mar. 2004. Web. 19 Mar. 2005.

Kauffman, Clark, and Tony Leys. "D. M. Facility's Residents Removed over Safety Fears." *Des Moines Register*. Des Moines Register, 3 Apr. 2004. Web. 19 Mar. 2005.

Office of the State Long-Term Care Ombudsman. Iowa Department on Aging, n.d. Web. 28 Mar. 2005.

State of Iowa. House of Rep. *House File* 2290. H.J. 259.2. Des Moines: Iowa State Legislature. Web. 20 Mar. 2005.

Wood, Erica F. "Termination and Closure of Poor Quality Nursing Homes." *American Association of Retired Persons.* AARP Public Policy Institute, Mar. 2002. Web. 19 Mar. 2005.

Unhealthy Lunchrooms: Toxic for Schoolchildren and the Environment

Kati Huff

Lake Michigan College
Benton Harbor, Michigan

Kati Huff proposes a solution to the "deep-fried corn dogs and grease-saturated French fries on non-biodegradable trays" that are all too common in school cafeterias in the United States. She takes on two problems in this essay—unhealthy food and the generation of excessive waste. Two solutions in one essay is a tall order, but Huff sees the two problems as linked. Both the food and the waste are unhealthy—for us and for the environment—and unsustainable for the future.

Huff cites her sources in APA style and provides an annotated bibliography at the end of her essay, where, instead of just listing her references, she describes each source briefly, telling what information it contains and who produced it. For more information about annotated bibliographies, see Chapter 25 of the *St. Martin's Guide to Writing*, Ninth Edition.

America's waistline is bulging over its belt, and the environment is   1
slowly wasting away. The cause of both of these problems lies in the most unlikely of places. This is a place where all schoolchildren have roamed, gossiped, and played, and where they have been conditioned to gorge themselves with fat-ridden food while at the same time disregarding Mother Nature. Where is this nightmare taking place? In tens of thousands of elementary, junior, and senior high cafeterias across the nation. Fried foods and foam trays are prevalent in almost all public

schools. Schoolchildren, especially in elementary schools, are oblivious to what they are putting into their bodies and into the garbage cans that fill up landfill after landfill. Feeding children deep-fried corn dogs and grease-saturated French fries on non-biodegradable trays is doing nothing for two of the biggest concerns this country has: obesity and the environment. By using reusable trays and being provided with healthy food, students may become more environmentally conscious as well as aware of what they are putting into their bodies. Landfills and the ozone layer will be less impacted by the production and disposal of thousands of foam trays and students will get the nutrition their growing bodies need.

As an elementary school student, my friends and I used to have   2
contests to see who could squeeze the most grease out of their cheese pizza on pizza Fridays. Usually, whoever ended up with the juicy middle piece of the pizza won. Because we were children, and we were hungry, we would set the grease puddle aside and continue to eat the pizza. This is not the type of food that should be infecting future school kids' stomachs. Schools need to change the way kids eat. In a *Newsweek* article published in 2005, it becomes apparent that the meals schools serve often consist of French fries, breaded patties, and some sort of canned vegetable. This, in turn, makes kids want to buy cookies and other snacks that the a la carte section of the cafeteria may offer instead (Tyre & Staveley-O'Carroll, 2005). Though public schools are now offering healthier items, some of the schools still have too many unhealthy foods weighing them down (Ramirez, 2007).

Unfortunately, the cost of healthy food is skyrocketing. In a   3
2005 article in the *Food Service Director* (2007), C. Atwell, a director from California, says that he supports the use of healthy foods and making the transition to them is not the problem. California schools are required to ban fatty and sugary foods from their schools. And, a state program gives school districts 10 cents per meal served when the lunchroom offers two vegetable and fruit options (Shalfi, 2007). However, the cost of food has "risen 25% over the last four years while [funding] increases from the state and federal governments came in at about 13%. The difference seems to grow wider every year" (qtd, Shalfi, 2007, p. 24). Even with some help from the government, schools have trouble affording healthy food for all their students.

If students could choose healthier foods at lunch, they would still   4
be putting the food on foam lunch trays. The food might be better,

but what about what is good for the environment? Schools need to change their minds about the food they serve, and also about what kind of trays they are serving them on. Though the foam trays are often called Styrofoam trays, the name Styrofoam is a trademark of Dow Chemical Company. Dow.com (2007a) states that Styrofoam is not the substance used for these foam trays, cups, or containers. Polystyrene, a substance much like Styrofoam but less durable and less insulating, is used for school lunch trays (Dow.com, 2007b). According to an editorial written by members of the Committee for the Preservation of Wildlife of Northern Illinois University (2005), 1,369 tons of products made with polystyrene are carelessly dumped in our landfills every day in the United States. This number is only increasing due to the excessive use of polystyrene trays in schools. For example, there are approximately 600 students at Berrien Springs High School, a public school in Southwestern Michigan. Every day the cafeteria serves lunch to roughly 400 students. If they used 400 trays a day for five days a week, that would be 2,000 polystyrene foam trays waiting to be dumped somewhere at the end of the week. This number is only for the high school. The elementary schools and junior high in the Berrien Springs School district also use foam trays. The number of foam trays being dumped every day is astronomical.

P. Evans, the food service director for Berrien Springs Public 5
Schools, stated that almost every school district in the area uses polystyrene foam trays. The reason, she says, is that using foam trays is more economically feasible. "We buy foam trays in cases of 500 that are about three to four cents apiece," said Evans. "Buying these disposables [trays] is much cheaper than the labor we would have to pay for employees to wash dishes" (personal communication, November 15, 2007).

Another benefit to the disposable polystyrene trays is that they 6
are sanitary. With disposable trays, districts do not have to worry about cleaning trays two or three times to make sure they are up to code to serve food on again. However, an article by the Committee for the Preservation of Wildlife (2005) reports that polystyrene is made with petroleum and benzene. Both of these are known cancer-causing elements. In 1986 the EPA National Human Adipose Tissue Survey said that they had found styrene residues in 100% of samples of human tissues. Styrene (a part of polystyrene) exposure has been found to cause fatigue, low hemoglobin values, carcinogenic effects,

and nervousness (Committee for the Preservation of Wildlife, 2005). If these side effects from styrene exposure have been proven, why do schools continue to serve children food on trays made from those very elements? Schools must come up with a better solution.

One solution would be to use disposable trays that are better for the environment. Unfortunately, this plan has many problems. P. Evans said that the Berrien Springs School District had looked into buying more ecologically friendly trays. However, "Go Green" lunch trays cost three to four times as much as the foam trays, and few districts could afford that. The Boise, Idaho schools tried to use trays made of sugar cane fiber, even though the trays cost three times as much as the foam ones. This school district was willing to stretch the extra penny and try them. However, the trays needed to be composted in humidity and high heat, which is not likely weather in Idaho (Allen, 2007). 7

To reduce the number of trays in landfills, the foam trays that schools use now could be recycled. However, recycling polystyrene is not an easy process and is extremely costly (Myron 1995). Schools would lose money trying to recycle every single tray they use. P. Evans stated that if the Berrian Springs School District was to recycle the foam trays, they needed to be washed and cleared of food debris before the recycling company would take them. This would defeat the purpose of using the trays—they would still need people to wash them. And, the process to make polystyrene produces chemicals that pollute the ozone, so it would still be bad for the environment (Myron, 1995). 8

Extra labor, special facilities, and healthy foods are certainly not cheap. Though these costs seem outrageous, they can be managed. When using reusable trays, schools have to pay once for the trays and also for occasional replacement trays. There are ways to eliminate extra labor as well. Berrien Springs School District food service program is trying out touch screens that will let students order their meal. This will eliminate the time it takes for cafeteria workers to fill out an order slip for each student. With this extra time, cafeteria workers will have time to wash dishes without going overtime (personal communication, November 15, 2007). According to M. Shalfi of *Food Service Director* (2007), a school district in Ohio is looking at investing in a combi-oven. The oven cooks with steam and adds crispness without deep frying. Since they won't be deep frying, the 9 school will not have to pay for oil or wash out fryers. They say that the oven will pay itself off in time because they will be saving about $3,000 a year. Another option for washing the trays would be to use students. Students at the high school level are, in most states, required to complete a certain number of community service hours. What better way to get those hours in than during the lunch period without taking the time to leave campus? Also, incentives for helping, such as a free lunch, can be used to get students to help wash the trays. In this way, there would be no extra cost for cafeteria labor.

While food service directors are trying to find a cost-effective, "green" approach to the trays, they must also try to get students to eat healthier. Sneaking the new ingredients into the foods is one option. Unfortunately, students sometimes turn away from foods that look the same as the unhealthy ones but taste different. According to a Liberal Democrat report, 250,000 fewer meals are eaten in secondary schools after mandating nutrition guidelines (Druce, 2007). Requiring a course on nutrition might help students make better food choices at lunch, but hiring and training new teachers would be costly, and students might not make the right decisions anyway. 10

There is, however, a light at the end of this toxic tunnel. It is simple to get students to eat healthier food. Slowly introducing fresh fruits and vegetables is a great way to start. Offering a well-balanced meal with a touch of the old food is the way to get the students to eat new foods. Children do not like change, so the transition to healthier foods needs to be a slow and continuous process. Skim milk, fresh fruits and vegetables, and whole grains should be easily accessible at each meal. The main course does not have to be made of soy beans, but healthy options need to be available for students to fill up their reusable trays with. If done properly, at a slow and steady pace, healthy foods will catch on and become just as popular as grease-pizza Friday. 11

By implementing this simple and effective plan, several groups of people will benefit. Food services will save money and time for not having to buy foam trays or pay for labor. Schoolchildren will be making the right food choices and will have less chance of becoming obese in the future. Finally, the environment will be cleaner and less impacted by millions of polystyrene foam trays polluting it. Although these solutions would require some changes to the current school food system, they would be worth it for their benefit to students and to the environment. 12

ANNOTATED BIBLIOGRAPHY

Allen, A. (2007, October 30). Boise schools pushing for eco-friendly lunch trays: Community urges schools to use materials that can be recycled or composted. *Idaho Statesman*. Retrieved from http://www.idahostatesman.com

The Boise Idaho school district shows their concern about foam trays used in the school cafeteria. Some of the schools in the district are equipped with facilities to use plastic trays while others tried a new tray made of sugarcane fiber that can be composted. Although these trays cost three times as much as the foam ones, students seemed to prefer them. Problems like recycling or composting the fiber trays arose. PTO groups are now offering to put dishwashers into the schools. Alternatives to the foam trays are still being discussed.

American Chemistry Council Plastics Food Processing Group (PFPG). (2007). *Polystyrene facts*. Retrieved from http://www.americanchemistry.com

The Plastics Food Processing Group is a business group of the American Chemistry Council and supplies the public with resin and polystyrene while responding to inquiries from the public. PFPG explains why polystyrene is sanitary, sturdy, efficient, economical, and convenient. The PFPG advocates the use of polystyrene products while relating them to our daily lives. The arguments for using polystyrene products are clearly stated here.

Committee for the Preservation of Wildlife. (2005, February 11). Students should choose Styrofoam alternative. *Northern Star*. Retrieved from http://www.star.niu.edu

This article, written by members of the Committee for the Preservation of Wildlife, explains some dangers of the use of polystyrene. The article ties in the dangers of its use with students' lives at the Northern Illinois campus. This article also reflects the views of the students on the foam trays.

Dow Chemical Company. (2007a). *What is STYROFOAM?* Retrieved from http://www.dow.com

Dow Chemicals explains that Styrofoam is not used in plates or trays that are commonly used in school cafeterias. Styrofoam is a trademarked name.

Dow Chemicals Company. (2007b). *Polystyrene*. Retrieved from http://www.dow.com

Dow Chemical explains what polystyrene is and what it is used for.

Hackes, B., & Shanklin, W. (1999). Factors other than environmental issues influence resource allocation decisions of school foodservice directors. *Journal of the American Dietetic Association, 99*(8), 944–946. Retrieved from http://www.adajournal.org

Respondents to an extensive survey give an insight into school food service recycling programs. Also, recommendations are made to conserve environmental resources and cut down on pollution.

Myron, H. (1995). *Polystyrene foam recycling.* Retrieved from http://www.newton.dep.anl.gov/newton/askasci/1995/environ/ENV138.HTM

"Ask a Scientist" offers some insight into recycling and alternatives to polystyrene (used for foam trays in school cafeterias). Recycling the foam is costly and not many companies are interested in buying back the recycled material. Also, ozone-destroying chemicals are used to make foam products.

Ramirez, E. (2007, August 16). Do school cafeterias make the grade? *U.S. News & World Report.* Retrieved from http://www.usnews.com

Creative ways to bring in more healthy foods to schools and the expenses of those healthy foods are discussed.

Shalfi, M. (2007, August 15). Taking back school lunch: Operators meet the challenges of the increased costs of healthier foods with creative solutions and an outcry for federal funding. *Food Service Director, 20*(8), 24–27. Retrieved from http://www.fsdmag.com

Transitioning to healthier lunch items is something that all schools agree on, but healthy food is expensive and not all school districts get the funding for it. "Sneaking" healthy foods into entrees has proven successful but nutrition education in the schools is still missing. Creative solutions such as buying combi-ovens, bringing back salad bars, creating more ethnic cuisines, and using whole grains are presented.

Tyre, P., & Staveley-O'Carroll, S. (2005, August 8). How to fix school lunch: Celebrity chefs, politicians and concerned parents are joining forces to improve the meals kids eat every day. *Newsweek, 146,* 50.

As the number of children who are obese or have diabetes grows, it is becoming apparent that school kitchens need to be reevaluated. Meals provided by untrained workers in understaffed cafeterias do not give children the nutrition they need. Also, money from vending machine sales has declined because of the implementation of healthy foods; therefore, schools find it hard to pay for fresh fruits and vegetables.

Justifying an 8
Evaluation

You are already very familiar with evaluations. In fact, if you're like most of us, you depend on them on a weekly or even a daily basis. Before spending more-than-fast-food-money to dine out, you probably ask for suggestions from friends who know the local restaurant scene or read restaurant reviews online or in your local newspaper. And you probably don't watch movies cold; instead, you're more likely to go to the theater on a friend's recommendation or read brief descriptions of what's playing in a free weekly or on a movie-review site before buying a ticket. For a major purchase like a car or truck, cell phone, digital camera, or even a pair of running shoes, you're likely to look for a recent, authoritative review of the product, perhaps in *Consumer Reports*—a magazine whose comprehensive evaluations have catapulted its parent organization, the Consumers Union, into the national consciousness.

Quite clearly, reviews are wide ranging. Student writers in this chapter evaluate quite different subjects: a painting, a magazine, a movie, and a book. Like any reviewers, these writers judge their subjects, but they go well beyond giving them just a thumbs up or down: they give reasons for their judgments and then support each reason with definitions, examples, descriptions, and comparisons to similar subjects. They may even anticipate readers' reservations or alternative judgments.

Judgments are easy to make—so much so that they are sometimes referred to as "snap judgments." When you evaluate, you test your snap judgments, turning them into reasoned evaluations. In doing so, you develop your powers of attention to details and the ability to discriminate among them. When evaluating a subject and writing up your evaluation of it, you must look closely, attentively (that is, without noisy distractions), look again, think hard and rethink, justify—all the while extending and refining your understanding of subjects like the one you are evaluating. To evaluate, then, is to engage in thoughtful, responsible, discriminating work—work that is worth your time.

Watchmen
Matthew Fontilla
Chaffey College
Rancho Cucamonga, California

Watchmen, a 2009 movie based on Alan Moore's graphic novel by the same name, is about a group of superheroes in an alternate-reality version of New York City in 1985. In this brief, exuberant review, Matthew Fontilla expresses his admiration for the style, characters, and overall intensity of the film. His review is designed for an audience who might see the movie based on his enthusiasm, and perhaps also for one that will identify as either "intellectual" or "geek." As you read, notice how Fontilla supports his judgment in each paragraph of his essay. Does it succeed in making you want to see *Watchmen*?

The film *Watchmen* is a "must see" for intellectuals and geeks alike; its visual style surpasses that of all other comic book films. There is never a dull moment during the film because the cinematography is phenomenal and the philosophy, although slightly arcane, is scathingly profound; your eyes will never leave the screen and your mind will never stop deciphering the meaning of the film. A second viewing is highly recommended if you wish to grasp all the information and the metaphors; the only problem with this is the fact that you will have spent six hours and twelve minutes watching it twice. However, if you take a lesson from Doctor Manhattan, you should be able to regard time as meaningless, which will allow you to appreciate this film without worrying about the hours passing by. *Watchmen* is a masterpiece because of its elucidation of the plight of society, the pains of superiority, and the limits of time. The characters illustrate these points by their vigilance, noncompliance with authority, and wisdom.

Watchmen alludes to fear in society being like a wildfire; it spreads   2
rapidly and the masses do nothing to impede its spread. Only a few
vigilantes will, sometimes foolishly, put their lives on the line in an effort to put a stop to something bigger than themselves. The Watchmen are these few vigilantes in a fire that is the fear of, among many
other issues, a seemingly inevitable nuclear war. Vigilantes are not
always heroes, though. This moral complexity is one of the reasons
why *Watchmen* is such a great film. While the Watchmen are superheroes, their actions aren't always justifiable. A recurring theme in the
film is the question: "Who watches the Watchmen"? This suggests
that the public is not always grateful for the actions of the Watchmen.
They are frequently violent, occasionally destroy public property, and
cannot always help the society they are a part of.

A brilliant aspect of the film lies underneath the costumes; a cer-   3
tain degree of noncompliance is at the heart of all vigilantes. Each one
is reluctant to follow the rules of society or even to follow a leader
within the group. Although the Watchmen have a history as a public
group, they are not always willing to comply with the public's demands.
At the time the film is set, their superpowers have been made illegal;
only two Watchmen are active, with government approval. However,
each member of the Watchmen exemplifies this noncompliance in his
or her own way. Rorschach, the member of the Watchmen who narrates the film, is perhaps the least compliant of the group. He is an independent, hardly a member of the group at all. His bitterness about
the immorality of society leads him to kill those whom he considers im-
moral; the viewer must consider whether his actions are morally just.

A notable quote from the film that will give some insight on the   4
wisdom of each character is: "My father was a watch maker. He abandoned it when Einstein discovered time is relative. I would only agree
that a symbolic clock is as nourishing to the intellect as a photograph
of oxygen to a drowning man." (The "symbolic clock" in the quote is
the nuclear doomsday clock, which indicates symbolically how close
the world is to nuclear war.) The Watchmen have cultivated wisdom
by analyzing the malice of society, and the people who contribute to
it, throughout their decades of existence. Thus, fearful symbols like
the doomsday clock mean little to them. They each hold steadfast beliefs on how to remake a malevolent society, even if that means de-
stroying it.

If you are looking to view an intellectually stimulating thriller, a   5
compelling superhero action film, or both, watch *Watchmen*. The deep

symbolism throughout the film will leave you in awe, and the action sequences will have your palms sweaty in no time. Your imagination will be grateful that you did so, as long as you are willing to dedicate your undivided attention to the screen for almost three hours.

Evaluation of Nickel and Dimed

Jane Kim

University of California, Riverside
Riverside, California

For this essay, Jane Kim chose to evaluate *Nickel and Dimed,* Barbara Ehrenreich's firsthand investigation into the lives of the working poor. In her very first paragraph, Kim presents the reader with enough information about the book to understand her position on the book and its argument. Then, Kim easily leads us through her well-organized argument, using relevant quotations from the book to support her judgments. As you read, notice the criteria Kim sets up for evaluating Ehrenreich's work.

Barbara Ehrenreich, a journalist with a PhD in biology, reports her experience in the world of the working poor in her book *Nickel and Dimed.* As an investigative reporter and scientist, she creates an experiment, sets some limits, takes a few necessities, and detaches herself from the upper-class world, which she is familiar with, and inserts herself into the society of the impoverished. She gains firsthand experience in what it feels like to live on a barely livable wage, always hoping to have shelter and nourishment the next day. She works as a waitress, a maid, a dietary aide, and an employee of Wal-Mart, while trying to sustain herself off just what she makes at these jobs, minus the advantages she came in with in her experiment (car, extra cash, and health). Ehrenreich, through her hands-on experience, evinces the difficulty and almost impossibility of living off the wages such workers make (as of 2001). Overall, Ehrenreich does a fair job of revealing the situation of the working poor and making it clear that something must be done to relieve this "state of emergency" (Ehrenreich 214).

Ehrenreich presents her argument that it is very difficult to "live   2
on the wages available to the unskilled" as "many people earn far less
than they need to live on" through excellent uses of supporting evidence (Ehrenreich 1, 213). Furthermore, to persuade her readers
that her claim is important, Ehrenreich shows the wage rise over the
years, saying "wages at the bottom are going up, [but] they're not
going up very briskly" and "they have not been sufficient to bring
low-wage workers up to the amounts they were earning twenty-seven
years ago, in 1973" (Ehrenreich 203). The author clearly presents her
position and argument through effective diction and by revealing the
seriousness of the issue, which should not be ignored, as the experiences of low-wage workers "are not part of a sustainable lifestyle, even
a lifestyle of chronic deprivation and relentless low-level punishment"
(Ehrenreich 214).

By doing firsthand field research to add to her extensive library   3
and Internet research, the author makes an especially convincing argument. Describing the daily lives of low-wage workers makes her evidence authoritative. For example, in the second chapter, Ehrenreich
shares the experience she went through working two jobs: a weekend
position as a dietary aide at a nursing home ($7 an hour) and a 40-
hour per week maid position ($6.65). Even when working two jobs
and being thrifty, she reveals the difficulty of managing to pay for rent
and food. In terms of rent, she explains that "when the rich and the
poor compete for housing on the open market, the poor don't stand a
chance" and essentially "the poor have been forced into housing that
is more expensive, more dilapidated, or more distant from their places
of work" (Ehrenreich 199). Furthermore, to increase the effectiveness
of her argument that wages must be higher, the author reveals that
even when the low-wage worker receives aid, it is difficult to get it.
When she tried to obtain food from food pantries and emergency aid,
it took her seventy minutes of calling and driving to get around seven
dollars worth of food, with limited choices (Ehrenreich 103).

In addition to her personal experience, Ehrenreich uses other au-   4
thoritative sources to enhance her reliability, integrating statistical
sources within her text and citing those sources in footnotes. For example, to explain why wages don't rise, Ehrenreich refers to a report
by Louis Uchitelle in the *New York Times* on how "many employers
will offer almost anything—free meals, subsidized transportation, store
discounts—rather than raise wages" (Ehrenreich 204).

Without Ehrenreich's investigative reporting, it would be hard 5
for people outside of the low-wage working class to grasp the reality
of the problem. Through firsthand experience, Ehrenreich effectively
reveals the dark world of the daily life of the low-wage worker. She
acknowledges that some readers could argue that she didn't truly experience "poverty," as she went in with some advantages: a car (her
own) or a rental vehicle (paid with credit card instead of earned
wages), the cushion of relying on her credit card for food if she ever
thought she wouldn't have food the next day, and knowing she
could end the project at the particular location if she ran out of
money for rent (Ehrenreich 5–6). Ehrenreich concedes this objection
to her experiment, explaining that "there was no way [she] was going
to 'experience poverty' or find out how it 'really feels' to be a long-
term low-wage worker" (Ehrenreich 6). Furthermore, she makes it
clear that there are people who endure much worse conditions than
she does during her experiment: "this is in fact the best-case scenario:
a person with every advantage that ethnicity and education, health
and motivation can confer attempting, in a time of exuberant pros-
perity, to survive in the economy's lower depths" (Ehrenreich 10).
Ehrenreich lets readers know through such comments that she is not
portraying herself as having experienced exactly what the impoverished face every day.

Another kind of objection Ehrenreich anticipates is that she 6
should not speak for others, but let them speak for themselves.
Although she concedes it would be better if they did speak and act
for themselves, Ehrenreich provides some information to support her
speaking out on behalf of the low-wage workers. She makes the point
that workers are often hesitant to form unions for fear of getting
fired because "the poorer they are, the more constrained their mobil-
ity usually is." She also notes that "help-wanted signs and want ads
coyly refrain from mentioning numbers" so workers can't compare
wages, and of course their employers may "make it hard to air [their]
grievances to peers or to enlist other workers in a group effort to
bring about change" (Ehrenreich 205, 206, 209). Ehrenreich effectively argues that low-wage workers do not have many opportunities
to safely speak for themselves, so she is justified in attempting to
speak for them.

Overall, Ehrenreich's *Nickel and Dimed* is well written and effec- 7
tively enlightens readers on a situation facing members of their own
community. The author's use of personal experience and authoritative

resources gives her argument strength and believability. Her inclusion of personal ethical indignation combined with effective rhetoric gives her argument an intensity that has the potential to move readers to action. She may not provide solutions to the problem she so vividly presents, but Ehrenreich achieves her goal of opening readers' eyes to the hardship of those who make the lives of others more comfortable at the expense of their own well-being.

WORK CITED

Ehrenreich, Barbara. *Nickel and Dimed*. New York: Metropolitan Books, 2001. Print.

May I Have This Dance?

Robert Nava

Riverside Community College
Riverside, California

We have all had the experience of coming away disappointed from an art exhibition or performance. After attending several "dreary and uninspiring" exhibits at his college's art gallery, Robert Nava was beginning to tire of such disappointments. Then one show—and one painting in particular, *Dance VII* by Gina Han—caught him pleasantly by surprise. Nava particularly liked the way *Dance VII* evoked movement. Of course, justifying an evaluation means more than just pointing out what you did or didn't like about a work. Evaluative authors should also provide reasons for their opinions and be able to support those reasons, and that means knowing their subject well. Experience helps, as do close or repeated viewings and, in some cases, additional research.

Nava is an experienced judge of visual art—he establishes his authority as an evaluator of *Dance VII* by noting his past experience at his college's art gallery. But he has also done his homework. Much of his essay is devoted to an examination of how color and texture work together in the painting to create the impression of movement. That examination required both a sustained viewing of the piece and an understanding of color theory, a concept Nava explains to his readers. We come away from Nava's essay with both a desire to see the painting in person and a new appreciation for color theory and its usefulness as an artist's strategy. It is a gift to the reader when an evaluation combines critique with insight or instruction, as Nava's does. Could your evaluation essay lend itself to such an approach?

A visit to the Riverside Community College art gallery can sometimes   1
be dreary and uninspiring. Having seen the faculty art show before, I
have found that the pieces on display become repetitive and tiresome,

154

with the same artists displaying new pieces with the same style and technique they've used every year before. However, this year the faculty artists have produced quite a few surprises, one of which is *Dance VII* by Gina Han. At first glance, I disregarded the oil painting, thinking little or no effort had gone into creating it. What could be so special about a canvas covered in random blotches of color? On a second look, I discovered what was so exciting about *Dance VII*: the creation of movement through color, placement, and texture.

But to better appreciate *Dance VII,* a brief explanation of color theory is necessary. An important tool for any artist is the color wheel, an arrangement of primary (red, yellow, and blue) and secondary (orange, green, and violet) colors that logically blend into one another in a circle, or wheel. From the combination of the primary and secondary colors, all other colors are created. The primary colors, those colors that cannot be created by mixing other colors, are equidistant from each other on the wheel. Secondary colors are those colors created by mixing two primary colors—for example, combining red and blue to create violet. There are also tertiary colors, which are made by mixing a primary color with its adjacent (on the color wheel) secondary color—for example, red (primary) mixed with orange (secondary) will create red-orange (tertiary). The color wheel in Figure 1 shows primary, secondary, and tertiary colors.

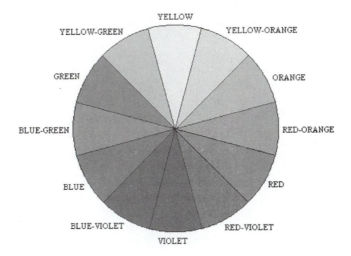

Figure 1. The color wheel.

With the color wheel, we can also identify different color combi-   3
nations that, oddly and without any notable explanation, are pleasing
to the eye. One of these combinations is called *complementary,* which
is a pairing of two opposing or contrasting colors—such as red and
green, blue and orange, or yellow and violet—that are positioned directly across from each other on the color wheel. These complementary relationships also extend to secondary colors, so that red-orange,
for example, is complementary to blue-green. Another relationship
on the color wheel involves harmonious colors, which are colors in
the same section of the color wheel. The closest relationship, however, exists between a primary color and its secondary color.

Initially, *Dance VII* strikes the viewer as merely a colorful piece,   4
but one of its functions is as a testing ground for color theory, creating radical—but acceptable—color combinations. In Figure 2, the
majority of the color blotches are purple, violet, pink-violet, and red-
violet, all of which are harmonious colors. The complementary color
to violet is yellow, hence the background color. Another use of complementary colors is in the color blotches themselves. Each blotch
consists of two "disks" of color, one overlapping the other. On occa-
sion, these colors are complementary: green on top of red, violet on
top of yellow, etc. On other occasions, however, the complementary

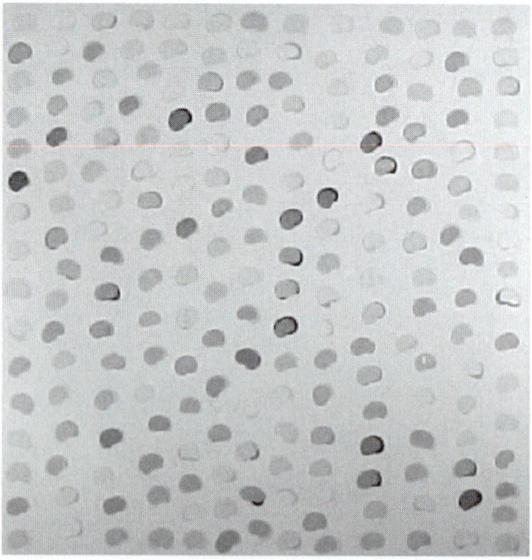

Figure 2. *Dance VII* by Gina Han. Oil on canvas (Han).

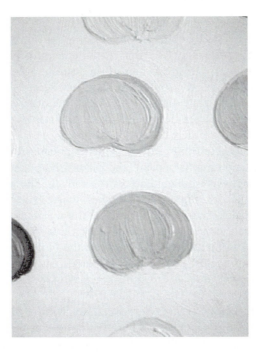

Figure 3. A visual relationship can be found between adjacent blotches (Han).

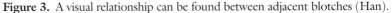

colors are implied or less direct. For example, a little bit of green can be mixed into red to produce a new, toned-down version of red that complements green in an interesting and fresh way.

Another noticeable element in *Dance VII* is that each color blotch   5
is in some way related to one or more color blotches immediately surrounding it. The two blotches in the center of Figure 3 have a color in common: pink. Han uses exactly the same pink for the top "disk" of the lower blotch as she does for the bottom "disk" of the upper blotch. The upper blotch relates to the one above it because Han has used the same greenish color on each blotch's top "disk." The uppermost blotch in Figure 3 is linked to the blotch on the right because Han has used harmonious violet colors for the uppermost blotch's bottom "disk" and the right-hand blotch's top and bottom "disks." The violet-on-violet right-hand blotch is linked to the lower blotch because the lower blotch's bottom "disk" is also a shade of violet. These playful relationships appear throughout the entire piece, creating paths of color for the viewers' eyes to follow.

In addition to the clever use of color, the placement of the individual blotches is key to the painting's composition. Focusing on the perimeter of *Dance VII*, we see that the blotches are, for the most part, lined up neatly. Toward the center of the painting, the blotches begin to break up and "move around," forcing our eyes to wander around without focusing on any single blotch. Once the orderly relationship of blotches begins to break down, the color relationships come into play, bringing order to a largely chaotic environment.

Texture also contributes to movement. The entire piece is smothered in thick applications of paint, and the brushes' bristles carved deep grooves as they were dragged across the canvas. The most noticeable elements of the painting are the blotches, which have the densest application of paint (see Figure 4), but in the negative space, or background, we can see peaks and valleys in the thick layers of paint. These textured strokes intentionally flow around the blotches like ocean currents sweeping against a collection of islands, suggesting movement. The background's fluid-like texture keeps viewers' eyes moving, cunningly redirecting them, again and again.

Dance VII is an exciting surprise. The painting disguises itself as an unexciting, effortless piece and then jumps out at the viewers if they dare to examine it more closely. The exploration of color relationships

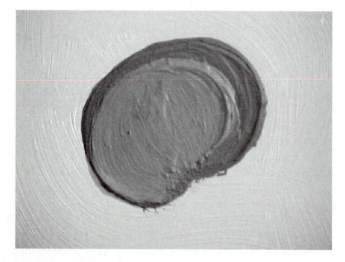

Figure 4. Thick applications of paint create texture, adding to the suggestion of movement (Han).

initially draws in the viewers, inviting them to participate. But over time, the viewers will begin to see the relationships between the blotches of color. Their eyes begin to move, and they are swept away in a whirling assortment of color and texture. As suggested by the painting's title, *Dance VII* conveys a fluid, harmonious movement among its colors, well-placed blotches, and textures.

WORK CITED

Han, Gina. *Dance VII*. N. d. Oil on canvas. Riverside Community College Art Gallery, Riverside, CA.

Buzzworm: *The Superior Magazine*

Ilene Wolf

University of California, San Diego
La Jolla, California

There's nothing worse than thumbing through a magazine that bangs you over the head with its one-sided rhetoric. Student author Ilene Wolf introduces readers to one that doesn't: *Buzzworm,* which approaches the controversial subject of the environment from an objective point of view. Wolf begins her essay both by explaining how the title *Buzzworm,* from the Old West term for a rattlesnake, reveals the magazine's purpose—"to create a reaction in its readers" —and by championing *Buzzworm* as a standout among other, less objective environmental magazines. As you read, notice how Wolf moves from a broad political perspective—presenting *Buzzworm* as a vehicle for change, and a better one than its rivals—to a focus on the magazine's technical aspects, including its visual appeal, subfeatures (sidebars), and captions. Does Wolf's attention to these details add to or detract from her evaluation of the magazine's overall effectiveness?

Many people today exist within their environment without really 1
knowing anything about it. If this ignorance continues, we will undoubtedly destroy the world in which we live. Only by gaining a better understanding of our planet will we be able to preserve our fragile
environment from pollution, hazardous waste, endangerment of
species, and ravaging of the land. A new magazine is dedicated to enlightening the general public about these important issues. It is called
Buzzworm.

What makes *Buzzworm* superior to other magazines dealing with 2
the same subject is that it not only fully explores all of the aspects of
the environment but does so in an objective manner. *Buzzworm* effec-

tively tackles the controversial question of how best to protect our planet and conveys the information in a way that all audiences can understand. In fact, the term *Buzzworm,* borrowed from the Old West, refers to a rattlesnake. The rattlesnake represents an effective form of communication, for when it rattles or buzzes, it causes an immediate reaction in those who are near. Thus the purpose of *Buzzworm* is to create a reaction in its readers regarding the conservation and preservation of the environment.

One of *Buzzworm*'s most striking features is its visual appeal.   3 Excellent photographs complement the articles. Contrasted with the photography in *Sierra,* another environmental magazine, the superb photographs in *Buzzworm* seem more striking. The summer 1989 issue of *Buzzworm* features a dramatic, full-page color picture of a gray wolf, which catches the reader's eye and draws attention to the article concerning the endangerment of the gray wolf's habitat. An issue of *Sierra* from the same year also has a picture of a gray wolf, yet it is smaller and the colors are not as clear—resulting in a less effective picture. Whereas both photographs of the animal pertain to their corresponding articles, it is the one in *Buzzworm* that makes the reader stop and discover the plight of the gray wolf.

A photograph must be of excellent quality and be placed cor-   4 rectly in the layout to enhance the article. The reader should be able to look at the picture and receive some information about the article it corresponds to. *Buzzworm*'s pictures of the East African Masai convey specific information about the tribe. Startling photographs depict the Masai in their traditional dress, focusing on the elaborate beadwork done by the women and the exquisite headdresses worn by the warriors. Looking at one picture of a young warrior wearing a lion's mane headdress, the reader gets a sense of the importance of the ritual and of the great respect that is earned by becoming a warrior. Another picture depicts a mother intently watching her daughter as she learns the art of beading. The look on the woman's face displays the care that goes into the beadwork, which has been an important part of their heritage for many generations. Thus, even before reading the article about the Masai, readers have some understanding of the Masai culture and its traditions.

Another functional and informative aspect of *Buzzworm*'s layout   5 is the use of subfeatures within an article. A subfeature functions in two ways: first by breaking up the monotony of a solid page of print, and second by giving the curious reader additional information. An article entitled "Double Jeopardy," for example, gives the reader an option of learning more about the subject through two subfeatures. The article itself describes the detrimental effects that excessive whale watching and research are believed to have on the humpback whale. To find further information about what might be contributing to the already low numbers of the humpback whale, one can read the sub-feature "Humpback Whale Survival." Furthermore, for the reader who is not familiar with the subject, there is a second subfeature, en-titled "Natural History," which gives general information about the humpback whale. No such subfeatures can be found anywhere in *Sierra*.

In addition to being an effective way of adding pertinent informa-   6
tion to the article, the subfeatures also add to the unity of the maga-zine. The subfeatures in *Buzzworm* all share a common gray back-ground color, adding to the continuity in layout from one article to the next. This produces a cleaner, more finished, and visually appeal-ing magazine.

Once again, *Buzzworm* shows superior layout design in keeping   7
the articles from being overrun by advertisements. I realize that ads do generate necessary revenue for the magazine, but nothing is more annoying than an article constantly interrupted by ads. *Buzzworm*'s few ads are all in the back of the magazine. In fact, not once does an ad interrupt an article. On the other hand, *Sierra* is filled with adver-tisements that are allowed to interrupt articles, which only frustrates the reader and detracts from the articles.

Buzzworm is unique in that it focuses on more than just one aspect   8
of the environment. In contrast, *Sierra* devoted its entire September/ October 1989 issue to one subject, the preservation of the public lands in the United States. Although it is a topic worthy of such dis-cussion, readers prefer more variety to choose from. The content of *Buzzworm* ranges from the humpback whale to the culture of the Masai to a profile of three leading conservationists. The great variety of issues covered in *Buzzworm* makes it more likely to keep the reader's attention than *Sierra*.

Buzzworm's ability to inform the reader is not limited to the in-   9
formation in its articles. Captions also play a large part. Readers who are too lazy to read an entire article will most often look at the pic-tures and read the captions. Thus *Buzzworm*'s long and detailed cap-tions are like miniature paragraphs, giving out more details than the terse captions in *Sierra,* which usually consist of only a few words.

The difference in the amount of information in the two magazines is obvious from a look at a typical caption in *Buzzworm* — "Finding relaxation of a different kind, Earthwatch participants spend a vacation patrolling beaches and assisting female turtles in finding a secluded nesting area" — compared to one in Sierra — "Joshua tree with Clark Mountain in background." Both captions give a description of their corresponding pictures, but only the caption found in *Buzzworm* gives any indication of what the article is about. The captions in *Buzzworm* supplement the articles, whereas the captions in *Sierra* only give brief descriptions of the pictures.

Finally, *Buzzworm* is objective, a rare quality in environmental magazines. An article on tourism versus environmental responsibility focuses on both the environmental and economic aspects of tourism, stating that while tourism generates income, it often destroys places of natural beauty that are so often visited. In contrast to this point of view, the article also cites examples where tourism has actually helped to preserve the environment. For every argument presented in *Buzzworm*, the counterargument is also presented. This balance is important, for readers must have all of the facts to be able to make well-informed judgments about controversial issues.

Despite all of its wonderful aspects, *Buzzworm* does have its flaws. Some of its graphics pale next to the color photographs. Also, the photographs should be more varied in size to create a more visually appealing layout. Except for these minor flaws, *Buzzworm* achieves its goal of appealing to its readers. In informing the general public about conservation and protection of our environment, *Buzzworm* is far more effective than *Sierra*.

9 *Speculating about Causes*

Beginning your day, you wonder why your car is increasingly hard to start. Driving to campus, you puzzle over why you seem unable to make better use of your study and homework time. Arriving on campus, circling the parking lot looking for a space, you fret about what could be holding up ground breaking for the promised multistory parking structure. This kind of thinking is so natural that your brain does it for you, without any urging or pushing. You couldn't really stop yourself from thinking about the whys and hows of things—even if you wanted to.

But fretful and even obsessive as this kind of thinking may be sometimes, you wouldn't want to shut it off because it could save you time if it inspires you to remove some obstacle; it could make you wiser if it leads to new understanding about yourself, other people, or the world at large; it could make you happier if it results in reaching a long-sought goal or finding romance. Nevertheless, this daily causal thinking—about how something you notice came to be the way it is, or why something happened or continues to happen—is idle and unsystematic.

Yet this kind of thinking is the basis for a more demanding, sustained kind of causal thinking, the kind you will find in the essays of this chapter—essays that speculate about the possible causes of phenomena or trends. (To *speculate* means to conjecture, wonder, or guess, or even to hypothesize or theorize. It can imply risk, play, uncertainty, and chance. A *phenomenon* is something noticeable that occurs or happens. This kind of essay can also speculate about a *trend*—something that has changed or is changing over time.) The student essay writers in this chapter speculate about these phenomena: Why are more people right-handed than left-handed? Why would an immigrant to the United States choose not to learn English? What could motivate a person to commit serial murder? Why is a successful multinational company starting to fail? These phenomena are the students' subjects, which are well defined and described in the essays. But that's usually the easy part.

The hard part is the speculation about the causes of these phenomena, which is a challenge because you are no longer idly speculating. Instead, you are trying to convince readers that your speculations—your proposed causes—are plausible or likely. The causes you propose may come from your own experience, from research, or both. The writing engages you in sustained, systematic thinking to answer a significant social, cultural, or political question—sustained because it's going to take you a while; systematic because you will need to select the most likely of many possible causes, sequence them logically, and support them so that they seem plausible, all with the aim of convincing particular readers to take your speculations seriously.

The rewards are great. Along with the other kinds of argument writing in this book, speculating about causes enables you to become the kind of person who confidently inquires deeply into events. You expect there is usually more to know than first appears. Adopting this stance, you join a new culture of debate, reflection, initiative, and knowledge seeking. Gaining confidence, you shake off old constraints and limits.

Left Out

Virginia Gagliardi

Lebanon Valley College
Annville, Pennsylvania

Being ambidextrous herself, Virginia Gagliardi found herself easily drawn into speculating about why people tend to favor one hand over the other, and why most favor their right. While doing research on this subject, Gagliardi uncovered some surprising answers. "Probably the area that I learned from the most was the area of parental influence," she says. "Nurture really does play an important role in the development of handedness."

Her biggest challenge was incorporating all the causes she had discovered during her research. She solved the problem by organizing the causes into three main subject areas: genetics and physiology; general influences, such as religion and language; and local influences, such as childhood training from parents who are right-handed, or the availability of only right-handed tools in school and at home. "These ideas were the ones I wished to convey to my unmindful, right-handed audience and to those people who question the origin of handedness," Gagliardi says.

As you read, notice that Gagliardi relies on research for both her proposed causes and her support for those causes. Altogether, she makes good use of six different sources, all of which are books published between 1981 and 2002, their dates confirming the continuing fascination with handedness, its causes and results. Instead of merely patching the sources together, she imposes her own plan and selectively paraphrases and quotes the sources only as they are relevant to the three main causes she addresses.

Behavioral differences that cause one limb or sense organ to be preferred for certain activities, despite the apparently insignificant differences in their morphology, constitute a problem that . . . has fascinated scientists and laymen for centuries. (Coren 2)

Opening a can, drawing a straight line, and writing a sentence are   1
three basic activities that display our *handedness,* or the "differential
or preferred use of one hand in situations where only one can be
used" (Coren 2). Handedness presents itself in two well-known categories—right- and left-handedness. But what causes each of us to be
either right- or left-handed? Why are there so many fewer left-handed
people than right-handed people? For years, scientists thought handedness was genetic; however, no genetic theory accounts for the ratio
of right- to left-handers, and the exact contribution of factors to predisposition to one side remains unknown. Genetic models propose
many different ideas about the roles of genes in handedness, but as
McManus writes in *Right Hand, Left Hand: The Origins of Asymmetry
in Brains, Bodies, Atoms and Cultures,* "what they cannot do is tell us
exactly what it is that makes us right- or left-handed" (163). A combination of factors in physiology, history, and society explains why genetics plays only a minor role in a Western bias toward one side—the
right side—of the body.

Perhaps the most basic explanation of handedness is the initial ge-   2
netic theory, which states that genetics determines handedness through
a specific gene inherited from parents. If both parents have the right-
handed gene, the children will all become right-handed; in contrast, if
both parents have the left-handed gene, the children would all become left-handed. Since there are fewer lefties in the world than right-
handed people, the model appears to fulfill conceptions for why
handedness occurs and why left-handedness occurs less often than
right-handedness. In the book *Left Brain, Right Brain,* however,
Sally P. Springer and Georg Deutsch elaborate on the extensive biological studies of this genetic model. The biologists who conducted
those studies quickly discovered that in comparison with obtained
data about handedness, "this [genetic] model cannot account for the
fact that 54 percent of the offspring of two left-handed parents are
right-handed" (108). So how does this possible cause fail? If the genetic model were accurate, reported data would show that two left-
handed parents would only have left-handed children. Therefore, new
studies began in an attempt to repair this theory with a complementary, yet more complex, model.

After many studies attempting to salvage this basic genetic theory,   3
the idea of "variable penetrance" arose. Variable penetrance means
"that all individuals with the same genotype [pattern of genes] may
not express that genotype in the same way" (Springer and Deutsch

108). Simply put, the statement suggests that although the genes make the parents left-handed, the combination that passes to the child may not cause left-handedness in the child. This speculation provides the explanation for two left-handers having right-handed children; however, "even with variable penetrance built into the [allele] model, the [variable penetrance] model's 'goodness of fit' to actual data is less than satisfactory" (Springer and Deutsch 108). The probability of left-handedness increases as the number of left-handed parents increases. However, the real-life data does not coincide with the theory. According to McManus, the fact that handedness "runs in the family" (156) remains distinguishable, but exactly how remains a mystery.

A third theory suggests that nurture determines handedness, not nature—or genetics—itself. Scientists base the theory on how handedness appears, not on which side it appears. In this case, genetics would determine handedness, just not a particular side to the handedness. Simplified, the design suggests, "If your mother and father are strongly handed [very reliant on one side], although we can't predict on the basis of their handedness whether you will be right- or left-handed, we can predict that you will be strongly handed. It is the strength . . . that is genetically variable" (Coren 91). Of all the theories, this idea proves the most plausible.

While genetics undoubtedly participates in determination of handedness, the suggestion that nurture more likely decides the side of handedness continues as the most logical "genetic" explanation. As McManus explains, "there are many things that run in families that are not inherited through genes" (157), such as parents' influence on their children in the development of handedness. The explanation lies in the fact that parents "convey basic pattern[s] of behavior to children" (Porac and Coren 108). Probably the most fundamental behavior learned is in the use of utensils. Parents "teach them [children] to use their first tools, such as spoons, knives, and pencils . . ." (Porac and Coren 108), so if the child's predisposition favors left-handedness but he continually learns right-handed motions, he will essentially develop into a right-handed child. This situation provides yet another example of the formation of handedness and how right-handedness forces itself into culture. The most easily defined reason for handedness presents itself every day in society: many people adopt right-handedness for ease of life and teach their children to do the same. This thought about the influence of nurture extends into the fact that handedness incorporates history into its origins.

Religion, which tends to be derived from nurture, is one of the most controversial historical justifications for handedness in Western culture. This idea is obviously seen in biblical illustrations. Followers of many Christian religions resort to right-handedness as a result of beliefs or traditions. The notion that left-handedness engages the devil explicates this fact. Passages from the Bible further reinforce these principles, such as the verses found in Matthew 25:34–41 in the New Testament:

> Then shall the King say unto them on His right hand, "Come ye blessed of my Father, inherit the kingdom prepared for you from the foundation of the world." . . . Then shall He say also unto them on the left hand, "Depart from Me, ye cursed, into everlasting fire, prepared for the devil and his angels." . . . And these shall go away into everlasting punishment; but the righteous into life eternal. (qtd. in Springer and Deutsch 105)

The Creator's being associated with the right hand strongly biases Christians toward the right hand, or the right side in general. Thus, this preference flows into other aspects of Christian culture. The most prominent example is in the sign of the cross, performed only with the right hand; using the left hand is sacrilegious. Another example appears during Communion, when the communicant receives the wafer in the left hand so that the clean, right hand can transfer the wafer to the mouth (Fincher 32).

The bias, though, does not limit itself to the church; it also extends into portraits concerning religion. Why, then, does a "marked tendency in classical renderings of the Madonna and child" (Fincher 30) illustrate Mary holding Jesus on her left side? Analysts proposed several reasons. According to Fincher, some analysts of the portraits suggest that the cause lies in the idea of freeing the "right hand for other, better things" (30). On the contrary, Fincher himself distinguishes the motive as something else: "Putting the child on Mary's left puts Him on the viewer's—and the art work's—right, clearly the place of honor" (31). Essentially, religion provides incentive for left-handers to become right-handers; however, religion remains just one aspect of history that influences this partiality for one side of the body.

For those people who lack a religious affiliation, the simple act of speaking holds an effect equivalent to the effect of religion on handedness because language places a stigma on left-handedness. Consistently, favorable connotations referring to right-handedness emerge in several languages. Fincher illustrates this idea from the word "riht, Anglo-Saxon for straight, erect, or just" (37). He also uses the "French word for right, droit, [which] also means 'correct' and 'law'" (37), to further demonstrate the point of language as a root of favoritism in handedness. Springer and Deutsch point out that "the French word for 'left,' *gauche,* also means 'clumsy'" and that "*mancino* is Italian for 'left' as well as for 'deceitful'" (104). They also explain that the Spanish phrase "no ser zurdo," which means "to be clever," translates directly as "to not be left-handed" (104). As terrible as those definitions appear, most Western languages have them— including the English language.

In English the term "left-handed" has derogatory classifications. 9
For example, *Webster's Third International Dictionary* lists several definitions of the adjective "left-handed," including the following:

> a: marked by clumsiness or ineptitude: awkward; b: exhibiting deviousness or indirection: oblique, unintended; c: obs.: given to malevolent scheming or contriving: sinister, underhand. (qtd. in Springer and Deutsch 104)

Similarly, analysis of the English language reveals common phrases filled with bias. "For instance, a *left-handed compliment* is actually an insult. A *left-handed marriage* is no marriage at all. To be about *left-handed business* is to be engaged in something unlawful or unsavory" (Coren 2). On the contrary, "to be someone's *right-hand man* means to be important and useful to that person" (Coren 2). Over time, this tainting of a certain handedness carries over into everyday life and remains one of several reasons why left-handers may try to become right-handers or at least ambidextrous. Other motives to switch revolve around the impressions and pressures of social traditions.

One of the largest-scale examples lies in written language. The 10
system of the written English language solely supports right-handed people because "[written] alphabetic languages . . . were designed for right-handers" (Ornstein 83). Coren explains the differences in the mechanics of left- and right-handed writing as:

> Our left-to-right writing pattern is set up for a right-handed writer. The most comfortable and controlled hand movement is a pull across the body. For the right-hander it is a left-to-right movement, and for the left-hander it is reversed. (230)

Due to the way a left-hander pulls across his body, his hand will rub over words he has already written, whereas a right-hander always moves his hand away from the words he has already written. This problem forces left-handers into unnatural hand positions during writing; most primary school teachers attempt to persuade left-handed children into writing right-handed. In fact, the "Victorians even invented a vicious leather device with a belt and buckles for strapping the left hand firmly behind the back" (McManus 268). Writing, although the most obvious of problems, remains just one of many issues for a left-hander in a right-handed society.

Every day, left-handers encounter issues with common tools that 11 right-handers take for granted. A simple household item, such as a can opener, can become the most complex of items for a leftie. Because a can opener "is designed to be held with the left hand while the cutting gear is operated by rotating a handle with the right hand" (Coren 223), using the instrument left-handed "forces the left-hander into a set of ungainly contortions" (Coren 223). Another example surfaces in the use of knives, typically beveled on only one side—the right side. Having the knife designed as such aids the "right-hander by producing a force which holds the blade upright" (Coren 227), causing the slice to peel outward from the material, rather than toward it. Still other issues outside of household items exist only for lefties.

More problems affecting left-handers reside in locations such as 12 school and work. The simple process of using a ruler becomes a diffi-cult task for a left-handed individual. The ruler, designed with right-handers in mind, presents numbers in a left-to-right fashion, much like the written English language. "This [style] makes sense for the right-hander because the motion of drawing the line usually begins at the 'zero inch' location on the far left and continues . . . until it reaches the mark indicating the desired length, somewhere to the right" (Coren 231). For a leftie, however, this system poses several problems:

> [This process] requires the left-hander to cover the numbers while drawing the line with a pulling motion across the body from right to left. The left-hander also covers the end of the ruler . . . causing a ten-dency for the pen to suddenly drop off the end of the ruler if the line is drawn too quickly and the unseen "zero inch" point is reached before the pen is stopped. (Coren 231)

Saws create problems by exposing body parts dangerously close to the blade. "When the right hand is used, the arm and elbow flare out to the side, safely away from the saw blade" (Coren 237), protecting a right-handed person from injury. Yet "if a left-hander wants to use this equipment, he must either use his right hand to hold the work . . . or cross his body with his left hand which places his arm directly in line with the saw blade" (Coren 237). This design forces a left-hander to resort to right-handedness temporarily or even permanently in many factory and workshop settings. However, these mechanical influences cannot solely explain the phenomena of left-handedness.

The combination of these factors forms a basis for handedness in the world. Right- and left-handedness appear as common expressions in everyday life, but the existence of both presents a misconception. Due to factors in physiology, history, and society, handedness appears in two forms, but not in right- and left-handedness. Rather, handedness categorizes into right-handedness and ambidextrous handedness for the sole reason that "to survive in this right-sided world, left-handers soon learn to do with the right hand many things that the right-hander could never and will never do with the left. The end result is a degree of ambidexterity" (Porac and Coren 95). Perhaps only one form of handedness exists, since, according to Porac and Coren, essentially "the left-hander must become more right-handed" (95). This idea reinforces the reason why right-handedness appears more often than left-handedness. Therefore, even though the exact cause of handedness remains unknown, the residue of known facts points not toward a right- and left-handed world, but in the direction of a world that completely relies on one-sided handedness. 13

WORKS CITED

Coren, Stanley. *The Left-Hander Syndrome: The Causes and Consequences of Left-Handedness*. New York: Macmillan, 1992. Print.

Fincher, Jack. *Lefties: The Origins and Consequences of Being Left-Handed*. New York: Barnes and Noble, 1993. Print.

McManus, Chris. *Right Hand, Left Hand: The Origins of Asymmetry in Brains, Bodies, Atoms and Cultures*. Cambridge: Harvard UP, 2002. Print.

Ornstein, Robert. *The Right Mind*. New York: Harcourt Brace, 1997. Print.

Porac, Clare, and Stanley Coren. *Lateral Preferences and Human Behavior*. New York: Springer-Verlag, 1981. Print.

Springer, Sally P., and Georg Deutsch. *Left Brain, Right Brain*. San Francisco: W. H. Freeman, 1981. Print.

Hispanic Pride vs. American Assimilation

Stephanie Cox

Metropolitan Community College
Omaha, Nebraska

"Why would immigrants want to make their lives more complicated by having to rely on others to communicate for them?" Stephanie Cox asks, after learning that the Spanish-speaking mother whose missing toddler she had helped find—a woman who had trembled and perspired as she tried to communicate her desperate situation—had declined the offer of English lessons from the church where Cox worked. Cox is compelled to discover why. A little research reveals that the woman belongs to a growing group of Mexican immigrants to the United States who are choosing not to learn English. This is no isolated incident—it is a phenomenon, Cox realizes.

After Cox narrates the incident of the lost girl as a way to engage readers' interest, she presents her subject—the phenomenon of acculturation—which she defines as "adapting to American culture" while continuing to "uphold the values and traditions of Latin America." She then forecasts the three causes—the three explanations for the phenomenon—that she will argue for: cultural pride; the proximity of a native country, especially Mexico; and the unwillingness of some Hispanics to help new Hispanics assimilate. Her plan is simple and visible.

Notice that Cox takes a stand on a hot-button social and political issue. Many Americans would be unsympathetic to the woman's refusal to learn English. Cox, too, admits some preconceived ideas on the matter, yet she keeps an open mind. She wants to know more before she judges the woman's decision not to learn English. She is motivated by curiosity.

My heart ached for the woman. She was visibly distressed and seemed   1
to grow more agitated by the minute. Tiny beads of perspiration were
beginning to form on her brow, and the black purse she carried shook

173

in her trembling grasp. She was desperately trying to tell me something, but I was unable to understand. She spoke Spanish and I didn't. After many awkward attempts at communication, the woman's ten-year-old English-speaking son was located. His translation revealed her worry over her missing toddler. It seems the child had wandered off while her mother was visiting a pastor of the church I work for. With the woman's son's help, we gathered enough details about her daughter's disappearance to locate the child, who had been playing in an empty classroom.

Even though the situation seemed to have ended happily, I was still troubled by it. If only the woman had known some English. The church offered several excellent programs to help immigrants learn about American culture and practice the English language. Had she taken the help offered by the church, she would have been able to communicate effectively enough to convey her message and prevent unnecessary frustration and possibly dangerous delay. When I presented my concerns to one of the church pastors, I was surprised by his response. This woman was at the church to pick up her son from an English class. When she had been given the same opportunity, she quietly refused. While she felt strongly about the importance of English for her son, she herself was proud of her Mexican heritage and had no desire to become an English speaker.

I was shocked. Why would immigrants want to make their lives more complicated by having to rely on others to communicate for them? This woman must surely be an exception, I thought, but to my surprise, she is among many Hispanic immigrants in the United States who are acculturating rather than assimilating into American culture (Grow et al.). Many Americans still view the United States as an ideal nation, a model for the world, and assume everyone must surely want to "be like us," but there is a new phenomenon among many U.S. immigrants: active pride in their home cultures. This cultural pride is especially evident among Hispanic immigrants who choose to adapt to American culture without losing the traditions and values of their native countries.

Hispanics are one of the fastest growing and largest minority groups in the United States, and they are developing their own version of the "true" American. Nearly nine out of ten Hispanics have accepted the importance of adapting to American culture, while nearly nine out of ten also believe it is extremely important to continue to uphold the values and traditions of Latin America (Artze).

This phenomenon of Hispanic acculturation rather than assimilation can be witnessed in several cities and towns in the United States.

Perhaps one of the best examples of how Hispanics are striving 5 to maintain their own culture can be seen in Los Angeles. As early as 1950, Los Angeles contained the largest Hispanic population in the country, and the conflict between assimilation and acculturation was already beginning. Immigrants were forced to choose between American cultural traditions and the distinctive values of Latin America. Today, you will find groups of new immigrants along with second- and third-generation Hispanics all with the same goal in mind: to successfully thrive in an ethnocentric culture without losing their own identity (Rodriguez).

While there may be quite a few reasons immigrants are reluctant 6 to assimilate, forgetting old traits and adopting new ones, three are most prominent. First is the strong feeling of pride Hispanics have for their native countries and cultural values, and the security they feel when segregated from American society. Second is the close proximity of Hispanics, especially Mexican Americans, to their native country. Third, and most startling, is the seeming lack of support from many Hispanic Americans to help new immigrants assimilate.

With the ever-increasing number of immigrants from Latin Amer- 7 ica, it is not uncommon to find entirely Hispanic communities within American towns and cities. These communities help to reinforce cultural traditions and pride, and make it unnecessary for immigrants to adopt new cultural traits or learn the English language. Many Hispanic Americans not only feel comforted by their segregation but also are wary of the negative influences American society may have on their families (Branigin).

The self-segregation of many Hispanic immigrants in America can 8 be compared to that of Americans who live and work abroad but remain quite isolated from their host culture. A classmate of mine described living in Japan while her husband was stationed at a military base there. Day-to-day life revolved around American customs. Her children attended American schools on the military base; she shopped at military stores geared toward the wants and needs of Americans; and her family socialized with a close-knit group of American friends. On the rare occasions that she and her family left the military base, she was startled by the numerous stares and suspicious glances she and her family received from Japanese citizens. While confident that she and her family had done their best to adhere to Japanese societal norms, the reaction of the Japanese left her with the acute feeling that she was still very different, and the isolation of the military base offered her family a feeling of security.

My classmate's experience is mirrored by the experiences of many   9
Hispanics living in the United States. In response to unsubstantiated fears of America becoming "Mexicanized," some politicians and government officials are being urged to speak out against Hispanic immigration. Most notably, border states such as California and Arizona are openly opposing immigration from Latin America by developing new anti-immigration bills. California's Proposition 187 and Arizona's Proposition 200 would limit the public benefits received by illegal immigrants, and politicians acting on public support of these bills and hoping to seek reelection are motivated to develop even more anti-immigrant legislation (Judis). While these propositions are much more aggressive than suspicious stares, the message is the same: if you are different, you must be a threat.

In addition to feeling more comfortable within their own com-   10
munities, many Hispanic immigrants see isolation as a way to hold on to their cultural values. In California, where bilingual education is no longer the norm, children from Hispanic families are immediately submerged into the English language and thus into American culture. Many Hispanics feel that this immersion forces their children to choose between the values taught by their parents—such as the importance of family—and those of their new country (Rifkin).

Reluctance to assimilate is strengthened even more when tradi-   11
tional, conservative Hispanic families witness their children adopting negative aspects of American culture. Many Hispanics cite American gang violence when defending their decision to keep their children away from American culture. Alarmingly, Hispanic youth may actually be propelled toward gang life by the attitudes and stereotypes of Americans who mistakenly assume that most Latinos are illegal immigrants (Branigin). A quest for group identity and a sense of belonging can be a strong lure for Hispanic teens trying to find their place in an unsympathetic society.

Fear of negative influences impacting traditional cultural values is   12
not the only reason Hispanics have hesitated to adopt American culture. Unlike the majority of immigrants from other locations, Hispanics—especially Mexican Americans—have the privilege of living fairly close to their native country. It is not uncommon for many Hispanics to travel between their native and adopted countries on a regular basis.

These frequent visits help reinforce the customs, values, and language of Latin America (Grow et al.).

This reinforcement of Hispanic customs and values is evidenced 13 not only by immigrants' attitudes toward American society but also by the many cultural traditions Hispanics bring to the United States. One tradition that is growing in popularity in America is the Quinceanera, the celebration of a Latina girl's fifteenth birthday. Historically rooted in Aztec and Roman Catholic customs, the Quinceanera is a time to celebrate a young girl's entrance into adulthood. While this lavish celebration is primarily a Hispanic one, which begins with a Roman Catholic Mass and ends with a reception in which the girl performs a dance with her father and members of her court, it is also showing signs of adaptation to American society. This can be seen in the celebrations held by Hispanics who are not members of the Roman Catholic Church, and who tend to invite friends of different ethnic heritages (Miranda). Once primarily a closed ceremony for family and close friends, the Quinceanera is expanding beyond its Latin American roots and replanting itself into Hispanic American culture.

Another example of a Hispanic cultural tradition celebrated in 14 the United States is Cinco de Mayo. Celebrated on the fifth of May, this holiday commemorates the 1862 Battle of Puebla, one of the most glorious victories in Mexico's military history. When France attempted to take control of Mexico by force, a poorly equipped Mexican army was able to halt the invasion of the French powerhouse despite being outnumbered by thousands. This celebration, with its message of success despite overwhelming obstacles, inspires Hispanics to be proud of their heritage (Vargas).

Finally, many new immigrants to the United States may feel 15 more comfortable within their own cultural group and hesitate to adapt to American culture because of discouragement from their own peers. Mexican Americans born and raised in the United States, called Chicanos, often humiliate new immigrants who are attempting to learn English. One immigrant teen, who despite three years in an English as a second language course still did not speak fluent English, believed the other students were laughing at her when she attempted to speak English (Branigin). This kind of teasing can lead to feelings of insecurity among newly arrived immigrants.

Not only are Hispanic children and teens experiencing discour- 16 agement from Mexican Americans, but so are many new immigrant adults who are seeking jobs in the United States. An immigrant named Antonio experienced this harsh reality when he found himself assigned to do one of the most laborious jobs in a meatpacking plant, while his cultural counterpart, a Chicano, was displaying the title of supervisor and taunting immigrant workers like him. In fact, in this particular meatpacking plant, it was quite common to see new immigrants from Mexico performing arduous tasks while enduring snide comments from their Chicano supervisors, who would make statements such as "Go back to Mexico, wetback!" or "Chicanos numero uno!" (Campo-Flores). Humiliation like this can cause many immigrants to stay within their own communities, where they feel accepted.

The feelings of isolation felt by the immigrant teen and the feelings of frustration felt by the immigrant worker Antonio shed new light on the complexities Latin American immigrants must face every day. Distrust of an unfamiliar culture mixed with strong pride in their own heritage has led to immigrants' longing to maintain the traits of their native country. As I remember the distraught woman who quietly yet proudly refused the pastor's offer to help her learn English, I can now respect her decision. She was quoted as saying, "I was Mexican at birth, I am Mexican today, and I will be Mexican forever."

17

WORKS CITED

Artze, Isis. "To Be and Not to Be." *Hispanic* Oct. 2000: 32–34. *EBSCOhost.* Web. 22 Jan. 2006.

Branigin, William. "Immigrants Shunning Idea of Assimilation." *Washington Post* 25 May 1998: A1+. Print.

Campo-Flores, Arian. "Brown against Brown." *Newsweek* Sept. 2000: 49–50. *EBSCOhost.* Web. 25 Jan. 2006.

Grow, Brian, Ronald Grover, Arlene Weintraub, Christopher Palmeri, Mara Der Hovenesian, and Michael Eidam. "Hispanic Nation." *Business Week* Mar. 2004: 58–70. EBSCOhost. Web. 10 Jan. 2006.

Judis, John B. "Border War." *The New Republic* 16 Jan. 2006: 15–19. Print.

Miranda, Carolina A. "Fifteen Candles." *Time* July 2004: 83. *EBSCOhost.* Web. 27 Jan. 2006.

Rifkin, Jane M. "Locked in Conflict with Mainstream America." *Hispanic Times* Dec. 1998–Jan. 1999: 40–41. *EBSCOhost.* Web. 22 Jan. 2006.

Rodriguez, Gregory. "Don't Mistake the Parts for the Whole in L.A." *Los Angeles Times* 6 July 2001: B15. Print.

Vargas, Roberto. "Cinco de Mayo: An Opportunity to Inspire Courage." *Hispanic* May 1999: 48. EBSCOhost. Web. 25 Jan. 2006.

La Donna Beaty

Sinclair Community College
Dayton, Ohio

Chances are there will never be a serial murder in your neighborhood, but there are more serial killers at large in the American population than you might imagine—close to 350, according to La Donna Beaty's research. While there's nothing we can do to avoid serial killers—their lack of telltale physical characteristics makes them impossible to peg—we can speculate about the forces that conspire to make them the monsters they are. Beaty offers several possible triggers that, taken together, might turn a child into a serial killer, including psychological abuse, frequent moves, and genetic abnormalities. As in most essays speculating about causes, Beaty's conclusions must be tentative. And yet speculating about the reasons serial killers develop may be our best approach to the problem: the scientists and psychologists who continue such speculative work may one day find a humane way to treat them or, even better, keep potential killers from becoming violent in the first place. As you read, notice how visibly Beaty signals her move from one cause to the next as the argument progresses.

Jeffrey Dahmer, John Wayne Gacy, Mark Allen Smith, Richard Chase, Ted Bundy—the list goes on and on. These five men alone have been responsible for at least ninety deaths, and many suspect that their victims may total twice that number. They are serial killers, the most feared and hated of criminals. What deep, hidden secret makes them lust for blood? What can possibly motivate a person to kill over and over again with no guilt, no remorse, no hint of human compassion? What makes a serial killer? [1]

179

Serial killings are not a new phenomenon. In 1798, for example, Micajah and Wiley Harpe traveled the backwoods of Kentucky and Tennessee in a violent, yearlong killing spree that left at least twenty— and possibly as many as thirty-eight—men, women, and children dead. Their crimes were especially chilling, as they seemed particularly to enjoy grabbing small children by the ankles and smashing their heads against trees (Holmes and DeBurger 28). In modern society, how-ever, serial killings have grown to near epidemic proportions. Ann Rule, a respected author and expert on serial murders, stated in a seminar at the University of Louisville that between 3,500 and 5,000 people become victims of serial murder each year in the United States alone (qtd. in Holmes and DeBurger 21). Many others esti-mate that there are close to 350 serial killers currently at large in our society (Holmes and DeBurger 22). 2

Fascination with murder and murderers is not new, but researchers in recent years have made great strides in determining the character-istics of criminals. Looking back, we can see how naive early experts were in their evaluations: in 1911, for example, Italian criminologist Cesare Lombrosco concluded that "murderers as a group [are] bio-logically degenerate [with] bloodshot eyes, aquiline noses, curly black hair, strong jaws, big ears, thin lips, and menacing grins" (qtd. in Lunde 84). Today, however, we don't expect killers to have fangs that drip human blood, and many realize that the boy next door may be doing more than woodworking in his basement. While there are no specific physical characteristics shared by all serial killers, they are almost always male, and 92 percent are white. Most are between the ages of twenty-five and thirty-five and often physically attractive. While they may hold a job, many switch employment frequently, as they become easily frustrated when advancement does not come as quickly as ex-pected. They tend to believe that they are entitled to whatever they desire but feel that they should have to exert no effort to attain their goals (Samenow 88, 96). What could possibly turn attractive, ambi-tious human beings into cold-blooded monsters? 3

One popular theory suggests that many murderers are the prod-uct of our violent society. Our culture tends to approve of violence and find it acceptable, even preferable, in many circumstances (Holmes and DeBurger 27). According to research done in 1970, one out of every four men and one out of every six women believed that it was appropriate for a husband to hit his wife under certain conditions (Holmes and DeBurger 33). This emphasis on violence is 4 especially prevalent in television programs. Violence occurs in 80 percent of all prime-time shows, while cartoons, presumably made for children, average eighteen violent acts per hour. It is estimated that by the age of eighteen, the average child will have viewed more than 16,000 television murders (Holmes and DeBurger 34). Some experts feel that children demonstrate increasingly aggressive behavior with each violent act they view and become so accustomed to violence that these acts seem normal (Lunde 15, 35). In fact, most serial killers do begin to show patterns of aggressive behavior at a young age. It is, therefore, possible that after viewing increasing amounts of violence, such children determine that this is acceptable behavior; when they are then punished for similar actions, they may become confused and angry and eventually lash out by committing horrible, violent acts.

Another theory concentrates on the family atmosphere into 5 which the serial killer is born. Most killers state that they experienced psychological abuse as children and never established good relationships with the male figures in their lives (Ressler, Burgess, and Douglas 19). As children, they were often rejected by their parents and received little nurturing (Lunde 94; Holmes and DeBurger 64–70). It has also been established that the families of serial killers often move repeatedly, never allowing the child to feel a sense of stability; in many cases, they are also forced to live outside the family home before reaching the age of eighteen (Ressler, Burgess, and Douglas 19–20). Our culture's tolerance for violence may overlap with such family dynamics: with 79 percent of the population believing that slapping a twelve-year-old is either necessary, normal, or good, it is no wonder that serial killers relate tales of physical abuse and view themselves as the "black sheep" of the family (Holmes and DeBurger 30; Ressler, Burgess, and Douglas 19–20). They may even, perhaps unconsciously, assume this same role in society.

While the foregoing analysis portrays the serial killer as a lost, 6 lonely, abused little child, another theory, based on the same information, gives an entirely different view. In this analysis, the killer is indeed rejected by his family but only after being repeatedly defiant, sneaky, and threatening. As the child's lies and destructiveness increase, the parents give him the distance he seems to want in order to maintain a small amount of domestic peace (Samenow 13). This interpretation suggests that the killer shapes his parents much more than his parents shape him. It also denies that the media can influence a child's mind and turn him into something that he doesn't already long to be. Since most children view similar amounts of violence, the argument goes, a responsible child filters what he sees and will not resort to criminal activity no matter how acceptable it seems to be (Samenow 15–18). In 1930, the noted psychologist Alfred Adler seemed to find this true of any criminal. As he put it, "With criminals it is different: they have a private logic, a private intelligence. They are suffering from a wrong outlook upon the world, a wrong estimate of their own importance and the importance of other people" (qtd. in Samenow 20).

Most people agree that Jeffrey Dahmer or Ted Bundy had to be "crazy" to commit horrendous multiple murders, and scientists have long maintained that serial killers are indeed mentally disturbed (Lunde 48). While the percentage of murders committed by mental hospital patients is much lower than that among the general population, it cannot be ignored that the rise in serial killings happened at almost the same time as the deinstitutionalization movement in the mental health care system during the 1960s (Lunde 35; Markman and Bosco 266). While reform was greatly needed in the mental health care system, it has now become nearly impossible to hospitalize those with severe problems. In the United States, people have a constitutional right to remain mentally ill. Involuntary commitment can only be accomplished if the person is deemed dangerous to himself or others or is gravely disabled. However, "[a]ccording to the way that the law is interpreted, if you can go to the mailbox to pick up your Social Security check, you're not gravely disabled even if you think you're living on Mars"; even if a patient is thought to be dangerous, he cannot be held longer than ninety days unless it can be proved that the patient actually committed dangerous acts while in the hospital (Markman and Bosco 267). Many of the most heinous criminals have had long histories of mental illness but could not be hospitalized due to these stringent requirements. Richard Chase, the notorious Vampire of Sacramento, believed that he needed blood in order to survive, and while in the care of a psychiatric hospital, he often killed birds and other small animals in order to quench this thirst. When he was released, he went on to kill eight people, one of them an eighteen-month-old baby (Biondi and Hecox 206). Edmund Kemper was equally insane. At the age of fifteen, he killed both of his grandparents and then spent five years in a psychiatric facility. Doctors determined that he was "cured" and released him into an unsuspecting society. He killed eight women, including his own mother (Lunde 53–56). The world was soon to be disturbed by a cataclysmic earthquake, and Herbert Mullin knew that he had been appointed by God to prevent the catastrophe. The fervor of his religious delusion resulted in a death toll of thirteen (Lunde 63–81). All of these men had been treated for their mental disorders, and all were released by doctors who did not have enough proof to hold them against their will.

Recently, studies have given increasing consideration to the genetic makeup of serial killers. The connection between biology and behavior is strengthened by research in which scientists have been able to develop a violently aggressive strain of mice simply through selective inbreeding (Taylor 23). These studies have caused scientists to become increasingly interested in the limbic system of the brain, which houses the amygdala, an almond-shaped structure located in the front of the temporal lobe. It has long been known that surgically altering that portion of the brain, in an operation known as a lobotomy, is one way of controlling behavior. This surgery was used frequently in the 1960s but has since been discontinued as it also erases most of a person's personality. More recent developments, however, have shown that temporal lobe epilepsy causes electrical impulses to be discharged directly into the amygdala. When this electronic stimulation is re-created in the laboratory, it causes violent behavior in lab animals. Additionally, other forms of epilepsy do not cause abnormalities in behavior except during seizure activity. Temporal lobe epilepsy is linked with a wide range of antisocial behavior, including anger, paranoia, and aggression. It is also interesting to note that this form of epilepsy produces extremely unusual brain waves. These waves have been found in only 10 to 15 percent of the general population, but over 79 percent of known serial killers test positive for these waves (Taylor 28–33). 8

The look at biological factors that control human behavior is by no means limited to brain waves or other brain abnormalities. Much work is also being done with neurotransmitters, levels of testosterone, and patterns of trace minerals. While none of these studies is conclusive, they all show a high correlation between antisocial behavior and chemical interactions within the body (Taylor 63–69). 9

One of the most common traits that all researchers have noted among serial killers is heavy use of alcohol. Whether this correlation is brought about by external factors or whether alcohol is an actual 10 stimulus that causes certain behavior is still unclear, but the idea deserves consideration. Lunde found that the majority of those who commit murder had been drinking beforehand and commonly had a urine alcohol level of between .20 and .29, nearly twice the legal level of intoxication (31–32). Additionally, 70 percent of the families that reared serial killers had verifiable records of alcohol abuse (Ressler, Burgess, and Douglas 17). Jeffrey Dahmer had been arrested in 1981 on charges of drunkenness, and before his release from prison on sexual assault charges, his father had written a heartbreaking letter pleading that Jeffrey be forced to undergo treatment for alcoholism — a plea that, if heeded, might have changed the course of future events (Davis 70, 103). Whether alcoholism is a learned behavior or an inherited predisposition is still hotly debated, but a 1979 report issued by Harvard Medical School stated that "[a]lcoholism in the biological parent appears to be a more reliable predictor of alcoholism in the children than any other environmental factor examined" (qtd. in Taylor 117). While alcohol was once thought to alleviate anxiety and depression, we now know that it can aggravate and intensify such moods; for serial killers, this may lead to irrational feelings of powerlessness that are brought under control only when the killer proves he has the ultimate power to control life and death (Taylor 110).

"Man's inhumanity to man" began when Cain killed Abel, but 11 this legacy has grown to frightening proportions, as evidenced by the vast number of books that line the shelves of bookstores today — row after row of titles dealing with death, anger, and blood. We may never know what causes a serial killer to exact his revenge on an unsuspecting society, but we need to continue to probe the interior of the human brain to discover the delicate balance of chemicals that controls behavior; we need to be able to fix what goes wrong. We must also work harder to protect our children. Their cries must not go unheard; their pain must not become so intense that it demands bloody revenge. As today becomes tomorrow, we must remember the words of Ted Bundy, one of the most ruthless serial killers of our time: "Most serial killers are people who kill for the pure pleasure of killing and cannot be rehabilitated. Some of the killers themselves would even say so" (qtd. in Holmes and DeBurger 150).

WORKS CITED

Biondi, Ray, and Walt Hecox. *The Dracula Killer.* New York: Simon, 1992. Print.

Davis, Ron. *The Milwaukee Murders.* New York: St. Martin's, 1991. Print.

Holmes, Ronald M., and James DeBurger. *Serial Murder.* Newbury Park: Sage, 1988. Print.

Lunde, Donald T. *Murder and Madness.* San Francisco: San Francisco Book, 1976. Print.

Markman, Ronald, and Dominick Bosco. *Alone with the Devil.* New York: Doubleday, 1989. Print.

Ressler, Robert K., Ann W. Burgess, and John E. Douglas. *Sexual Homicide— Patterns and Motives.* Lexington: Heath, 1988. Print.

Samenow, Stanton E. *Inside the Criminal Mind.* New York: Times, 1984. Print.

Taylor, Lawrence. *Born to Crime.* Westport: Greenwood, 1984. Print.

A Grande Trend at Starbacks

Shane Sohail

University of California, Riverside
Riverside, California

Shane Sohail wrote this essay in 2008, when he learned that Starbucks—the chain behind the seemingly ubiquitous retail coffee shops—was reportedly experiencing a precipitous drop in profits. Although the economic situation in the United States has changed since then, as have Starbucks' fortunes, his essay is still an excellent model of speculating about causes. After researching the plausible causes for Starbucks' decline, Sohail chose the one he found most convincing, and argues for it using data he found in his sources. For every competing cause he brings up, Sohail has a clear, logical, and supported counterargument.

As you read, think of other national trends, in business or otherwise, that you have wondered about recently. What might some of their causes be, and where could you look for more information to determine which one is most plausible?

Thirty-seven years ago, no one would have expected that Starbucks 1
Coffee Company would be as ubiquitous and prominent as it is today. For such a massive corporate empire, Starbucks has modest roots. In 1971, the company opened up its very first store in Seattle's Pike Place Market as a whole bean coffee seller ("Company"). Fast forward to 2008, and it is evident that the company has experienced massive maturation. In just six short years, from 2002 to 2008, Starbucks has increased its number of stores from 5,886 to over 15,000 (Barbaro and Martin). CEO Howard Schultz has set a monumental goal for the company: to open 40,000 stores worldwide within the

next few years, a task which "no food or beverage chain has ever achieved" (Barbaro and Martin). Starbucks has become a worldwide phenomenon, and with almost seven new stores opening every day, the world's "finest purveyor of gourmet coffee" has shown no signs of significant weakness . . . until now (Barbaro and Martin).

For the first time since Starbucks went public in 1992, customer   2
traffic has decreased by over one percent and same-store sales have declined significantly beginning last summer (Darguste). While this decline may seem trivial, it has led to a forty-two percent fall in Starbucks stock since the end of 2007, "making it one of the worst performers on the NASDAQ exchange" ("Coffee Wars"). Stock market analysts and company executives have been dissecting this recent financial trend over the past year to determine who or what is to blame. Is Starbucks Coffee creating its own financial burdens due to overexpansion and the creation of a saturated market? Are the consequences of such a rapid expansion, most notably increased competition and a decline in overall customer experience, having an effect on the company? Or, are trends in consumer spending the main source of the coffee giant's recent economic woes? While a combination of both company-related causes and consumer-related causes account for the financial problems of Starbucks, overexpansion and its consequences are truly responsible for the regression in Starbucks' customer traffic and tumbling stock prices.

Whenever any company grows as rapidly as Starbucks has, over-   3
expansion becomes a possibility that cannot be ignored. Market analysts agree that the main problem for Starbucks is overexpansion and "growing too fast in a mature market" ("Coffee Wars"). As more and more coffee shops are built, there comes a point when growth exceeds profits. This is caused by store cannibalization, a situation in which profits at one store dwindle due to business at another nearby store. Starbucks is experiencing this situation, as "Weaker growth in traffic and same-store sales reported in the first half of 2007 raised investor concerns that Starbucks' recent expansion has been too aggressive and was beginning to result in cannibalization" (Darguste). Chicago analyst Dean Haskell notes, however, that "Rapid development on an already large store base hurts comparable sales at existing units, but increases total sales" (Buck and Millman). Although this may hold true for a while, it cannot be overlooked that "as cannibalization continues, the investment in new stores outpaces the profits earned from increases in total sales" (Buck and Millman).

Furthermore, Starbucks may be creating an oversaturated mar-   4
ket. Market saturation occurs when a particular product or brand has
become too rapidly dispersed in the market. Starbucks is notorious
for opening several stores within blocks of each other, a strategy that
is possibly saturating the market and exceeding demand (Darguste).
Investors say that "signs of saturation at Starbucks would include
lackluster same-store sales" (Allison). The fact that "Starbucks posted
its weakest same-store sales in years" in 2007 raises much concern
among executives and bolsters the theory that saturation is causing
the company's financial hardships (Darguste). However, there are
some economists who firmly believe that Starbucks is not saturating
the market and that the company's goal of opening 40,000 stores is
possible. Starbucks Chief Financial Officer Michael Casey has confidence that "despite the common view . . . that Starbucks stores are
everywhere, there remain plenty of opportunities for growth" (Allison). Whether or not market saturation is causing economic difficulties
for Starbucks remains an issue for debate, but the possibility is certainly
a cause for concern.

Another consequence of Starbucks' immense expansion and an-   5
other probable cause of the company's dubious financial situation has
been a newly developed rivalry with another corporation just as well-
known as Starbucks: McDonald's. A so-called "Coffee War" has
begun between the two and it is beginning to take its toll on Starbucks. Investor Charles Mizrahi believes that "as [Starbucks'] expansion swept the U.S., Starbucks also began adding drive-through
window service and selling breakfast sandwiches. By doing this, Starbucks encroached on McDonald's territory, and it was only a matter
of time before 'war' would be declared" (Halpern). The more that
Starbucks began to resemble McDonald's, the more of a threat the
company became to the fast food pioneer. In retaliation, "McDonald's began taste testing its coffee and in February 2007, *Consumer
Reports* magazine rated McDonald's drip coffee as better tasting than
Starbucks'" (Halpern). As if this weren't a large enough blow, Mc-
Donald's announced that it will build coffee bars in 14,000 of its
stores in 2008 that will serve beverages similar to Starbucks' but at
lower prices (Halpern). This "coffee war" is truly monumental, as
Starbucks has not seen any substantial competition since its inception.
With more variety in the coffee market, customers are realizing that
there are more choices available. The fact that McDonald's drip coffee
is sold "for as little as a quarter of the price of a fancy Starbucks brew"

has drawn in customers turned off by Starbucks' relatively high prices ("Coffee Wars"). Why pay more for a cup of Starbucks coffee that was voted worse-tasting than McDonald's coffee? This is the question many consumers have asked themselves, and they have answered it by flocking to the new coffee connoisseurs at McDonald's.

Although Starbucks clearly views McDonald's as the opposition, several lessons can be learned by looking at the situation the fast food giant was in back in the late 1990's. For more than a decade, Mc-Donald's opened four stores a day and began expanding worldwide. The company's profits and stock rose, but eventually "McDonald's stalled" (Allison). Starbucks seems to be in a similar situation today, and "plenty of Starbucks investors fear their stock darling will endure a similar plunge" as it grows "toward its goal of opening [over] 30,000 shops—the number McDonald's had when it hit the wall" (Allison). McDonald's was plagued with market saturation and loose control of its stores, difficulties Starbucks currently faces. However, there are financial analysts and Starbucks executives who feel that the two companies cannot be compared. Starbucks vice president of business development Ken Redding states that "we're in a position to have far more outlets than [McDonald's] could ever have. By way of example, how many people are going to walk into McDonald's every day and buy a Big Mac and fries? Not many. But a lot of people walk into Starbucks four or five times a week and get a cup of coffee" (Allison). McDonald's downfall had also been attributed to a "stale menu" and lack of innovation, a situation Starbucks is nowhere near as the corporation is constantly releasing new promotional beverages and offering more non-coffee products such as CDs and books (Allison). As irrelevant as it may seem for Starbucks to look to McDonald's for history lessons, it would not hurt the company to learn about the possible causes of its recent predicaments by looking at the situation McDonald's was in not too long ago.

The recent "watering down" of the Starbucks customer experience caused directly by the company's enormous growth may be another cause for Starbucks' decline in customer traffic and same-store sales. The mission of Starbucks is not only to provide customers with quality beverages, but also to create a "third place" environment in each of its stores. The "third place" is an escape from the hassles of life, a dwelling between home and work that anyone can escape to. When CEO Howard Schultz took back the reins of the company in 2007, he voiced his main concern with the corporation as "the watering down of the Starbucks experience" and the deterioration of the "third place" atmosphere caused most directly by hasty expansion ("Text"). In a memo to Starbucks executive Jim Donald, Schultz laments that the company has overlooked the "theater" once associated with Starbucks coffee. Efficiency and speed have been placed ahead of the customer's experience, highlighted by additions such as automatic espresso machines and monotonous cookie-cutter store designs ("Text"). The customers are also noticing the atmosphere, as one customer comments that Starbucks "has lost its mom-and-pop home-away-from-home feel . . . it feels more corporate now" (Barbaro and Martin). Once viewed as an escape from the turmoil of life, Starbucks stores have become more like assembly lines as the company has grown. Cutting down long lines in the fastest amount of time has become priority number one, and the focus has shifted away from customers' experience.

On the other hand, many economists and Starbucks executives feel that the negative trend in the company's finances and customer traffic has to do with an overall decline in consumer spending, not the company's expansion. There is "strong evidence . . . emerging that consumer spending, a bulwark against recession over the last year even as energy prices surged and the housing market sputtered, has begun to slow sharply at every level of the American economy" (Uchitelle). Compared to 2007, companies such as Macy's and Kohl's, which are used as barometers for the retail market, have seen an eight percent drop in sales (Uchitelle). Gasoline prices are not helping retailers, as the average price of gasoline was $3.15 at the beginning of January 2008; this has caused severe "cutbacks in other purchases" (Uchitelle). As uncertainty in the American economy grows and Americans are cutting back on their spending, it is not surprising that "caramel macchiatos are among the first luxuries to go when times get a little tougher" (Kirby). Starbucks has become susceptible to any kind of change in consumer spending, and market analysts at Bear Stearns Financial "attribute this new sensitivity to the success [Starbucks] has had in past years broadening its customer base to include more blue-collar, less-affluent customers who are more likely to react to economic pressures by scaling back visit frequency" (Kirby). Consequently, companies that sell more reasonably priced cups of coffee, such as McDonald's and Dunkin' Donuts, have seen an increase in sales as Americans become more price conscious

(Kirby). Once again, the company's recent growth can be pinpointed as the main culprit in the dwindling number of customer visits to Starbucks. Recent consumer spending trends have had adverse effects on the company's business, but ultimately colossal development can be speculated as the true perpetrator. Starbucks has become available to a wider range of consumers who have responded to current economic situations by squelching their need for Starbucks.

Once thought of as nearly invincible and immune to any kind of   9
decrease in sales or customer visits, Starbucks Coffee is beginning to look like a mere mortal as it has experienced a trend in decreased customer traffic, same-store sales, and a slide in its stock. While gasoline prices and the weak housing market have caused consumers to limit their spending, more damaging causes exist for the coffee giant. Expansion at lightning speed has fostered competition with companies offering lower-priced coffee. Furthermore, Starbucks' growth has caused the company to put customer experience on the back burner, a move that has generated discontentment among longtime patrons. Although many feel that the fiscal rut McDonald's was in a few years ago is not comparable to the one that Starbucks is currently in, it would not hurt the company to look at the similarities between the two corporations. Without reformed business and growth strategies, each of these causes will continue to mount against Starbucks, and the company will continue to lose momentum as quickly as it obtained it.

WORKS CITED

Allison, Melissa. "Super Sizing Starbucks." *Seattle Times.* Seattle Times, 12 Sept. 2008. Web. 21 Feb. 2008.

Barbaro, Michael, and Andrew Martin. "Overhaul, Make It a Venti." *New York Times.* New York Times, 30 Jan. 2008. Web. 21 Feb. 2008.

Buck, Genevieve, and Nancy Millman. "A Chain Devours Its Own." *Chicago Tribune.* Chicago Tribune, 2 Mar. 1997. Web. 22 Feb. 2008.

"Coffee Wars." *The Economist.* The Economist, 10 Jan. 2008. Web. 21 Feb. 2008.

"Company Fact Sheet." *Starbucks.* Starbucks Coffee Co., Feb. 2008. Web. 21 Feb. 2008.

Darguste, Valerie. "Starbucks Coffee: Expansion in Asia." Case study. *Global Marketing Management.* 3rd ed. By Mike Kotabe. Hoboken: Wiley, 2003. Web. 20 Feb. 2008.

Halpern, Steven. "The Coffee Wars." *BloggingStocks.* BloggingStocks, 12 Feb. 2008. Web. 21 Feb. 2008.

Kirby, Jason. "Grande Trouble at Starbucks." *Maclean's.* Maclean's, 9 Jan. 2008. Web. 21 Feb. 2008.

"Text of Starbucks memo." *Wall Street Journal.* Wall Street Journal, 24 Feb. 2007. Web. 21 Feb. 2008.

Uchitelle, Louis. "Americans Cut Back Sharply on Spending. *New York Times.* New York Times, 14 Jan. 2008. Web. 21 Feb. 2008.

Interpreting Stories 10

Interpreting a story requires you to make inferences, something you do in your everyday life when you arrive at insights about people and relationships, whether in real life or in fiction. You make inferences when you gossip with one friend about a mutual friend, or judge the motives of a TV or movie character. Rather than being final verdicts, your judgments in these situations are more likely to be invitations to further discussion. The same goes for story interpretations, which can be logical and even insistent without being final or comprehensive. In a classroom in which every student offers a different interpretation of the same story, no one student need be right; sharing and discussing the interpretations will result in a fuller understanding of the story for everyone.

Using your gossiping and character-judging experience as a starting point, interpreting a short story can lead you someplace different and, to be honest, harder to get to. After all, unlike gossiping or discussing a movie, interpreting a short story is a solitary experience, not a social one. It's textual, not conversational. And it is unbending in its demands on your time because it's usually associated with a deadline and requires that you choose every word, shape every phrase and sentence, and visibly and logically connect every sentence to the one before and after it.

Though it may seem daunting, this kind of writing can bring great satisfaction. It teaches you strategies that enable you to deepen and extend any interpretation you wish to make, whether in real life or in the arts, and to support your insights in ways your readers or listeners will find plausible and enlightening. It gives you more confidence in asserting and supporting your insights about anything at all with different kinds of people in various kinds of situations. Most important to you personally, it will help you decide which of your insights are worth keeping—which insights, added to your store of hard-won personal knowledge, will lead you to a place of greater understanding of yourself and your world. Along with the other kinds of argumentative writing in chapters 6–9, thesis-centered interpretations—logically organized and well supported—can take you there.

Synopsis: D. H. Lawrence's "In Love"

D. H. Lawrence's story "In Love" was published in *The Woman Who Rode Away and Other Stories* in 1928. You can search for the book in your college library or, better yet, access it online through Google Book Search (http://books.google.com). When you have the book in your browser, simply enter the keyword "Hester" into the search bar to skip ahead to "In Love" on page 138. Or, for a quick orientation to the story, read the synopsis below.

"In Love," a short story by D. H. Lawrence, opens with twenty-five-year-old Hester anxiously fretting about a weekend visit to the farm cottage of her fiancé, Joe. On this day a month before the wedding, Hester's younger sister, Henrietta, confronts her and tells her point-blank that she needs to snap out of her pout and "either put a better face on it, or . . . don't go." Although Hester does make the trip, she is never comfortable with her decision. 1

The crux of Hester's problem is that she and Joe had been good friends for years before she finally promised to marry him. Hester had always respected Joe as a hardworking, "decent" fellow, but now that they are to marry, she finds him changed. What she detests is the fact that, in her view, he seems to have made "the wretched mistake of falling 'in love' with her." To Hester, this notion of being in love, accentuated by all of Joe's "lovey-dovey" attempts to cuddle and snuggle and kiss, is completely idiotic and ridiculous. 2

After she arrives at Joe's farm cottage, Hester avoids his advances by asking him to play the piano. As he concentrates on his fingering, she slips outside into the night air and, when Joe comes looking for her, remains hidden in a tree. Alone in the dark, Hester falls into a fit 3 of internal questioning, doubt, and upset concerning "the mess" her life seems to have become. Then suddenly, in the midst of her anxiety, who should arrive but Henrietta, claiming she is in the neighborhood on a visit to a friend down the road. Hester leaps at the chance to join Henrietta and thus escape her entrapment with Joe. When Joe hears this, however, he responds angrily, accusing the two sisters of playing a "game."

In the confrontation that follows, Hester and Joe, for the first time, speak honestly of their feelings. Hester tells Joe she detests his "making love" to her. Joe responds that she's mistaken, that he was in fact not "in love" with her but was behaving in such a manner only because he thought that "it was expected." In the conversation, Joe goes on to reveal his dilemma and his true feelings about Hester: "What are you to do," he says, "when you know a girl's rather strict, and you like her for it?" 4

In speaking the truth of their hearts to each other for the first time, the couple is able to reveal the depth of their feelings. They recognize that they've betrayed the intimacy of their relationship because they've acted on the basis of expectations rather than on the basis of genuine emotion. By acknowledging these facts, the couple is able to reach a new understanding. Seeing Joe's honest love, Hester feels herself responding to him and, in the end, decides to stay with him. She will accept whatever he does, she says, as long as he really loves her. 5

In Love
Sarah Hawkins
University of California, San Diego
La Jolla, California

By the end of paragraph 3, Sarah Hawkins' interpretation is clear; in the last paragraph, she repeats it. In between, she focuses on details of the relationship between Hester and Joe, with Henrietta speaking for the predictable social expectations and constraints Hester and Joe must struggle against. Hawkins stays extremely close to the story throughout her essay, following through consistently with what is called a "close reading" to support her interpretation. The story offers only a small cast of characters and a small scene, and only a few hours pass; yet Hawkins has more than enough material to select from to support her interpretation.

As you read, notice that Hawkins is not merely retelling the story. Instead, she's organized her essay around the stages of the argument supporting her interpretation. The first sentences of her paragraphs—where readers look for cues to the staging or sequence of an argument—keep readers focused and on track. Notice also Hawkins' careful choice of words to help readers understand the personal and social conflicts at the center of the story. Here is a sample:

game vs. genuine feelings
love game vs. love me really
hypocritical vs. pure and true
wooden vs. intimate
social imposition vs. unique bond of love

For most people, the phrase *in love* brings many rosy pictures to mind: a young man looking into the eyes of the girl he loves, a couple walking along the beach holding hands, two people making sacrifices to be together. These stereotypes about what love is and how lovers should 1 act can be very harmful. In his short story "In Love," D. H. Lawrence uses the three main characters to embody his theme that love is experienced in a unique way by every couple and that there isn't a normal or proper way to be in love.

Hester; her fiancé, Joe; and her sister, Henrietta, all approach and respond to love in different ways. Hester is unwilling to compromise what she really feels for Joe, but she is pressured by her own notions of how a young woman in her situation should feel. Joe appears to be the typical young man in love. He seems at ease with the situation, and his moves are so predictable they could have come straight from a movie script. But when he is confronted and badgered by Hester and Henrietta, he admits that he was only putting on an act and feels regret for not being honest with Hester. Henrietta is the mouthpiece for all of society's conceptions of love. She repeatedly asks Hester to be normal and secretly worries that Hester will call off the wedding. Henrietta is like a mother hen, always making sure that Hester is doing the right thing (in Henrietta's opinion, anyway).

Hester and Joe are, in a sense, playing a game with each other. Both are acting on what they feel is expected of them now that they are engaged, as if how they really feel about each other is unimportant. It is only when Hester and Joe finally talk honestly about their relationship that they realize they have been in love all along in their own unique way.

Hester, ever the practical one, becomes more and more frustrated with "Joe's love-making" (650). She feels ridiculous, as if she is just a toy, but at the same time she feels she should respond positively to Joe, "because she believed that a nice girl would have been only too delighted to go and sit 'there'" (650). Rather than doing what she wants, enjoying a nice, comfortable relationship with Joe, Hester does what she feels she ought to. She says that she ought to like Joe's lovemaking even though she doesn't really know why. Despite her practical and independent nature, Hester is still troubled by what society would think.

Lawrence seems to be suggesting a universal theme here. If Hester, with such firm ideas about what she wants, is so troubled by what society dictates, then how much more are we, as generally less objective and more tractable people, affected by society's standards? Hester's is a dilemma everyone faces.

At the heart of Hester's confusion is Joe, whose personality was so different before they became engaged that Hester might not have gotten engaged if she had known how Joe would change: "Six months ago, Hester would have enjoyed it [being alone with Joe]. They were so perfectly comfortable together, he and she" (649). But by cuddling and petting, Joe has ruined the comfortable relationship that he and Hester had enjoyed. The most surprising line in the story is Hester's assertion that "[t]he very fact of his being in love with me proves that he doesn't love me" (652). Here, Hester makes a distinction between really loving someone and just putting on an act of being in love. Hester feels hurt that Joe would treat her as a typical girl rather than as the young woman she really is.

Hester is a reluctant player in the love game until the end of the   7
story when she confronts Joe and blurts out, "I absolutely can't stand your making love to me, if that is what you call the business" (656–57). Her use of the word *business* is significant because it refers to a chore, something that has to be done. Hester regards Joe's love-making as if it were merely a job to be completed. When Joe apologizes, Hester sees his patient, real love for her, and she begins to have the same feelings for him again. When she says, "I don't mind what you do if you love me really" (660), Hester, by compromising, shows the nature of their love for each other.

Lawrence uses Joe to show a typical response to society's pres-   8
sures. Joe obediently plays the role of the husband-to-be. He exhibits all the preconceived images one may have about a man about to be married. In trying to fit the expectations of others, Joe sacrifices his straightforwardness and the honesty that Hester valued so much in him. Although Joe's actions don't seem to be so bad in and of themselves, in the context of his relationship with Hester, they are completely out of place. His piano playing, for example, inspires Hester to remark that Joe's love games would be impossible to handle after the music he played. The music represents something that is pure and true—in contrast to the new, hypocritical Joe. Joe doesn't seem to be aware of Hester's feelings until she comes forward with them at the end of the story. The humiliation he suffers makes him silent, and he is described several times as wooden, implying stubbornness and solidness. It is out of this woodenness that a changed Joe appears. At first the word suggests his defensiveness for his bruised ego, but then as Joe begins to see Hester's point about being truly in love, his woodenness is linked to his solidness and stability, qualities that represent for Hester the old Joe. Once Joe gets his mind off the love game, the simple intimacy of their relationship is revealed to him,

and he desires Hester, not in a fleeting way but in a way that one desires something that was almost lost.

Henrietta serves as the antagonist in this story because it is through her that society's opinions come clear. In almost the first line of text, Henrietta, looking at Hester, states, "If I had such a worried look on my face, when I was going down to spend the weekend with the man I was engaged to—and going to be married to in a month—well! I should either try and change my face or hide my feelings, or something" (647). With little regard for Hester's feelings, Henrietta is more concerned that Hester have the right attitude. Although Henrietta herself is not married, the fact that Hester, who is twenty-five, is soon to be married is a relief to her. Not wanting her sister to be an old maid, Henrietta does all she can to make sure the weekend runs smoothly. She acts as though Hester were her responsibility and even offers to come with Hester to take the "edge off the intimacy" (648). Being young, Henrietta hasn't really formed her own views of life or love yet. As a result, she easily believes the traditional statements society makes about love. When Hester says that she can't stand Joe's being in love with her, Henrietta keeps responding that a man is supposed to be in love with the woman he marries. She doesn't understand the real love that Joe and Hester eventually feel but only the "ought-tos" of love imposed by society. It is unclear at the end of the story if Henrietta really recognizes the new bond between Hester and Joe.

What society and common beliefs dictate about being in love isn't really important. In order to be happy, couples must find their own unique bond of love and not rely on others' opinions or definitions. Joe and Hester come to this realization only after they are hurt and left unfulfilled as a result of the love game they play with each other. Hester knew how she really felt from the beginning, but pressure about what she ought to feel worried her. Joe willingly went along with the game until he realized how important their simple intimacy really was. In the end, Hester and Joe are in love not because of the games they play but because of an intimate friendship that had been growing all along.

WORK CITED

Lawrence, D. H. "In Love." *The Complete Short Stories*. Vol. 3. New York: Penguin, 1977. 540–47. Print.

Synopsis: Susan Glaspell's "A Jury of Her Peers"

You can read Susan Glaspell's story "A Jury of Her Peers" online at the Electronic Text Center at the University of Virginia Library. Go to http://etext.lib.virginia.edu/modeng/modeng0.browse.html and look under "G" for "Glaspell." Or, for a quick orientation to the story, read the synopsis below.

Susan Glaspell's short story "A Jury of Her Peers" begins when three men and two women—Mr. Peters, the county sheriff; Mr. Henderson, the county attorney; and Mr. Hale, a farmer; along with two wives, Mrs. Peters and Mrs. Hale—begin to investigate the death of a farm neighbor, John Wright, who they believe was murdered the previous day by his wife, Mrs. Wright. Although there is no direct evidence linking her to the crime, Mrs. Wright is nevertheless jailed on suspicion of murder.

At the Wright farmhouse, the county attorney asks Mr. Hale, the man who by chance discovered the murder, to recount his experience at the farmhouse. Mr. Hale describes how he found Mrs. Wright sitting in a rocking chair as she calmly told him that Mr. Wright was upstairs dead with a rope around his neck.

As the three men search the farmhouse for evidence that might establish a motive for the crime, Mrs. Peters and Mrs. Hale sit in Mrs. Wright's kitchen. With attentive eyes, they keenly observe domestic details that begin to reveal a pattern of meaning that the men overlook. As they continue to look around, the details begin to speak volumes about the emotional lives and marital relationship of Mr. and Mrs. Wright. Mrs. Peters and Mrs. Hale notice the uncharacteristic dirty pans and towels in the kitchen, neither of which fit Mrs. Wright's

201

character as a careful housekeeper. They note a half-full bag of sugar that, again, is uncharacteristic, suggesting an interrupted task. They find a single square on Mrs. Wright's quilt that is raggedly sewn—just one, amid a field of perfectly sewn pieces—which suggests the seamstress had to be out of sorts.

As these domestic details add up, they gain significance for the women while the men scoff and dismiss their concerns as simplistic and typical of women. Finally, when the women discover a birdcage with its door broken and then—at the bottom of the sewing basket—a dead canary wrapped in silk, its neck wrung, they realize they have stumbled upon the motive for the murder. Bound up in the details of violence and dishonor—the husband killed the wife's canary—Mrs. Peters and Mrs. Hale discover the joyless horror Mrs. Wright endured in her marriage to her hard, uncaring husband. They realize John Wright was the man who killed not only a canary but also the spirit of his wife, a woman who had been a beautiful singer—a songbird—in her youth. Mrs. Peters and Mrs. Hale draw on personal experiences to empathize with Mrs. Wright. Mrs. Peters recalls the raging desire to hurt the boy who killed her kitten when she was a girl, and Mrs. Hale recalls the stillness she felt when her first baby died, likening it to the stillness that Mrs. Wright must have endured in her loveless marriage.

In the end, Mrs. Peters' and Mrs. Hale's empathy for Mrs. Wright is so deep that when the men return to collect them to leave, the women look at each other quickly and Mrs. Hale stuffs the dead bird into her coat pocket. Without concrete evidence to establish a motive for murder, they know a jury will not convict the woman. Mrs. Peters and Mrs. Hale act as Mrs. Wright's first jury—a true jury of her peers, relying on experience, intuition, and empathy rather than legal reasoning to find justice in their world.

Irony and Intuition in "A Jury of Her Peers"

Margaret Tate

DeKalb College
Decatur, Georgia

Margaret Tate begins by briefly establishing the historical context and setting of "A Jury of Her Peers"—the early years of the twentieth century in the U.S. Midwest. Her key terms are *intuition* and *irony*, her theme, the differences between men's and women's intuitions. She does not leave you waiting for her thesis: you will find it at the end of her first paragraph. As you read, notice how she selectively and repeatedly quotes and paraphrases the story without retelling it. Instead, she uses the details of the story to support each stage of her argument.

————————

Though men and women are now recognized as generally equal in talent and intelligence, when Susan Glaspell wrote "A Jury of Her Peers" in 1917, it was not so. In this turn-of-the-century, rural midwestern setting, women were often barely educated and possessed virtually no political or economic power. And, being considered the weaker sex, there was not much they could do about it. Relegated to home and hearth, women found themselves at the mercy of the more powerful men in their lives. Ironically, it is just this type of powerless existence, perhaps, that over the ages developed into a power with which women could baffle and frustrate their male counterparts: a sixth sense—an inborn trait commonly known as women's intuition. In Glaspell's story, ironic situations contrast male and female intuition, illustrating that Minnie Wright is more fairly judged by women than by men.

"A Jury of Her Peers" first uses irony to illustrate the contrast between male and female intuition when the men go to the farmhouse

1

2

203

looking for clues to the murder of John Wright, but it is the women who find them. In the Wright household, the men are searching for something out of the ordinary, an obvious indication that Minnie has been enraged or provoked into killing her husband. Their intuition does not tell them that their wives, because they are women, can help them gain insight into what has occurred between John and his wife. They bring Mrs. Hale and Mrs. Peters along merely to tend to the practical matters, considering them needlessly preoccupied with trivial things and even too unsophisticated to make a contribution to the investigation, as illustrated by Mr. Hale's derisive question, "Would the women know a clue if they did come upon it?" (289).

Ironically, while the men are looking actively for the smoking gun, the women are confronted with subtler clues in spite of themselves and even try to hide from each other what they intuitively know. But they do not fool each other for long, as Glaspell describes: "Their eyes met—something flashed to life, passed between them; then, as if with an effort, they seemed to pull away from each other" (295). However, they cannot pull away, for they are bound by a power they do not even comprehend: "We all go through the same things—it's all just a different kind of the same thing!...why do you and I understand? Why do we know —what we know this minute?" (303). They do not realize that it is intuition they share, that causes them to "[see] into things, [to see] through a thing to something else . . ." (294). Though sympathetic to Minnie Wright, the women cannot deny the damning clues that lead them to the inescapable conclusion of her guilt.

If it is ironic that the women find the clues, it is even more ironic that they find them in the mundane household items to which the men attribute so little significance. "Nothing here but kitchen things," the men mistakenly think (287). Because of their weak intuition, they do not see the household as indicative of John's and Minnie's characters. They do not see beyond the cheerless home to John Wright's grim nature, nor do the dilapidated furnishings provide them with a clue to his penurious habits. Minnie's depression and agitation are not apparent to them in the dismal, half-cleaned kitchen; instead, they consider Minnie an inept, lazy housekeeper. Oddly, for all their "snoopin' round and criticizin'" (290), the three gentlemen literally do not have a clue.

The women, on the other hand, "used to worrying over trifles" (287), do attach importance to the "everyday things" (299), and looking around the cheerless kitchen, they see many examples of the miserably hard existence of Minnie Wright. Knowing the pride a woman takes in her home, they see Minnie's kitchen not as dirty but as half-cleaned, and the significance of this is not lost on them. And, upon discovering the erratic quilt stitching, they are alarmed. Also, they cannot dismiss the broken birdcage as just a broken birdcage. They instinctively know, as the men do not, that Minnie desperately needed a lively creature to brighten up such a loveless home. Upon finding these clues, ironically hidden in everyday objects, the women piece them together with a thread of intuition and create a blanket of guilt that covers the hapless Minnie Wright.

Though there is irony in the fact that the women, not the men, 6 find the clues, and irony in the fact that they are found in everyday household things, most ironic is the fact that John Wright meets the same fate he has inflicted on the poor bird, illustrating that he is perhaps the least intuitive of all the men in the story. John Wright never sees beyond his own needs to the needs of his wife. He does not understand her need for a pretty creature to fill the void created by her lonely, childless existence. Not content to kill just Minnie's personality ("[s]he was [once] kind of like a bird herself. Real sweet and pretty" [299]), he kills her canary, leaving her with the deafening silence of the lonesome prairie. Minnie has endured many years of misery at the hands of John Wright, but he pushes her too far when he kills the bird. Then, ironically, he gets the "peace and quiet" (283) he values over her happiness.

John Wright lacks the intuition to understand his wife's love of 7 her bird, but the two women do not. They understand that she needed the bird to fill the still air with song and lessen her loneliness. After discovering the dead bird, they do not blame her for killing John. The dead bird reminds Mrs. Peters of a traumatic episode from her childhood:

> "When I was a girl," said Mrs. Peters, under her breath, "my kitten—there was a boy took a hatchet, and before my eyes—before I could get there . . . If they hadn't held me back, I would have . . . hurt him." (301–02)

The women see the reason for Minnie's murderous impulse, but they know that the men lack the insight to ever fully understand her situation or her motivation; therefore, in hiding the bird, by their silence, they acquit Minnie Wright.

Through the ironic situations in "A Jury of Her Peers," Glaspell   8
clearly illustrates a world in which men and women vary greatly in
their perception of things. She shows men as often superficial in the
way they perceive the world, lacking the depth of intuition that
women use as a means of self-preservation to see themselves and the
world more clearly. Without the heightened perspective on life that
this knowledge of human nature gives them, women might not stand
a chance. Against the power and domination of men, they often find
themselves as defenseless and vulnerable as Minnie's poor bird.

WORK CITED

Glaspell, Susan. "A Jury of Her Peers." *Lifted Masks and Other Works.* Ed. Eric
    S. Rabkin. Ann Arbor: U of Michigan P, 1993. Print.

A Note on the Copyediting

We all know that the work of professional writers rarely appears in print without first being edited. But what about student writing—especially essays that are presented as models of student writing? Do these get edited too?

While it's easy to draw an analogy with professional writing and simply declare that "all published writing gets edited," there are some important differences between student and professional writing. For one thing, student writing is presented as student writing. That is, it's offered to the reader as an example of the kind of writing students can and do produce in a writing class. And since most students don't have the benefit of a professional editor, their work may not be as polished as the models they see in textbooks.

For another, unlike professional writers, students rarely have the opportunity to participate in the editorial process. Companion readers like this one are compiled while the main text is being revised, at a time when the authors and editors are immersed in the work of the text and don't have time to also supervise twenty-five or more student writers. For this reason, students are usually simply asked to sign a statement transferring to the publisher all rights to their essays, subject to final editing, and don't see their work again until it appears in print. For these reasons, editing student writing is problematic.

But publishing student essays without editing is equally problematic. Every composition teacher knows that even the best papers, the A+ essays, aren't perfect. But readers of published prose, accustomed to the conventions of edited American English, aren't always so generous. The shift in tense that may be seen as a simple lapse in a student narrative becomes a major distraction in a published piece. Rather than preserve that tense shift in the interest of absolute fidelity to the student's work, it is more in keeping with the spirit and purpose of the enterprise to edit the passage. After all, the rest of the evidence indicates that the student is a strong writer and that he or she would likely accede to the change if it were called to his or her attention.

The editing of a student essay is not a violation of the student's work, then, but really a courtesy to the writer. True, some essays require more editing than others—perhaps because some students did not have much opportunity to revise—but none in this collection has been altered significantly. In fact, every attempt has been made to respect the students' choices.

To give you an inside look at the editing process, we reproduce here the originally submitted version of Sheila McClain's essay "Proxemics: A Study of Space and Relationships," along with the Bedford/St. Martin's editor's changes. You might use this sample as an opportunity to consider the usefulness and necessity of editing. What changes were made, and why? Which of them improved the essay? Were all of them necessary? If you are a writer whose work has undergone editorial revision—perhaps as part of peer review—you might think about how the process felt to you. Did you appreciate your editor's work? Resent it? What did you learn from it? If you're like most of us, you probably realized that it's natural to resist, but necessary to accept, criticism. In other words, you learned to think like a writer.

Sample Copyediting

Proxemics: A Study of Space and Relationships

by

Sheila McClain

Everyday we interact and communicate, sometimes without even saying a word. Body language, more ~~correctly~~ formally known as nonverbal communication, speaks volumes about who we are and how we relate to others. As ~~noted by~~ Lester Sielski, an associate professor at the University of West Florida, writes "Words are beautiful, exciting, important, but we have over-estimated them badly 1/m since they are not all or even half the message." He also asserts that "beyond words lies the bedrock on which human relationships are built 1/m nonverbal communication" (Sielski). ~~As related by author Roger E. Axtell~~ A group of psychology students at the University of Texas recently ~~discovered~~ demonstrated just how

209

profound an effect nonverbal communication can have on people. The students conducted an experiment to test the unspoken rules of behavior on elevators. Boarding a crowded elevator, they would stand facing and grinning at the other people on board. Understandably, the people became uncomfortable; and one person even suggested that someone call 911 (Axtell 5-6). Why all the fuss? Unspoken elevator etiquette dictates that one should turn and face the door in a crowded elevator, being careful not to touch anyone else and honoring the sacred personal space of each individual by staring at the floor indicator instead of looking at anyone else. Although they are not written down, strict rules govern our behavior in public situations. This is especially true when space is limited as on elevators, buses, or subway trains (Axtell 5-6). Patricia Buhler, an expert in business management and associate professor at Goldey-Beacon College, confirms the large role nonverbal communication plays. She asserts that as little as 8 percent of the message we communicate is made up of words. We communicate the rest of our message, a disproportionately large 92 percent, with body language and other nonverbal forms of communication (Buhler). According to a professor of

~~social work,~~ while researchers have long known that

nonverbal cues play a large role in communication, for

many years they made no efforts~~9~~ to learn more about

them (Sielski).

~~this component of language.~~ Amid rising public

interest, several scientists pioneered new research in

the field of nonverbal communication in the 1950s.

Among these experts was anthropologist Edward T. Hall.

focused

He ~~pioneered research~~ on a specific type of nonverbal

(ital)   (rom)   **is**

communication called *Proxemics. Proxemics* ~~defined as~~

the study of how people use personal space to

communicate nonverbally, plays a major role in

our everyday interactions with others, whether we are

conscious of it or not, **our use of space**

and   **A review of some of Dr. Hall's main terms will help us.**
appreciate   ~~Proxemics carries great importance because it~~
just how
~~affects our relationships with others. To~~ better
much our
use of   understand ~~the impact~~ proxemics ~~can have on~~
space
affects   relationships, ~~we need to know the meanings of two key~~
our   **For example,**
according to   **in our everyday interactions, we choose to**
~~terms used by~~ Dr. Hall. ~~A professor from University of~~ **position**

~~St. Thomas summarizes Dr. Hall's terms. The first term~~ **ourselves**
                                                          to create
"~~S~~ociopetal space"~~9~~ invites communication. ~~The second~~ **either**
                                      1   **"sociopetal"**
~~term~~ "~~S~~ociofugal space"~~9~~ is the opposite ~~of the first.~~ **or**
                                                                  "sociofugal"
~~I~~t separates people and discourages interaction **space.**

                                          a
(Jordan). ~~For example,~~ a student in a school lunchroom

may ~~choose to~~ sit alone at an empty table in ~~the~~
                                        creating
                              the
corner, away from others~~9~~ students ("~~S~~ociofugal space"),

or ~~he may choose to sit~~ directly across from a person
he would like to befriend ("sociopetal space"). ^creating^ ~~As the
examples show, our use of space could greatly impact
our social relationships.~~

~~Falling under both "sociopetal" and "sociofugal
space,"~~ three ~~main types of space~~ in which we ~~interact
are defined by Dr. Hall. These include~~ "fixed-feature
space," "semi-fixed feature space," and "informal
space" (Jordan). ~~Fixed-feature spaces are~~ hard, if
not impossible, for us to control or change. ~~"Fixed
feature" refers to the permanent aspects of the space
in which we interact. A "fixed-feature" problem exists
in~~ my college English class ~~where the room~~ is too
small for the number of students attending. ~~Consequently,
we have a hard time finding a place where~~ we can ~~see~~ the
overhead projections. We cannot make the walls of the
classroom bigger or the ceiling higher, and the
overhead screen is likewise "fixed" in place. We must
work within the constraints of this space. A "semi-
fixed feature space" is ~~somewhat adjustable allowing
for space to be~~ defined by ~~more~~ mobile objects. ~~Couches
and chairs in a living room may be oriented to~~ face
only the television, thus discouraging conversations
and relationship building. ~~Reorientation of the couch
and chairs, so that they face each other, may~~ create a

Inserted handwritten edits: "Dr. Hall identifies" · "kinds of general spaces with" · "can create either sociofugal or sociopetal space. These are" · "a" (Jordan) · "For example, because" · "positioning ourselves so that (all)" · "e" (this) · "usually" · "such as furniture. The" · "for example" · "But we are able to reposition the furniture" · "to"

more social and conversational environment. Informal space is by far the easiest to manipulate. We each ~~have~~ control ~~of~~ our personal "bubble," and we can set distances between ourselves and others ~~which best suit~~ that reflect our relationships with them. ~~To illustrate this~~ Take for example the way that, people ~~may~~ approach their bosses ~~in various ways depending upon how they feel about their boss. If people are~~ A man who is afraid of or dislikes his ~~their~~ boss ~~they~~ may communicate with ~~them~~ her from as far away as possible. ~~They~~ He might stand in ~~their~~ her doorway ~~and not enter the boss' office~~ to relay a message. Conversely, ~~people~~ a woman who ~~have~~ has known ~~their~~ her boss for many years and ~~are~~ is good friends with ~~their bosses~~ him may come right in to his office and casually sit down in close proximity to ~~their bosses~~ him. ~~Thus they show by their use of space that they feel comfortable and have a good relationship with their bosses.~~ Individually, we have a great deal of control over our informal space, and how we use this space can speak volumes about our relationships with others.

~~As one source explains,~~ After observing many interactions, Dr. Hall ~~further~~ broke down ~~this~~ informal space ~~by~~ further, identifying four ~~separate~~ distances commonly used by people in their interactions with others: "intimate distance," zero to one and a half feet;

"personal distance," one and a half to four feet; "social distance," four to twelve feet; and "public distance," twelve feet and beyond ~~all distinguish zones we use for different interactions~~ (Beebe, Beebe, and Redmond 231). "Intimate distance," as the name suggests, is generally reserved for those people closest to us. Lovemaking, hugging, and holding small children all occur in this zone. The exception to this rule comes when we extend our hand to perfect strangers in greeting, allowing them to briefly enter our intimate space with a handshake. "Personal distance," while not as close as intimate, is still reserved for people we know well and with whom we feel comfortable. This zone ~~is~~ usually occupies an area relatively close to us. It can at times be applied, however, to include objects we see as extensions of ourselves. For instance, we [while driving] may feel ~~that someone is invading~~ our personal space [being invaded] ~~when we are driving a car if the~~ [by a] car (behind us) follow[ing] too closely [our own]. We see ~~the~~ car as an extension of ourselves and extend our "personal bubble" to include it. "Social distance" is often considered a respectful distance and is used in many professional business settings as well as in group interactions. ~~To illustrate~~ [There is a] "public distance," ~~we might think of the distance used when~~ [between a] lectur[er]~~ing a~~

~~large group or~~ <ins>and a class, or someone</ins> speaking publicly from a podium. <ins>and his or her audience.</ins> ~~This distance can also include speakers who are not physically present, such as watching the President address the nation on television.~~

As we have seen, ~~proxemics, or how we use the space around us, has some impact on the multitude of interactions we have with others everyday.~~ <ins>in positioning ourselves in relation to others — especially in choosing nearness or distance — we communicate respect or intimacy, fear or familiarity.</ins> We can improve ~~or damage our social~~ <ins>a friendly</ins> relationships simply by using a "warm, personable" distance, ~~with friends,~~ or ~~we may~~ drive potential friends away by seeming "cold and distant," or getting quite literally "too close for comfort." We <ins>can</ins> put people at ease or make them uncomfortable just by our proximity to them. The study of nonverbal communication, and specifically proxemics, demonstrates the truth of the old adage, "actions speak louder than words."

Submission Form

We hope that this collection is one of many, and that we'll be able to include more essays from more colleges and universities in the next edition. Please let us see the best essays you've written using *The St. Martin's Guide to Writing; The Concise Guide to Writing; Reading Critically, Writing Well;* or *Sticks and Stones.* Send them with this submission form and copies of the agreement form on the next page (one for each essay you submit) to English Editor—Student Essays, Bedford/St. Martin's, 33 Irving Place, 10th Floor, New York, NY 10003. You can also submit essays online at bedfordstmartins.com/theguide.

Student's Name _____

Instructor's Name _____

School _____

Department _____

Course Text (circle one)

The St. Martin's Guide to Writing   *The Concise Guide to Writing*

Reading Critically, Writing Well   *Sticks and Stones*

Writing Assignment (circle one)

Remembering Events   Proposing a Solution

Writing Profiles   Justifying an Evaluation

Explaining a Concept   Speculating about Causes

Finding Common Ground   Interpreting Stories

Arguing a Position

Other: _____

Agreement Form

I hereby assign to Bedford/St. Martin's ("Bedford") all of my right, title, and interest throughout the world, including, without limitation, all copyrights, in and to my essay, _____, and any notes and drafts pertaining to it (the sample essay and such materials being referred to as the "Essay").

I understand that Bedford in its discretion has the right but not the obligation to publish the Essay in any form(s) or format(s) that it may desire; that Bedford may edit, revise, condense, or otherwise alter the Essay as it deems appropriate in order to prepare the same for publication. I understand that Bedford has the right to use and to authorize the use of my name as author of the Essay in connection with any work that contains the Essay (or a portion of it).

I represent that the Essay was completely written by me, that I have cited any sources I relied on, that publication of it will not infringe upon the rights of any third party, and that I have not granted any rights in it to any third party.

In the event Bedford determines to publish any part of the Essay in one of its print books, I will receive one free copy of the work in which it appears.

Student's Signature _____

Name _____ Date _____

Permanent Address _____

Phone Number(s) _____

_____

Email Address(es) _____

_____

A Note to the Student:

When a writer creates something—a story, an essay, a poem—he or she automatically possesses all of the rights to that piece of writing, no trip to the U.S. Copyright Office needed. When a writer—a historian, a novelist, a sportswriter—publishes his or her work, he or she normally transfers some or all of those rights to the publisher, by formal agreement. The form above is one such formal agreement. By entering into this agreement, you are engaging in a modern publishing ritual—the transfer of rights from writer to publisher. If this is your first experience submitting something for publication, you should know that you are in good company: every student who has published an essay in one of our books entered into this agreement, and just about every published writer has entered into a similar one.

Thank you for submitting your essay.